Profiles in Pennsylvania Sports

OTHER BOOKS BY AUTHOR—

     · *The Pennsylvania Sampler*

     Profiles From the Susquehanna Valley

Profiles in Pennsylvania Sports

*Athletic Heroes and Exploits
from Past and Present in the
Commonwealth Where Sports
Are Almost Everyone's Passion*

PAUL B. BEERS

Stackpole Books

PROFILES IN PENNSYLVANIA SPORTS

Copyright © 1975 by Paul B. Beers

Published by
STACKPOLE BOOKS
Cameron and Kelker Streets
Harrisburg, Pa. 17105

Printed in the U.S.A.

Library of Congress Cataloging in Publication Data
Beers, Paul B
    Profiles in Pennsylvania sports.

    Includes index.
    1. Athletes—Pennsylvania—Biography. 2. Sports
—Pennsylvania—History. I. Title.
GV697.A1B43   796'.092'2 [B]   75-19234
ISBN 0-8117-2046-2 pbk.

CONTENTS

> . . . Pennsylvania's interest in sports covers all classes of people, races and sexes. The ethnic groups took to sports in a big way, followed by black Pennsylvanians and now women. It is a state in which every community has had its heroes on the playing fields.

. . . Joe Namath's Hometown Builds Winners

There are many sports-minded communities in Pennsylvania, but Beaver Falls is something special. With a coach like Larry Bruno, the Tigers win in the toughest conference of Pennsylvania schoolboy football.

Ferocious Linebackers   115
. . . Take a Boy from a Small Pennsylvania Town

For defense, Pennsylvania produces linebackers. The names Bednarik, Schmidt, Michaels, Drazonovich, Pottios, Lucci, Conners and Ham are familiar.

Don't Knock the Rock   127
. . . Slippery Rock Isn't Funny

The name of this Western Pennyslvania college strikes many as humorous, but its brand of football is superb. In other sports too, the Rockets soar.

3 Golf   131

The Palmer Magic   131
. . . Arnie Is America's Most Successful Athlete

Latrobe's Huck Finn applied competitiveness with a lot of practice to make himself Pennsylvania's most famous native-born athlete.

4 Tennis   141

Blue-Blooded Bill   141
. . . Tilden Made Tennis a National Sport

He not only dominated the net game, but he also was an actor, playwright, novelist, expert in bridge, a homosexual, and always in the headlines.

5 Baseball   148

Mr. Mack   148
. . . The Grand Old Man Was Nobody's Fool

Philadelphia was enchanted and exasperated by the owner-manager who won and lost more ball games than anyone else in baseball. Connie Mack knew exactly what he was doing in his 76-year career.

The Flying Dutchman   156
. . . Honus Wagner Set the Style for Shortstops

The bowlegged working boy from Carnegie played for the Pirates 19 years, hit .329, and is baseball's all-time, all-around ballplayer.

Immortal Matty   162
. . . Christy Mathewson Was Baseball's First Superstar

The Giant by way of Factoryville and Bucknell gave a touch of class to the roughhouse American sports scene. Furthermore, he threw a baseball more accurately than perhaps any other man who ever lived.

Never thinking of himself as handicapped, Pete Gray used his speed, sharp eyesight, ingenuity and immense confidence to play ten years of professional baseball.

In the Golden Age of boxing, Pennsylvania had 19 world champions, one more if Joe Palooka qualifies.

The Pittsburgher fought his way up from the Fighting Zivics to be middleweight champ. Clean or dirty, but always polite, he was the workingman's fighter.

From the Lehigh Valley westward, the Commonwealth produces a bountiful crop of champion wrestlers. There are the three Peerys of Pittsburgh, Billy Sheridan of the Lehigh Engineers, Penn State, Clarion, Wilkes and others.

As the first of America's great women's collegiate basketball teams, the Macs and their coach, Cathy Rush, earned a national reputation. They also were very good.

ACKNOWLEDGMENTS

The subject of sports in Pennsylvania is endlessly complex and detailed. There are, and have been, millions of participants and followers. Every community has a cherished athletic legend or two. The myriad of names, dates, scores and championships boggles the mind. There simply is a staggering amount of sport facts in Pennsylvania.

Even the most intrepid writer of a book on Pennsylvania sports must concede that omissions will be his cardinal sin. It is as impossible to know and to include every outstanding Pennsylvania athlete and team of the past 100 years as it is to count the butterflies on a summer day in Fertility, Pa. Comparisons indeed are odious, especially in sports. The selection of articles, citations and lists of Pennsylvania stars and teams is not meant to imply that any omitted Pennsylvanian failed to qualify or that those mentioned indisputably were the most superb of all time. The point must be emphasized: the athletes and teams noted in this book were outstanding. Regretfully, not everybody could be named.

A lesson is learned early in researching sports that this is the most transitory of history. A new champion seemingly is crowned every day, while yesterday's hero is soon forgotten. With luck, the "boys of the summer of '42" will be remembered, but what about the deserving boys of the summer of '43?

Every sports fan has his special memories and those that are shared become common remembrances and evolve into legend, such as the exploits of the Pottsville Maroons or the romantic figure of Christy Mathewson. Only a few select individuals and teams earn reputations that endure beyond even five years, let alone a generation. Athletic glory is ruthlessly fleeting and ephemeral. Yet personal memories of fabulous athletes and feats last a lifetime, as they are especially linked to the joys of our youth, and sport fans treasure that part of the past they recall so vividly.

The author is grateful for what memories he can reinforce in his chronicle of Pennsylvania sports and for what success he might have "to communicate the meaning of what men have done," as the late Dr. Roy F. Nichols of the University of Pennsylvania said is the purpose of the historian.

The most urgent debt one must pay is to the working sportswriters. These editors and writers probably outdo all others in Pennsylvania newspapering. Not only is it often true that the coverage, the news value and the imaginative reporting is greatest on the sports pages, but it is here that the best writing usually is done. The public is apt to know the names of sportswriters more than any other newspapermen, and for good reason.

Sports editors like John Kunda of Allentown, Joe Tronzo of Beaver Falls and Fred Yost of Johnstown were especially helpful in the gathering of material for this book. Ron Christ, Charles Danasko, Skip Hutter, Bruce Whitman and Judi Patton of the Harrisburg *Patriot-News* were informative and generous in their assistance.

Thanks also is due to Murray Brown, Jim Campbell, Rusty Cowan, Bob Craig, Charles G. Gangaware, Doc Giffin, Tom Leask, Charles McCullough, John Millar, John M. Morris, Brent Hancock, Bill Northrop, Louis Rauco, John Redding, John Reese, Dick Sharbaugh and Michael L. Smith.

Profiles In Pennsylvania Sports is dedicated to two men who have given most of their adult lives to athletics in the Commonwealth. Al Clark is executive sports editor of the *Patriot-News* and John Travers is assistant editor. They were co-founders of the Pennsylvania Big 33. Clark, a native of Hanover, celebrated his 50th year as a sportswriter in 1974, and his 25th as a Harrisburg editor. Travers, originally of Lynn, Mass., came to Harrisburg in 1945 after serving in World War II. Clark has had a career that has taken him from the days of Jim Thorpe to the era of the Super Bowl. Creative, knowledgeable and spryly individualistic, Clark undoubtedly is one of the finest Pennsylvania sports editors of all time. Travers, a versatile writer, has been a perennial winner of awards and once was a Pulitzer Prize nominee. He is a fine football and golf reporter and certainly is one of the nation's top hockey writers. For almost 20 years, the author has found these two talkative gentlemen to be living, unindexed repositories of sports lore, occasionally even wisdom. Their contributions to Pennsylvania athletics, as well as to this book, have been immense.

P.B.B.

SUPERSPORTS

1

Pennsylvania is packed with sports—games, tournaments, leagues, championships. There are millions of athletes, mostly amateur and recreational, and there are millions of spectators and fans. The Commonwealth is engrossed by athletics. Sports, more than any other subject, seemingly preoccupies the most Pennsylvanians for the most time.

"Avid Fan of Pirates Dies at 110," the Pittsburgh *Press* reported in half-inch headlines on Nov. 11, 1974. By radio, Mrs. Alta B. Dilley had followed the Pirates' every hit, run and error for years.

When Gov. John K. Tener (1911–14) signed a measure he had fought for, possibly either the first historic Highway Act or the famed Education Code, an aide exclaimed, "Governor, that is the landmark of your career." The 6-foot-5 fastballer from Charleroi replied, "Don't forget, I once shutout the New York Giants."

The passionate devotion to sports in Pennsylvania has not diminished despite today's higher living standards, more education, the disintegration of many community bonds, and even the new life-styles. Perhaps the enthusiasm has increased for sports in contemporary times.

Everybody plays. Pennsylvania has 78,600 youngsters involved in competitive football on 549 varsity and junior high school teams. It has 33,700 on 638 varsity and 485 junior high basketball teams, and 31,300 on 475 varsity and 306 junior high wrestling squads. Yet, the fastest-growing sport is girls high school basketball, with 580 varsity teams.

1974 was not an exceptional year, but look how Pennsylvania stacked up in champions. Pro football: Pittsburgh Steelers. Lambert Trophy: Penn State. National League East: Pittsburgh Pirates. National Hockey League Stanley Cup: Philadelphia Flyers. American Hockey League Calder Cup: Hershey Bears. Ivy League basketball: University of Pennsylvania. National women's basketball: Immaculata College. Mid-Atlantic basketball: St. Joseph. U.S. pocket billiards: Joe Balsis of Minersville. Harness racing: all ten major stakes captured by Pennsylvania-sired or bred horses. Whitewater double canoeing: Al Harris and Dave Knight of Philadelphia. Gymnastics: Robert Rice, Joan Moore Rice, Ann Carr and the Philadelphia Manettes. U.S. amateur soccer cup: Philadelphia International. U.S. civilian smallbore shooting: William P. Schweitzer of Lancaster. Weightlifting: York champions in five of nine categories. Collegiate wrestling: Pennsylvania in two divisions. Squash senior doubles: Newton Meade of Philadelphia.

Of course there is universal interest in sports across the nation, but the fervor over athletics is particularly prevalent in Pennsylvania. Say any sporting phrase, such as "three strikes you're out," and you are speaking a common language in Pennsylvania. Appeal to Pennsylvanians to be good sportsmen, make a goal-line stand, go to the mat, or stage a rally, and the cliche is understood instantly. In fact, public speaking in Pennsylvania would improve immeasurably if much of the sports lingo were eliminated.

Sport Magazine in 1974 featured on a cover the three richest contemporary American athletes, all native-born Pennsylvanians— Arnold Palmer, Wilt Chamberlain and Joe Namath.

Jimmy the Greek, the nation's most celebrated oddsmaker on sporting events, is a Pennsylvanian. Jimmy Snyder was born Demetrios Synadinos in 1920 in Monessen, a red-hot sports town in the Monongahela Valley.

Pennsylvania's mania for athletics for more than 100 years has been so accepted as a social norm that it has not been studied, defined, classified or interpreted. It is odd, but no one has been puzzled as to why of all Pennsylvania's institutions, sports retains such widespread popularity. Athletics is the common denominator, not ethnic nor religious background, not occupation, political beliefs nor educational achievement. The dominant role of Pennsylvania sports was described best in *That Championship Season,* Broadway's top play of 1972. Playwright Jason Miller was a high school basketball player in Scranton. He has his coach spout pseudo-philosophy that many Pennsylvanians believe in, such as, "You quit on the field, you'll quit in life."

Pennsylvania athletic excellence runs the gamut of age. Jimmy Carr (Erie) was only 16 at the 1972 Olympics, the youngest American Olympic wrestler in history. He came back home to be the Pennsylvania schoolboy champ afterwards. John Williams (Cranesville) was the world's second-best archer at 15, the best at 17, and the 1972 Olympic gold medal winner at 18. Dan Seemiller (Carrick) at 20 in 1974 probably was the world's leading table tennis player. Eddie Ressler, of Allentown, won the 1975 American Bowling Congress masters championship with a 213.6 average. At 20 he was the youngest person ever to be the masters champ, and his annual earnings in the pin game exceeded $60,000. Eddie learned how to roll a bowling ball at 7. Yet Pennsylvania also produces senior stars. In 1974 Herman "Red" Klotz (Philadelphia) at 55 was playing pro basketball against the Harlem Globetrotters, George Blanda (Youngwood) at 46 was still kicking field goals in pro football, and Walt Chyzowych (Philadelphia) at 37 was a top pro soccer player.

Bob Hoffman at 75 in 1974 could press 200 pounds with one hand. Hoffman, a former outstanding canoeist and polka dancer, is a 260-pounder who turned York into the "Mecca of Muscledom." He was the U.S. Olympic weightlifting coach from 1948–64, succeded by his colleague, John Terpak, a native of Mayfield and twice world champ.

The annals of Pennsylvania sports make a rich history. The first recognized pro football game was played in Pennsylvania by Pennsylvanians. Two of the nation's seven collegiate basketball teams with more than 1000 wins are Penn and Temple. The nation's first powerhouse girls college basketball team is little Immaculata. The nation's most successful minor league franchise in any sport is the Hershey

Bears. The largest racehorse breeding ranch in the world is the Hanover Shoe Farms.

Jim Thorpe is regarded as the greatest American athlete of all time. He excelled in at least 18 sports, and learned most of them as a young man at the Carlisle Indian School.

Johnny Weissmuller was born in Windber and became Tarzan and the holder of 52 swimming titles. Yet the real Tarzan is probably Russell Chaffee, a math teacher in Sayre who at 44 in 1971 swam 214 miles of the Allegheny River from Olean, N.Y., right into the Golden Triangle.

On the National Football League rosters for 1974, there were 80 native Pennsylvanians, plus 26 on the coaching staffs. Penn State in recent years has produced more pro football players than any other university in the nation. It is accepted that the greatest quarterbacks of all time for length of their careers and flair of their playing are two Pennsylvanians, Johnny Unitas and Joe Namath. Similarly, it is true for linebackers, Chuck Bednarik and Joe Schmidt. And no one in history has played in more pro football games than the incomparable George Blanda.

Pennsylvania decided to take on the nation in schoolboy football in 1958 with the Big 33 Game. Through 1974 in ten contests against the high school All-Americans and the all-stars from Ohio and Texas, Pennsylvania was ahead in the series, 6-3-1.

With the thought that even pro, college, high school, junior high and amateur athletics were not enough, Little League Baseball Inc. was founded in Pennsylvania. Carl Stotz got it going on the sandlots of Williamsport in the 1940s.

Pennsylvania has long been enthusiastic about baseball. Alfred J. Reach, a Philadelphian, was the first paid pro ballplayer back in 1865. John Montgomery Ward (1860–1925) came out of Bellefonte to win fame in the early days as a pitcher, shortstop and manager. Ward as a student at Penn State developed one of the first curveballs in the hallways of Old Main. He went on to win 163 big-league games and make 2105 hits. In the 1879–80 seasons he pitched 117 complete games, won 82, struckout 469 and had a perfect no-hitter. Ward became John J. McGraw's personal lawyer and was a noted amateur golfer. Meanwhile, 66 Pennsylvania communities, including Carbondale, Patton, Punxsutawney and Stroudsburg, had minor-league baseball. Through

1968, Pennsylvania led the nation for putting its sons into the major leagues, 1142 of them or 275 more than its nearest rival, New York. Two of the first five immortals to the Hall of Fame were Pennsylvanians, Honus Wagner and Christy Mathewson. Both the football and baseball Halls of Fame are studded with Pennsylvanians.

Pennsylvania has had the top in coaching and management: Pop Warner, Jock Sutherland, Joe Paterno, Bert Bell, Art Rooney, Connie Mack, Joe McCarthy, Danny Martaugh, Harry Litwack, Doc Carlson, Eddie Gottlieb, Ken Loeffler, Cathy Rush, Ed McCluskey, Fred Shero, Frank Mathers, Bob Hoffman, Lawrence B. Sheppard, Rex Peery, Billy Sheridan, Hubert Jack, Bill Jeffrey, and many more.

George Ulmer and Paul Tomasovich are among the all-time champs in the world of softball. Ulmer, born in 1937, won about 600 games, including 120 no-hitters, and struck out more than 7000 batters in 15 years of pitching for the Flatiron team of the Fishtown section of Philadelphia. A grocer by occupation, he once whiffed 101 batters in four days. Tomasovich, born in 1936, is a truck driver in Pittsburgh and a recognized great at third base in softball. In the Greater Pittsburgh League, he whacked a softball as far as major league home-run kings slug hard balls, but with greater frequency.

Pennsylvania leads the nation with 1.1 million hunters and 900,000 licensed fishermen. Almost 10 million pieces of game are shot a year and 6 million trout caught. There are more deer in the forests today than when William Penn was here, and the Commonwealth has 45,000 miles of rivers and streams for fishing. The 250,000-member Pennsylvania Federation of Sportsmen's Club, the spokesman for all this outdoor life, is one of the most effective and powerful lobbies there is. Incumbent Sen. Joseph S. Clark credits his 1968 upset loss to getting on the wrong side of the sportsmen, who were livid at his suggestion of firearm controls.

Pennsylvania contributes its share to the roar of auto racing. Mario Andretti, brought to Nazareth from Trieste at 15, was national champ in 1965–66 and 1969. Mark Donohue, of Newtown Square, educated as a mechanical engineer, won the 1972 Indianapolis 500. Before retiring at 36 to become president of Penske Racing, Donohue had career earnings of more than $2 million. Kenny Weld, of Loganville, was the 1974 sprint car champ.

Bill "Grumpy" Jenkins, of Downingtown, is one of the nation's top drag racers. At 41 in 1972, the 5-foot-4 Jenkins won $260,000 with his lead foot on the pedal roaring down the asphalt.

Al Lippman and Ray Fischer of the Quaker City Darting Association are the most formidable twosome at the corkboard in the American colonies. "Al the Iceman" is the only person to win the U.S. Darting championship two consecutive years. Lippman and Fischer headed the Philadelphians who stuck the first defeat on a touring English professional dart team in 10 years.

Pennsylvania is outstanding in weightlifting, wrestling and pool-shooting. The name Willie Mosconi takes care of that last category. The Commonwealth has had some superb athletes in basketball, gymnastics, handball, squash and soccer. Coach Jim Elliott's Villanova track squad copped 15 indoor eastern titles between 1956–75, and Elliott, who started coaching in 1935 after he graduated from Villanova, has trained 22 Olympians, 14 outdoor world recordholders and 31 American indoor recordholders. Of course, in golf there is Arnold Palmer; in tennis, Bill Tilden, and in sculling, John B. Kelly Sr.—the three biggest names in the histories of their sports. And so it goes.

There must be explanations as to why Pennsylvanians are so devoted to sports, and so successful too.

The Opiate of All Classes

"Why are so many so deeply involved, so caught up in emotionally in athletic events?" asked Yale philosopher Paul Weiss in his 1969 book, *Sport, A Philosophic Inquiry*. He said it was strange that philosophers never raised that question. Neither have the historians, the sociologists and other scholars, particularly in Pennsylvania.

Professorial investigation into Pennsylvania's affliction with sports is almost nonexistent. Texts professing to describe life in Pennsylvania past or present might include a paragraph or two on Pennsylvania sports, but in the back of the book. It is not just that most researchers have failed to delve into the implications that Pennsylvania sports are linked to Pennsylvania values, politics, family life, labor, education, domestic tranquility, religion or even land-use planning, but few scholars have recognized what strong ties there are.

The relatively new discipline of ethnic studies in Pennsylvania has bumped abruptly into this sports mania, though older practitioners in the field skirted it as long as possible. It was difficult to write about

Pennsylvania Catholics and not parish basketball, Pennsylvania Slavs and not neighborhood football, and Pennsylvania blacks and not their emergence into athletic prominence, yet it was done. Even the scholars of the established elites managed to overlook that athletic accomplishment was a definite rite de passage to self-esteem, manhood and social leadership. Fox hunting was part of the scene, but so was scrimmaging without a helmet. Privileged lads with such sterling WASP names as McCormick, Brooke, Aukerman, Saxman, Hewitt, and Hickok were among the earliest of Pennsylvania's great athletes.

The lapse in scholarship is especially embarrassing because in the manner in which black achievement in sports has been ignored and the exclusion of women from Pennsylvania sports never acknowledged.

Sports had a major role in the development of Pennsylvania. The need—often the obsession—with athletics reflected the social and personal conditions of living in a state such as this.

No state in the nation has had such a variety of religious and ethnic groups as Pennsylvania. Furthermore, with the geography of separating mountains and streams, the Commonwealth became a network of hundreds of isolated communities, many of them one-industry towns. The state's two biggest cities are at its farthest ends. Some 3 million Pennsylvanians still live in communities under 20,000 population, and there are 30 cities and 112 boroughs with populations between 7000 and 25,000. It was in these pockets that the immigrants settled to work in the mills, mines, forests or on the railroad.

Management was tough and penurious. The political structure of Pennsylvania supported management flagrantly until the 1920s. Exploitation was all too common, upward mobility and acculturation difficult, and the annals of the Pennsylvania workingman drip with the blood of labor strife and occupational death and maiming.

Sports had a serious two-fold role to play—an emotional outlet from the workaday world and a bond for the community or ethnic group. If an occasional boy made it out to a professional athletic career and economic freedom, that was an added bonus.

When Stanley Coveleski, the spitball ace from Shamokin, was inducted into the Hall of Fame at Cooperstown in 1969, he recalled that in 1902 he "started working in the mines 11 hours a day, six days a week, for $3.75 a week." It was not strange for a 12-year-old Polish boy to be so employed. "What was strange," he said, "was that I even got out of there." Stanley and Harry Coveleski were the youngest of five boys, and the only two to make it into the middle class. Stanley won 216 big-league games and Harry, 84. To fit the boxscore, they changed their name from Kowalewski.

Joe McCarthy was a fatherless boy working for $6.50 a week in the textile mills near Germantown. He too headed into baseball and was a fair minor-league second baseman but a great manager in the big time, winning nine pennants. Stanley "Bucky" Harris, another New York Yankees manager, at 13 worked in the coal mines at Pittston. He took $2 to play semi-pro, lost his eligibility for the Sunday School League, but was signed on as a profesisonal by Hughie Jennings, also of Pittston. Jennings was an Irishman and Big Ed Walsh was a Polish boy from nearby Plains. When Walsh pitched for the Chicago White Sox and Jennings was manager and shortstop for the Detroit Tigers, Hughie would holler, "Your real name is Wallonski. You stole a good Irish name just as you stole the pennies out of the poor box." Then Walsh would uncork a spitball. In 1908—a year 678 Pennsylvania hard-coal miners were killed—Walsh won 40 games throwing spitballs.

Coveleski, McCarthy, Harris, Jennings and Walsh are in the Hall of Fame. The ambitious Jennings also is the only lawyer enshrined at Cooperstown.

For decades the railroads and steel companies, in particular, supported community and semi-pro athletic teams. The plutocracy enjoyed sports—as young men, they had been the leaders at college in baseball, football and wrestling. The executive suite also recognized that athletics served as an escape valve, a compensatory outlet, for the emotions and even violence of the steelworkers, miners and trainmen who, had they had idle time on their hands, might have taken action against their oppressors. Pennsylvania newspapers' in-depth coverage of sports and famous criminals up until World War II reflects the conscious effort there was by those in social authority to divert the attention of the common people from their tedious, arduous, dangerous and unwanted occupations. Many a politician played baseball with the boys, and then walked back into the legislative chambers to vote against a child labor restriction bill. Athletics unquestionably was a form of aggression transference in Pennsylvania. It still is. "That is what sports is all about—it takes the pressure off the front page," Joe Garagiola, the old Pirates catcher, exclaimed on television in 1974.

An impersonal clog at the factory or in the mine, condemned often to live in the most sordid steel and mining towns, Pennsylvania males took to athletics eagerly. The first generation thought their sons lazy and shiftless for putting so much effort into just play. The young saw sports, however, as a means for status, self-recognition, heroics and affiliation they could not get elsewhere. Their thinking was expressed best long ago by Homer in the *Odyssey*: "There is no greater glory for a man as long as he lives than that which he wins by his own hands and feet."

Just as games are self-contained time units, the process toward becoming an accomplished athlete invariably is a matter of combining training time with skill, strength and energy. The selection process can be ruthless, but usually it is fair. Models of excellence and expectations of performance are clearer in sports than in most of life. And, unlike laboring, playing sports can be highly personal and self-fulfilling. There is a sense of identity and destiny to becoming an accomplished athlete —and the careers of a Joe Namath, Wilt Chamberlain or Stan Musial have a sequential plot of achievement that makes their life stories, unlike those of their successful hometown classmates, so fascinating.

Art Rooney of the Steelers said Pennsylvania is good in sports simply because of "the type of people, the hard-working people, steelworkers and coal miners and people like that."

Hundreds of Pennsylvania communities immersed themselves in sports. Beaver Falls, Nanticoke, Mahanoy City, Lock Haven, the ethnic pockets of the big cities—certainly sports was as important an activity as anything else in town, unless the factory chimney stopped belching smoke. The communities took to athletics with an innocent avarice. Sport records and heroes—the district and state championship titles embellished on the back of varsity jackets in fading school colors— became the boast and the history, as well as the substance, of many towns. The home team was as important as the church, and much more vital than municipal beautification. The most cooperative people—towns like Ambridge, Steelton and Swoyersville—became the most competitive sports fans.

Jason Miller in *That Championship Season* portrays a town of dress factories, car lots, bars and empty mines, where a man's contentment was had in replaying the great games in his head. This fictional Lackawanna Valley community of 5,400 won the state basketball title in 1952 (actually, Farrell won Class A and Avalon won Class B that year, both Western Pennsylvania towns). Twenty years later at the team reunion the mayor sadly admits that nothing has been more gratifying, not even winning election, than having been a starter on that wonderful team.

In the twilight of his writing career, John O'Hara looked back at the real Gibbsville where he had grown up. "Most men settle for a routine interest in baseball, a conventional partisanship toward the alma mater football team, and a participation in golf during the good-weather months," he observed. "But in towns where sports generally are taken seriously, the boys never get cured. Boston is a good sports town, so is Buffalo, N.Y., and so is Pottsville, Pa."

When the Pennsylvania father knew his son would not follow him into the mill or the mines, sports became his link with the boy—often his tie by memories to his own youth. Athletic clubs and booster groups have a long history in Pennsylvania, each outdoing the other with even longer annual banquets.

A particular aspect of Pennsylvania sports is how it became so much a family tradition. The Skladanys of Larksville, the Michaelses of Swoyersville, the Namaths of Beaver Falls and the Blandas of Young-wood produced a tribe of brothers for the gridiron. Charley Gelbert Sr. was a great football player and Charley Jr. a major league shortstop. Leroy Kelly of Philadelphia starred in football and his brother Pat in baseball. Pennsylvania wrestling is filled with father-son or brother combinations. The Beck brothers were Harrisburg's most legendary athletes. Tony Orsini of Hummelstown was a fine back at Penn State and his three sons played at Notre Dame, Temple and Penn State. Bert Bell was a Penn quarterback who became football commissioner, brother John was an All-American soccer player and tennis star who became Pennsylvania's chief justice, and a sister married Hobey Baker the great Princeton halfback. Temple soccer coach Walter Bahr's son Chris became an All-American soccer player as well as the holder of Penn State's football field-goal record. Oney Doyle, of Swatara Town-ship, was the state's 100-yard dash champion, and 25 years later his daughter Angel Doyle tied the world's woman mark for the 60-yard dash. Steve Suhey was All-American guard for the Nittany Lions. His son Paul was the 1975 schoolboy heavyweight wrestling champion, while sons Matt and Larry both made the Big 33 team. In fact, in the 19 years of the Big 33, there have been 21 sets of Pennsylvania broth-ers outstanding in sports.

The John B. Kelly story of Philadelphia undoubtedly is Pennsylva-nia's most dramatic family athletic adventure. Bricklayer J. B. Sr. won three Olympic gold medals as an oarsman and held U.S. amateur championships in every phase of sculling. A handsome, 6-foot-2 athlete, he was called the "Adonis of the Schuylkill." He also excelled in ama-teur baseball and football, and as a businessman developed the nation's largest bricklaying firm. He revived the Philadelphia Democratic Party in 1935, but narrowly lost winning the mayorship.

Kelly Sr. was denied an opportunity to compete in the Royal Henley Regatta of 1920 because he was a workingman. Incensed at the insult, he trained his son Jack from childhood to win the Diamond Sculls. In 1945 at 18, Jack went to the Thames but lost. In 1947, wearing his dad's green cap, he went back and won. Then he won again in 1949, and meanwhile took the bronze medal in the Olympics and also snared the Pennsylvania bricklaying championship. Today he is a Philadelphia councilman.

The Kellys, with Princess Grace as Jack's sister, have been called the Kennedys of Pennsylvania. The Kennedys were better politicians, but the Kellys were better athletes.

The Brills had a different father-son story. Martin Brill entered Penn but could not make the football team as a sophomore. Many Philadelphians believed that the quick, little halfback was simply discriminated against because he was Irish. Marty transferred to Notre Dame, and on Nov. 9, 1930, the Fighting Irish played the Quakers before 80,000 at Franklin Field. Marty's father, J. Edward Brill, was a truck manufacturer and he told his son he would give him $1,000 for every touchdown he scored against his former team. Marty carried the ball just 10 times, but he dashed 25, 38 and 67 yards for scores and intercepted a pass in Notre Dame's 60–20 victory. That game earned Marty Brill $3,000 and All-American honors.

Pennsylvania's family tradition in sports has been strickly male. The women who earned recognition in athletics have been conspicuous, and it is only in the past few years that the absence of women athletes was noticed. "Historically, girls have had limited interscholastic opportunities," the Pennsylvania Department of Education reported Nov. 1, 1974, in issuing a directive of the State Board of Education. A new age is dawning. In the 1975–76 school year, districts must provide girls with equal access to all athletics, including coaching and funding. For the first time, no rules will be allowed that exclude girls from trying out, practicing or competing on boys' interscholastic teams.

In this heavy-industry, ethnic, workingman state, the woman's place was in the home, the office or the hospital ward, but not on the playing field. And the secondary, supportive and sedentary position of women in sports fits the Pennsylvania pattern, because they suffered similar discrimination in politics, business and other endeavors.

There were few exceptions to the rule of Pennsylvania women not even being seen in sports. The late Ruth McGinnis, of Honesdale, was the woman's pocket-billiards champion of the 1930s and 1940s. Eleanor Engle, of Shiremanstown, tried out with the Harrisburg Senators in 1952 as an infielder, but never broke baseball's sex barrier. Margaret Varner, Bette Meade and a few other Philadelphia area women have been outstanding squash players, and there were good field hockey players and amateur horse women. Cynthia Sullivan Anzolut, of Harrisburg, was president of the Ladies Professional Golf Association, 1969–73, and in 1974 Carol Semple, of Sewickley, won the British

Amateur title, Debbie Massey, of Bethlehem, the Canadian Amateur, and Lori Nelson, of West Chester, the World Junior crown. Occasionally there was a good tennis player, like Tory Fretz, but that was about the sum of Pennsylvania woman athletes.

The breakthrough came only in the 1970s, accompanying the national awareness of the gender problem. Immaculata College's string of national basketball crowns did as much as anything to spotlight the skill and excitement there can be in women's sports. Joan Moore Rice, of Philadelphia, went to the 1972 Olympics as a gymnast and Linda Myers, of York, as an archer. Gymnast Ann Carr, of Philadelphia, and sprinter Angel Doyle, of Swatara Township, are hopefuls for the 1976 Olympics. Miss Doyle, of Central Dauphin East High School, was only 16 when she tied a world 60-yard dash record in 1975. She could be Pennsylvania's first great black woman athlete.

Pennsylvania's ethnic groups played a large role in making sports a major educational function, as well as a community pastime. As a means of keeping their ethnic identities, the Slavs, Italians, Irish, Polish, Jews and others took to athletics in a big way. Dr. John E. Bodnar, head of the ethnic studies program of the Pennsylvania Historical and Museum Commission, found in his research how the Slavs, for example, created a statewide network of leagues. Steelton teams of ethnic groups would travel as far as Western Pennsylvania for games. The ethnic press was laudatory to its sports heroes. To this day, Pete Maravich, a native of Aliquippa, receives ample news coverage, as do other stars.

The ethnic dominance of sports was delayed. The Grundy-type manufacturers successfully fought off adequate child labor legislation for decades. It was not until World War I that a youngster was required to have six years of schooling before working papers could be issued. It took strong unionization—and in steel that was not until the late 1930s —before ethnic groups were into politics and their representatives were getting elected to local school boards and municipal councils. The historical mesh could not have been better coordinated. The second-generation immigrants, unlike their job-indentured fathers, were playing sports. The ethnic groups were assuming community power and the old-line elites were evacuating the cities and towns for suburban living. Acquiring authority, the ethnic groups emphasized school and community rivalry in varsity sports, and this is a major reason why Pennsylvania became notorious for its competitiveness.

Winning sports, it often seemed, became a major goal of the hometown high school. While physical education usually was ignored, the importance of varsity athletics was exaggerated. Training a promising boy to excel on the playing field was considered an aspect of vocational education, which in its strict sense for many Pennsylvanians it was. The schoolboy star was the town hero, and the coach usually was more well-known than the mayor and invariably was one of the highest paid educators. Coaches would even assume the role of the village secular priest, as the one in *That Championship Season* said: "Teaching the game was not just a profession, it was a vocation. Like a priest. Devoted my life to excellence, superiority. . . . You boys are my real trophies."

When Stan Musial was accepted into the Hall of Fame at Cooperstown in 1969, he introduced his mother, his family but then the mother of his old Donora coach. He praised Coach Michael Duda, as well as his own parents and the hometown, for making him what he became. Dr. Duda by then was president of California State College, which like Donora High, emphasized athletics.

In the last 20 years the mania for schoolboy sports has abated somewhat across Pennsylvania, or at least there are other schooltime diversions. Coaches, like Mike Duda, headed off into administration until it often seems that there are more old athletes in swivel chairs than there are in locker rooms. The teacher organizations having insisted that coaches be treated no better than other instructors. The job is not the plum it once was. Nor are all the girls enamoured by the star halfback. But this change, whether it is all for the good, has not been allowed to happen abruptly. In 1971 when the Philadelphia School Board sought to balance its tight budget by curtailing some competitive athletic programs, the populace was up in arms. Retired board president Richardson Dilworth called the public's reaction "revolting." A former oarsman, football player and Marine Corps hero, Dilworth said, "For three years, we announced cutbacks in the reading programs, educational improvement programs and activities programs without a complaint." Superintendent Mark Shedd huffed, "What this says is that the people who make the noise have a distorted sense of values." Distorted or not, varsity sports stayed in the budget.

Stanley Frank Musial was the product of a sports environment, and he didn't turn out too badly. The son of an immigrant Polish steelworker, Musial was born in 1920 and grew up on Donora's Heslep Avenue in the midst of the Depression. Even when he first started to play sports, he was a poised, natural athlete. He saw his first organized baseball on the sandlots when he was 15. Monessen was four runs ahead, so young Musial was sent in to pitch by Joe Barbao, a zinc worker who was coach. Stan fanned 13 batters in a few innings. In high school, the 6-foot 175-pound Musial was a star basketball player but the Pirates and Tigers scouted him and decided he could never make the

(National Baseball Hall of Fame)

Stan Musial

majors as a pitcher. Everyone overlooked his hitting, but his fellow first baseman, Joe Dzik, now police chief of Fallowfield Township. Dzik kept the team's bunting bat, because Stosh Musial used it as a kid. The bat is varnished and on display in Dzik's living room.

The Musial story is the American dream come true. He came from nothing but a good, hardworking family. He signed with the St. Louis Cardinals for $65 a month, and in his third minor league season at Daytona, where he won 18 games, he injured his shoulder making a diving catch as a temporary outfielder. Manager Dickie Kerr took Musial and his expectant wife into his home, converted Musial to a full-time outfielder and never fooled with his synchronized, uncoiling batting style. The next season, 1941, Musial hit .379 at Springfield, Mo., and .326 at Rochester before he went up to hit .426 with the Cards. He was 20 years old. In all, he played 22 years—made the All-Star squad in 20 of them. His 3630 hits and his 3026 games rank him just behind Ty Cobb and Hank Aaron.

Musial hit 475 home runs—seven more in All-Star games. He struck out less than an average of twice a week, was most valuable player three times, has a career average of .331, and received 93 percent of the votes to make the Hall of Fame the first time he was eligible.

Stan the Man retired from active ball in 1963, and a decade later a market research poll listed him first among sports personalities as the athlete the public liked best and trusted the most for endorsements. "Stanley was what every father wants his son to be," Branch Rickey once said. "His social habits were beyond reproach. His desire on the field was tremendous. His natural skills made him an effortless performer. He was the model player." Brooks Robinson is just one contemporary major leaguer who says his boyhood idol was Stan Musial.

A Musial, or a Namath or Blanda, made it up from an ethnic heritage through conventional channels. Other Pennsylvanians had to be just as enterprising in a less structured athletic system.

Eddie Gottlieb's Philadelphia Sphas—for the South Philadelphia Hebrew Association—lasted 29 years, winning basketball games up and down the East Coast. They were an ethnic-based powerhouse, with stars like Howard "Red" Rosan, Inky Lautman, Gil Fitch, Red Wolfe, Moe Goldman, Shikey Gotthoffer, Herman "Red" Klotz and Harry Litwack, who became the great Temple coach. David "Cy" Kaselman played 14 years, 1928–41, and in that time the Sphas won 11 Eastern or American Basketball League titles. Kaselman may have been the most accurate two-handed setshot artist and foul shooter who ever played basketball. One season he hit 247 of 261 free throws.

The Wilkes-Barre Barons of the postwar American Basketball League were another community-ethnic based team. With Cas Ostrowski and brothers Steve and Billy Chanecka, and the theme song, "I'm Looking Over a Four-Leaf Clover," the Barons won four straight ABL crowns. On March 20, 1949, they set a pro scoring record of 127 points against the Hartford Hurricanes, which had John Bach, the current Penn State hoop coach, as its star. The Barons beat the New York Knicks and the Syracuse Nationals, and all of Wyoming Valley fondly remembers them as invincible.

Soccer, stressing individual skill and teamwork, has been much like basketball as an outlet for the talented in ethnic communities. The Lighthouse Boys Club in Philadelphia was one of the early hotbeds, producing many stars such as Walt Chyzowych, who became a standout with Temple and the Philadelphia Atoms and is coach of the powerful Philadelphia Textile College team. At the high-school level, Girard College and Northeast were deadly rivals. By 1973, when a statewide scholastic championship at last was established, 167 schools had varsity soccer. West Snyder High took the crown the first year and its neighbor, Middleburg, in 1974. Collegiate teams like Philadelphia Textile, West Chester, Penn, Temple, East Stroudsburg, Penn State and Elizabethtown have had many winners in the postwar years, while the Ukrainian Nationals of Philadelphia and the Atoms were either the U.S. pro champions or contenders.

Pennsylvania has volumes of ethnic sport stories and heroes. Some go back to at least the 1890s. At that time Edward J. Abbaticchio was the kicker for his hometown Latrobe pro football team. He eventually became a big-league infielder for 10 seasons with the Phillies, Pirates and Red Sox. His name was the bane of sportswriters, and they usually misspelled it when he was booting points for Latrobe. Often the newspapers did not seem to care, as it was a "foreign name." On some occasions in print, the writers bluntly referred to him as "Awful Name." Little did they know that in their future sports pages would be such not-uncommon Pennsylvania names as Pierantozzi, Iacavazzi, Filipowicz, Biletnikoff, Kowalkowski, Hrivnak, Romaniszyn and Drazenovich.

Black Luster

The Pennsylvania sports scene before World War II was virtually all white. There was no written policy against having black athletes. At the schoolboy level, they did compete but only an occasional Negro boy made it to college. The most notable exception was in track. John Woodruff, of Connellsville, a 6-foot-3 freshman at Pitt, won the 1936 Olympic gold medal in the 800-meter race. "The Black Shadow of

Pittsburgh," Damon Runyon described him. A pulled muscle prevented Ben Johnson, of Plymouth, from making that 1936 team. Johnson, as a Columbia University track star, set four world records, including one for the 60-meter dash that still stands. Barney Ewell, of Lancaster, was renowned as a high school sprinter in the late 1930s. He went on to Penn State and in the 1948 Olympics, when he was 30, Ewell won three medals.

It was in the postwar years that the Pennsylvania blacks burst forth. Chuck Cooper, of Pittsburgh and Duquesne University, was one of the first four blacks to sign with the National Basketball Association in 1950. He went to the Boston Celtics, while New York and Washington put blacks under contract before the hesitant Philadelphia Warriors did. Cooper led the way for Wilt Chamberlain, Maurice Stokes, Dick Ricketts, Guy Rodgers and other black stars from Pennsylvania in the hoop game.

Chamberlain, and later baseball players Dick Allen and Reggie Jackson, quickly became national leaders in black assertiveness. These talented blacks' outspokenness was directed more for their own independence as individuals than for the black movement nationwide. As superstars, they willingly traded away popularity, but gained respect, sometimes grudgingly, in return. Interestingly, in the early 1970s, four of the five most controversial American athletes were Pennsylvanians— Joe Namath, Bill Hartack, Chamberlain, Allen and, of course, the fifth, Muhammad Ali, who trains in the Poconos. Not unexpectedly, the blacks seemed to receive more criticism for their independent life-style than the white unconventional stars.

Wilton Norman Chamberlain, of Overbrook, grew up in a family of nine children. His father was a handyman and his mother a domestic. At birth 29 inches long, Wilt emerged 7-foot-1 fully grown, the first well-coordinated giant in sport history, potentially capable of being an Olympic track star and heavyweight boxing champion as well as a great basketball player. A bright man, he once said that if he had been only 6-foot-2, he would have become a Philadelphia lawyer. His very size prejudiced the public's accepting the fact of how he dominated professional basketball. He holds the pro scoring record of 31,419 points, the highest lifetime average of 30.1, the most minutes played and the most rebounds. At the Hersheypark Arena on March 2, 1962, against the New York Knicks, Wilt set an all-time pro record of 100 points. A notoriously poor foul shooter, Chamberlain that night also set an NBA record of 28 foul points, missing only four tosses.

Pennsylvania's attitude toward the black in most endeavors, not only sports, long was one of more ostracism than outright hostility. Nowhere

(Harrisburg *Patriot-News*)

Wilt Chamberlain scoring 100 points at Hershey

was this more true than in pro baseball. Robert W. Peterson, a native of Warren, told the story in his excellent, 1970 book, *Only the Ball Was White.*

The first black professional ballplayer was Bud Fowler, who in 1872 played on a white team in New Castle. An occasional black could make a team until about 1900. A Harrisburg club in 1891, for example, was called the Polka Dots because it allowed black ballplayers. At the turn of the century, organized ball went all white. To play baseball before World War II, the blacks had to form their own leagues, and in Pennsylvania there were such teams as the Crawfords, Colored Stars and Keystones in Pittsburgh, the Homestead Grays, the Giants and Bacharach Giants in Philadelphia, the Harrisburg Giants and the Hilldale Daisies of Darby.

The Athletics, Phillies and Pirates coolly ignored such stars as Josh Gibson, Roy Campanella and William "Judy" Johnson, all now members of the Hall of Fame. Rap Dixon, a power-hitting outfielder from Steelton, played with the Harrisburg Giants, the Homestead Grays and the Pittsburgh Stars and Crawfords, but never got a chance in the big leagues. Johnson, from Snow Hill, Md., was with the Daisies, Grays and Crawfords and was a tremendous third baseman, but the best he could do for the white big leagues was scout for Connie Mack.

Cumberland W. "Cum" Posey Jr. died in 1946, just as Jackie Robinson entered the white man's game. Posey, a black, grew up in Homestead, was a basketball star at Penn State and Duquesne, and became an outfielder for the Grays. He took control of the club in 1912, at the same time he coached Homestead High basketball. Later he was a Homestead school director, a stockholder in the Pittsburgh *Courier,* and secretary of the Negro National League. His Grays and Gus Greenlee's Crawfords had such stars as Satchell Paige, Oscar Charlestown, Buck Leonard, Rap Dixon, Smokey Joe Williams, Cool Papa Bell, Judy Johnson and Gibson, yet they could only use Forbes Field when the Pirates were out of town.

It would have been interesting to see the 1931 Grays play Mack's World Series champion Athletics or the fifth and sixth placed Pirates and Phillies. The Grays that year had a touring record of 186–17, not a fluke because the following year they were 99–36.

Josh Gibson never earned more than $1,000 a month, but unquestionably he was one of the greatest baseball players who ever lived. He was born in Georgia in 1911, but at 12 he was brought to Pittsburgh's North Side. His father was a steel laborer. Josh dropped out of the ninth grade and from 1929–45 was a catcher.

Gibson hit at least 623 home runs in his career. One season he

(National Baseball Hall of Fame)

Josh Gibson

whacked 89, another season, 75. At 6-foot-1 and 215 pounds, he could ride a ball. He hit what is regarded as the longest ball ever in Yankee Stadium; in fact, it remains the only home run to leave the stadium. In Monessen, he knocked one and the mayor ordered the game stopped for a tape measure. The ball had traveled 512 feet. He drove one pitch over the centerfield fence of Forbes Field, something Willie Stargell never did. Yet when he died on Jan. 20, 1947, at only 35, he received a one-column headlined obituary in the Pittsburgh newspapers. The big sports story of the day was that the Pirates now owned two renowned sluggers, Ralph Kiner and Hank Greenberg.

"Henry Aaron, Mays, Musial, Williams, great hitters," said Roy Campanella once, "but Josh Gibson was the best hitter I ever saw."

There is a wonderful tall tale about Gibson's hitting one for the Crawfords that went so high in the Pittsburgh smog that it didn't come down and the umpire ruled it a home run. The next day the Crawfords were playing in Philadelphia, and out of the sky dropped the ball and the centerfielder caught it. Pointing to Gibson, the umpire shouted, "Yer out—yesterday in Pittsburgh."

Roy Campanella, ten years younger than Gibson, did make the big leagues. He was born Nov. 19, 1921, in Philadelphia, the son of an Italian fruit peddler and a black mother. As a kid, he started ball with the neighborhood Nicetown Giants, and at 14 he was a pro with the Bacharach Giants for $35 a weekend. After Robinson and Don Newcombe were signed by the Brooklyn Dodgers, Campanella was put under contract. He made it to the majors after two and a half years in the minors. Roly-poly No. 39 broke in with 9 hits out of 12 times at bat, including two home runs. In all, he spent ten years in the big time, hit .276, outdid every previous catcher with 242 home runs and was the most valuable player in 1951, 1953 and 1955. In one 51-game stretch, nobody stole a base against him. But Campanella's luck ran out the January after he retired. In 1958 he was severely paralyzed in an automobile accident and has remained confined to a wheelchair.

Dick Allen and Reggie Jackson are Pennsylvania blacks who followed Campanella with perhaps even greater natural talent. Both came from broken homes. Allen led Wampum to 82 straight basketball victories as a schoolboy. At 5-foot-11, he became baseball's strongest pocket-sized slugger since Jimmy Foxx. Jackson did the 100-yard dash in 9.7 seconds for Cheltenham High School. A tremendous football prospect, he chose pro baseball as his game to excel.

The racial sports record book should have one footnote. On Sept. 1, 1971, the Pirates in Pittsburgh unknowingly fielded the first all-black team in 102 years of major league baseball. Manager Danny Murtaugh,

(National Baseball Hall of Fame)

Roy Campanella

a native of Chester, started a line-up of Stennett, Clines, Clemente, Stargell, Sanguillen, Cash, Oliver, Hernandez and Ellis, and they defeated the Phillies, with two blacks in their line-up, 10–7. The Pirates happened to have a roster of 14 whites, six blacks and seven Latins. Murtaugh was unaware that he had made baseball history. "When it comes to making out the line-up, I'm color blind and my athletes know it," he said.

By the 1970s, Pennsylvania sports are farther ahead in racial integration than virtually any other institution in society. It is a genuine integration, a fact so accepted that it is not even mentioned. Similarly, the black's emergence to fame in the sporting world is taken for granted. This book lists 250 of the top native-born Pennsylvania athletes in baseball, basketball and football. By coincidence, 40 are black. That is 16 percent, and only 9 percent of Pennsylvania's population is black.

The Joy of Competing

With its tremendous love of athletics, Pennsylvania also is notorious for having "dumb jocks" and also having the worst fans this side of Latin America. Both charges should be put aside.

Very few Pennsylvanians who ever made it big in American sports were "dumb." The opposite could be said of Art Rooney, Joe Namath, Wilt Chamberlain, Arnold Palmer, Willie Mosconi, Christy Mathewson, Harry Greb and a host of others. If not prominent academicians, such outstanding athletes invariably outdo a vast majority of their contemporaries for their realistic, level-headed and emotionally controlled approach to tense, competitive situations.

Anyone with an acquaintanceship with athletes tires quickly of the unsubstantiated charges that even more than a handful end up boozehounds with scattered brains. Fritzie Zivic in boxing and Frank Mathers in hockey were not in the most gentle of livelihoods, but they are bright, alert, well-educated and respectable middle-age citizens today.

The indiscriminate charge of stupidity toward athletes often masks a dislike of ethnic or racial groups. "Gum-wacking yowsers" is one of the terms used in Western Pennsylvania, for example. Some critics get ridiculous enough to maintain there is a difference between "academic I.Q." and "athletic I.Q.," as if there were such criteria and they had been properly measured.

Genuine Pennsylvania sport fans can out-argue the "dumb" theory without much difficulty. Mansfield's star basketball player Tom McMillen was a Rhodes scholar. Wampum's great Don Hennon turned from basketball to medicine, as did Penn's great end from its glory days, Hunter Scarlett. Coach Harold "Red" Carlson of Pitt was an M.D. in the Pittsburgh Public Health Department for 32 years. Jock Sutherland, the football immortal, was a dentist. Basketball's great coach Ken Loeffler was a lawyer, as was football's four-time All-American, T. Truxton Hare. William E. Kerstetter, of Lykens, won letters in basketball and track and probably was Dickinson College's greatest soccer player. Today he is president of DePauw University. The list is endless.

Two of Pennsylvania's finest governors, John K. Tener and Gifford

Pinchot, were accomplished athletes. Pinchot played football and tennis and even when he was 60 loved to challenge anyone to a foot race. "The man who thinks about nothing but work is inevitably consumed by it," he wrote in a book on fishing. "In a sense, our best work is done in play time."

Curious about how "jocks" make out in the supposed "real game of life," J. Clyde Barton of the Pitt Athletic Department traced 1678 Pitt lettermen from 1900–60. He received 1391 replies to his survey, and found that 512, or 37 percent, had earned advanced degrees.

The more difficult complaint to handle is the charge that Pennsylvania breeds the nation's worst sport fans. The finger invariably is pointed at Philadelphia—"Boodom" of the American sporting scene. The Philadelphia fans booed President Herbert Hoover at the 1931 World Series. At an Eagles game, the fans threw snowballs at Santa Claus. On April 22, 1973, the Easter Bunny was presented at Veterans Stadium, and they booed him. It has been said that Philadelphians would boo an announcement that a cure for cancer had been discovered.

Pennsylvanias love winners. And they have had them—Connie Mack's old Athletics, Art Rooney's modern Steelers, the Philadelphia Sphas, the Homestead Grays, the Wilkes-Barre Barons, the Pottstown Firebirds, the Carlisle Indians, the Pottsville Maroons, so much of our college football to modern-day Joe Paterno's Penn State, Arnold Palmer, the great boxers, the Immaculata girls, and such high schools as Farrell, Sharon, Beaver Falls, New Castle, Mahanoy City, Camp Hill, Middletown, old Harrisburg Tech, Roman Catholic, Northeast, Schlenley, Westinghouse, Overbrook, Lancaster Catholic for girls basketball, Girard College for soccer, and other schools that in specific sports in given eras can't seem to lose for winning.

But Pennsylvanians also endure losers. And they have had them—Connie Mack's old Athletics, the Phillies and Eagles of yesteryear, the old Steelers, and the 1972 Philadelphia 76ers with a record of 9–73, the worst in NBA history. The 1926 Reading Keystoners of the International League probably were organized baseball's worst team. "Chronic losers," as the Reading *Eagle* termed them, they finished with a 31–129 mark, or .194, a baseball record of 75 games behind the pennant winner. But even the Keystoners did not kill baseball in Reading, for that city in 1975 remained the last Pennsylvania community with minor-league ball.

A super-intellectual, Norman Podhortz, wrote in 1973: "There are towns like Philadelphia that seem to be a curse on sports. No matter what anyone does, all the Philadelphia teams are a disaster." That was penned a few months before the Flyers won the Stanley Cup and 2 million Philadelphians jammed Independence Mall to toast the "Broad Street Bullies."

Perhaps the real complaint underneath the charge that Pennsylvanians are lousy sport fans is not that they are, but that athletics might be overemphasized in this Commonwealth. It is not unnatural that Pennsylvanians support winning teams more than they do losing teams, but it is a tribute to their devotion—and their civic restraint—that they keep their anguish in check as well as they do with some persistent losers.

The blunter question of overemphasis of Pennsylvania athletics is not easily answered. Pennsylvanians certainly do not stress physical education and lifetime recreation, but many other states vie with Pennsylvania in their affliction with varsity sports. That is a national obsession, if it is that.

Yet if there is a worship of sports in Pennsylvania—and that is exaggerating the description of "interest" far beyond what is the reality —are Pennsylvanians any the poorer for it?

Considering the awesome tasks down through the decades of raising children, of filling leisure time for youths and adults, of defusing human aggressiveness, of providing adequate emotional relief from empty occupations, subsistent living and discrimination, of finding neutral ground and perhaps understanding among races, religions, life-styles and incomes, and of avoiding social anomie—hasn't sports met the challenge as well, or better, than most other endeavors?

We might ask ourselves: If there weren't all that practicing, all those "big games," all that barroom and parlor talk, all that sports-page reading, all that simple but amazingly pleasant and thoroughly human chatter and curiosity about Pennsylvania sports, what would we have in its place? A void? Would the personal and social nihilism foreseen in science fiction be one step closer? Or would we be at each other's throats in more serious games of ideology, race or religion? Would the elimination of competitive athletics be a solution to anything?

Subtract sports and many Pennsylvania towns even today would sink back into a vague oblivion. They would lose a vital component of their identity. Their cohesiveness and their socialization capability to have all ages, incomes, races and ethnics live together, even as well as they do, would slip. Few divided communities have unified, thriving athletic programs.

Pennsylvanians have chosen to play the game.

It may well be a mark of our degree of civilization, our approach to maturity, that we Pennsylvanians are so athletic-minded. Our tears of disappointment are short-lived. Our enthusiasm, we hope, prevails.

2

FOOTBALL

Beaver Falls, Football Town

... *Joe Namath's Hometown Builds Winners*

"They got great soil for growing stars in my state," Joe Namath once exclaimed. "Great football country," he said of the steel-mill towns of Beaver County, "the home of more All-Americans per square mile, I'll bet, than any other section of the country."

At last count, Namath's native Beaver County, population 210,000 on the Western Pennsylvania line, had turned out 40 professional football players.

To the east and south of Pittsburgh, less than two hours' drive from Beaver Falls, lie the bituminous fields. "That coal country of Western Pennsylvania," said George Blanda in duplicating Namath, "has produced more fine athletes per square mile than any other part of the United States."

Local pride aside, Western Pennsylvania could be the sports capital of America. For football, anyway, it must be. One of the reasons Johnny Majors accepted the Pitt Panther coaching job was that it was in the middle of what he called "the bedrock of high school football."

The landscape is one of workshops, smokestacks, bridges and railroad tracks along the curving Ohio, Beaver, Monongahela, Allegheny and Youghiogheny rivers. Much of it isn't very pretty. "The low-downdest hole in the surface of the earth," said O'Henry. "Appalling desolation," remarked H. L. Mencken, of "unbroken and agonizing ugliness . . . the most loathsome towns and villages ever seen by mortal eye."

The sun is "a filtered dull gold haze," observed Theodore Dreiser when he worked on the old Pittsburgh *Dispatch*. But there is a beauty of sorts in the reflection of the blaze of furnaces in the ripples of contaminated rivers. "Six months residence here would justify suicide," the British philosopher Herbert Spencer remarked to capitalist Andrew Carnegie in 1886.

Ernie Pyle wasn't the first to visit Western Pennsylvania and notice the strange pride taken in having a dirty collar, because enough of them indicate prosperity in steel and coal towns. Out of the hearth of the

(New York Jets)

Joe Namath

Pittsburgh area has come the nation's hardware—its steel plate, wire, tools, farm implements, glass, aluminum, industrial machinery, and armaments. When helmets were first used in World War I, Pittsburgh made more than half of them.

"What a place for a realist to work and dream in," asserted Dreiser. It is "most agreeable" for anyone interested in the unpretentious, he added.

It is also fantastic football country.

Every autumn, tremendously rough and often quite skillful football is played in the Western Pennsylvania Interscholastic Athletic League, founded during World War I and now having 133 schools in 14 conferences surrounding Pittsburgh. A similar high brand of football is played by the 14 teams in the Pittsburgh City League.

The best of this football is in the Class AA Midwestern Conference centered in Beaver County, according to Beaver Falls Coach Larry Bruno. "You just don't get many easy games in this 10-team conference," said Bruno. "You can go through a season and have your back up against the wall on every one. You get taken to lunch if you have to play more than one or two sophomores, it's that tough. Every college coach in the country knows what we've got here. When we say a boy can play in this league, he's good." Dr. Roger B. Saylor, the Penn State statistician who has been rating Pennsylvania high school football teams since 1947, agrees. "I scale the quality of the opposition, and Beaver Falls is in the toughest conference in the state," he said.

Bruno was born in nearby East Liverpool, Ohio, in 1922, but he attended Geneva College in Beaver Falls. A 5-foot-10, 170-pound halfback, he was All-State in 1947 for the Covenanters and played in that season's East-West Shrine Game in San Francisco. He was drafted by the Pittsburgh Steelers, but instead took a coaching job at Monaca. In 11 years he had a record of 52–33–5. In 1959 Bruno came back to Beaver Falls, where a tall, skinny junior by the name of Joe Willie Namath was just working his way into the quarterback position. Bruno suffered a losing season in 1959, and one more in 1964, but that is it. When the 1974 campaign was over, Bruno's mark at Beaver Falls was 106–43–8, and lifetime he has won 67 percent of his games as coach.

It was in 1960 that Beaver Falls got going. Namath was taking a false step on the snap, and Bruno corrected that. What a year it was, 9–0, with even a 39–0 victory over arch-rival New Castle. Until 1960, Beaver Falls had an embarrassing 3–16–3 record with the Lawrence County powerhouse. The two had last played in 1943. New Castle had 12 straight wins over the Tigers, 10 of them shutouts and in the other two contests Beaver Falls had scored just one touchdown a game. So in

(Author)

Larry Bruno, Beaver Falls coach

the 1960 splurge when Namath put his club over the goal, it was the first time since 1939 that Beaver Falls had tallied against New Castle.

Namath went into the New Castle game with a twisted ankle, but he completed 9 out of 13 pass attempts, ran for 63 yards and scored twice himself. He made the national All-High School Team that year, along with guard Don Croftcheck and quarterback Fred Mazurek, both of Republic in Fayette County. It was a banner year. Among the backs with Namath and Mazurek were John Huarte, Dick Butkus, Mike Curtis and Tucker Frederickson.

Even after Namath went on to the University of Alabama, the Beaver Falls Tigers kept winning. Bruno's team had an amazing 10–0 record in 1961, the Western Pennsylvania schoolboy championship, and, by the time it was all over, a 23-game winning streak. Namath acknowledges that the studious, undramatic Bruno is as capable a coach as any he has ever met in the collegiate or professional ranks. "He knows football. He works hard. He knows how to handle people," he said of

Bruno who was chairman of Beaver Falls's "Joe Namath Day" in 1969.

The coaching must be good. The 1974 Tigers were 7–1–1, again among the top Pennsylvania teams. In a town of 14,375, the high school has 958 students. Fifty-six came out for football, none quit. As usual, the Orange and Black was physically small. This is true of much of Pennsylvania football, where gigantic players are rarities. Beaver Falls has not fielded a big team since 1968. The top weight on the 1974 club was 201 pounds in the line and 190 pounds in the backfield. Bruno had to make do with determination, speed and teamwork, the ingredients he wants anyway. Typically, a Bruno team is offensive-minded. There are 83 pass patterns, and the Tigers never run the exact play twice in a game.

As much as the coaching, it is what Beaver Falls as a community puts into sports that makes it excel in football. It "creates the opportunity for the potential to mature," said Bruno. It provides boys who are not only natural athletes, but have an ingrained spirit to compete. And Beaver Falls has had that spirit since its first recorded schoolboy contest in 1904, a 16–0 win over Beaver.

"Those who stick will be champions," Bruno told his 1974 squad, noticing that on the first day of practice, July 15, that all 56 of his players already were in condition to scrimmage. In the pre-season workouts, the Tigers suffered one injury—a twisted knee. That record is almost traditional, though one of the earliest accounts of Beaver Falls football was back in 1895 and the newspapers reported a star on the YMCA team had his collarbone broken in play. Under modern high school conditions, few of the Tigers have ever gotten seriously hurt in a game.

The players come up to the varsity from a junior high squad, coached by three qualified assistant coaches. Bruno regards his junior high assistants on par with his varsity assistants, for these are the men who teach the fundamentals of the game. Beaver Falls junior high ball usually is excellent, but oddly enough the town does not have the competition in midget football that some of its neighbors have.

Beaver Falls takes its sports, especially football, as a form of vocational education.

"We think of it in that way," said Bruno. "They say we coaches in this conference work harder at college entrance for our boys than guidance counselors. But that's a big part of our job. The boys learn the game here and if they attend to their studies, their football gets them to college, and from there it can be the pros. Joe Namath had exceptional ability, but the pattern of his career could be the same for others who have skill and apply themselves."

That is not idle talk. Out of Beaver Falls came not only Namath, but Joe Walton, the great end for the Pittsburgh Panthers and New York Giants, and Jim Mutscheller, another top end for Notre Dame and the Baltimore Colts. Ken Loeffler, the great LaSalle basketball coach, grew up in the town. Beaver County, furthermore, has produced Babe Parilli, Mike Ditka, Mike Lucci, John Skorupan, Po James, Bill Koman, Tony Dorsett, basketball stars Norm VanLier and Mickey Davis, and New York Yankees pitcher George "Doc" Medich. When Namath, a C-student, went off to Alabama in 1961, ten of his teammates got athletic scholarships and all finished college. Few legitimate vo-tech courses, or academic ones for that matter, have such a superb record.

Bruno makes a college scouting roster of his seniors. It lists academic ranking, college board scores, size, speed and comments like a handicapper's. A particularly good student and 200-pound center on the Tigers, for example, was rated by Bruno and his staff as "blue chipper, best in league." A 6-foot, 200-pound linebacker was judged ready for the "big time." One small guard was rated a potential for only small-college competition. The athlete with the highest college board scores unfortunately was only 5-foot-7 and 131 pounds, but he was good enough to play for the Tigers because his rating was "small but tough."

The prevalent social and personal values of Beaver Falls gives an unusual community importance to athletics. Football doesn't make Beaver Falls. Beaver Falls makes football.

George Blanda noted about his hometown of Youngwood. "In the coal country," he said, "nobody has a whole lot, right? So they learn the pleasures of competing, and that's what produces great athletes. Did you think it was an accident that Stan Musial came from Donora, 20 miles from Youngwood, or that Arnie Palmer came from Latrobe, nine miles down the road? The list is endless."

Both Namath and Blanda have pointed out the sociological implications of their coming from poor, ethnic, seemingly physically depressing small Western Pennsylvania towns.

"I'm glad I grew up in Beaver Falls," Namath told sportswriter Dick Schaap. "It was a great place to grow up, with good people, real people, and a river and woods and athletic fields and swimming pools and rock fights and junkyards, everything a kid could want. I remember funny things, and sad times."

Said Blanda to sportswriter Jack Olsen, "As a training ground for competitiveness, you couldn't beat Youngwood. We had people subdivided into more nationalities, classes, religions and types than any sociologist ever imagined, and every group competed with every other group."

Namath's father immigrated from Hungary and spent 51 years in the mills, starting off at 23 cents an hour for a 55-hour week. Before he retired, he was measuring white-hot strips of steel in the No. 2 hot mill of Babcock and Wilcox. He wore thermal underwear all the time, because in the summers it was 120 degrees and in the winters 80 degrees.

Blanda's dad, a Slovak, mined coal 10 hours a day. He too vowed that none of his boys would follow his occupation.

George Blanda had 6 brothers and 4 sisters, and he was the number 8 child. Tom Blanda was quarterback for Army and Paul Blanda was a Pitt linebacker. "I'm known as the fourth-best kicker in the Blanda family and the third-best quarterback," George once joked.

Joe Namath was the fourth and youngest son in his family. All were fine athletes. When Joe was 6, his second brother, Bob, was the junior high quarterback. Bob taught his kid brother how to grip a ball and throw it from back of the ear. Joe credits this useful instruction for his ability to get a quick release, throw a long ball, and never have a sore arm in his entire career. When Joe signed his $427,000 bonus contract with the New York Jets, part of the deal was to include brothers Bob and Frank, as well as the husband of his adopted sister, on the Jet payroll as scouts. The Namaths, the Blandas and most others in these mill towns stick together as families, in part because of the community's long-time emphasis on economic survival, but mainly because of the common household bonds of affection.

Beaver Falls, 25 miles north of Pittsburgh, in many ways typifies the sports-fervid atmosphere of Western Pennsylvania. Yet even for the steel and coal valley towns, Beaver Falls is renowned for its unusual ardor for athletics.

The Tigers draw well, at $1.50 a head. There are police escorts to the football field, and firecrackers pop when the home team scores. For the pep rallies at school, the girls wash their hair the night before and don their best clothes. With some exceptions, athletes date the prettiest girls. There's enthusiasm for victories and dismay, but not rancor, at losses. Yet the day of the football hero as the big man in school is fading. At Beaver Falls, as it is everywhere, players, as well as coaches, are not the privileged characters they were 20 years ago. They don't get automatic esteem from fellow students and faculty as they used to.

It is easy to satirize the sports scene in such communities, but it can be grossly inaccurate to be one-dimensional about it.

A fine early postwar novel, *No Country For Old Men*, by Warren Eyster, was set in his hometown of Steelton, Central Pennsylvania's version of Beaver Falls. Eyster was highly critical of the football talk and betting in poolrooms, the service clubs' feting of star ballplayers

(Oakland Raiders)

Old Folks George Blanda

and the entire aura of glory that surrounded the exploits on the gridiron. In such an atmosphere, the fun of games was distorted. "They made victory too important and too ruthlessly sought. They could not accept victory, let alone defeat. They could not find sufficient expression for the dissatisfaction in their lives, and their eyes watched the field with the squint of hatred," wrote Eyster. One mother in the stands stood up and screamed at her son on the field, "You play hard. You don't, I get your brothers beat hell out of you. You hear, you lazy sonofabitch, you hear your mother?" In Eyster's view, the overemphasis on sports produced hollow men still in their twenties, widespread self-hatred, and a has-been town that despised intelligence and was doomed by its people's common narrowness of thinking.

Perhaps Eyster was right in the 1930s, but even then he could have misread emotions for reality. His is not a picture of today's Steelton nor, for that matter, Beaver Falls nor many of the other communities in Pennsylvania that are football-minded.

What sports does is give Beaver Falls a community identity and a cohesiveness. It is a tangible part of the town's socialization, of its convivium.

Hemmed in by mills in the heart of the 30-mile-long Beaver Valley, the community has a static population. Even now a third of its youngsters can trace their parents or grandparents back to Europe. In a nation where social centrifugation is a major urban concern, sports gives Beaver Falls a focus, and a very human one.

It is interesting in Beaver Falls, for example, that there is a minimum of social hierarchy. Even the country-club set is not that far removed. In fact, the management of the mills sends its children to public school to mingle, not self-consciously either, with the Namaths. In many mill towns, with the rise of the labor unions and lower middle class' initial participation in politics in the late 1930s, the older ethnic establishment fled the community. The spelling of names got longer on the school board and the football team. But this did not happen in Beaver Falls to any extreme degree. The town still has its representation of Presbyterian Covenanters, whose ancestors started Geneva College. The town also has a good ethnic mix, with 10 percent black and many whites of Polish, Italian, Hungarian and Croatian stock.

The school principal, Charles Pietro, is the son of Italian immigrants. He is not a former athlete either, but was music director, and Beaver Falls has a strong music program. Since all of Beaver County has only one secondary Catholic high school, Beaver Falls High is not religiously segregated either.

The school system is highly regarded by the residents of the town.

The high school was built in 1930 and a new one is planned, but it will be constructed right next to the present school, which is a block off the town's main drag. The community wants its school in the center of town, geographically as well as in importance.

"The parents respect education and property," said Pietro. "Most own their own homes, and I would say the average value is about $14,000. To us in education, the parents give great backing and understanding. They are very close, in attitude and proximity. And that is true of the teachers, too. Many of our teachers were once students here. Many still live in the neighborhoods. They know the students they teach and they know their parents. They walk to work, in fact."

Beaver County has 473 persons per square mile, so there is little crowding. Its prison rate is half Pennsylvania's and its crime rate a sixth. Beaver Falls in 1972 and 1973 had no murders, one rape and only 20 aggravated assaults. It may be as tough as its steel, but it is law-abiding. The civilities that go with citizenship are accepted. Even politics is not abrasive. A wholesome sense of freedom exists and considerable outward, at least, individuality. Persons who have worked in the town and moved on, such as Lt. Gov. Ernest P. Kline, maintain friendships back where they came from.

John O'Hara in his 1960 novel, *Ourselves to Know*, dealt with a similar Pennsylvania town. He noted the "compact, continuous conventionality" of such a place as its dominant characteristic. Its "eccentrics or their caprices" were not its boast. He observed, as is true in Beaver Falls, that "the upper class and its close connection, the middle class, successfully maintained the appearance of respectable normality."

The man who succeeded Joe Namath as the Tigers' quarterback for another undefeated season was Karlin "Butch" Ryan, a converted halfback who went on to the University of Iowa and is now one of Bruno's assistant coaches. "It's a great place," said Ryan, one of the county's 11,600 blacks.

The great Joe himself gets to Beaver Falls twice a year to see his father and mother. "He still messes around with the kids when he comes back," said his father. "I can remember when he was their age. He always wanted to be bigger. He was gifted in sports, we knew that even then, but we never thought he'd go as far as he did. I don't think Beaver Falls realized it until people saw their Joe on the television screen beating the Colts in the Super Bowl. That made an impression on this place. He was bigger than the President that day. It's funny, because Joe as a kid was always better in baseball. But, sure, he gets back. And he always asks how we did against New Castle, Aliquippa and the rest."

Pottsville Maroons and Other Heroes

... *Pennsylvania's Gridiron Glory Came Early*

"Such enthusiasm has never been recorded in Pottsville on the good side of thc ledger," the Pottsville *Republican* commented in 1925 after its Maroons dumped the Cardinals in Chicago for the world's professional football championship. And when the Maroons opened the following season to defend what they considered their rightfully won title, the *Republican* asserted, "Nowhere in the world can better football be witnessed."

These were glorious days for coal-smudged Pottsville, otherwise famous for the Molly Maguires. When the "Queen City of the Anthracite," as its devotees called it, held a testimonial for the victorious Maroons, some 300 persons attended, including one of the most ardent fans, 20-year-old John O'Hara, then a beginning reporter on the Pottsville *Journal*. The locals assailed the character of National Football League president Joe F. Carr, and then they toasted themselves and their team. The exuberance knew no end, and O'Hara later wrote that most of the town thought that "football madness" was normal behavior.

In legend, and perhaps in fact, nobody could play football quite like the Pottsville Maroons. And in actuality, no team has ever been robbed of a championship quite like the Maroons either.

The story has a significance beyond just the glory and anguish of Pottsville. For historically, the Maroons were at the end of a 30-year, exceedingly rough but exciting, and certainly disorganized infancy of professional football, much of which took place in Pennsylvania. After the Maroons, the NFL organized into a big-city, franchised league which, with the exception of the Green Bay Packers, bore slight resemblance to its upstart, humble beginnings.

Pottsville had a population of 24,300, or almost 4600 more than today. Through the initiative of local entrepreneurs with a love for football, it got into the play-for-pay game after World War I. It had a fine team in 1923, and in 1924 copped the Anthracite League championship with a 14–1 mark. It was no wonder that the 15-man Maroon squad was good, with players like Fats Henry, Doggie Julian, Barney Wentz, Vic Emanuel and the Beck brothers. Wentz, of Shenandoah, had been a halfback on Penn State's 1923 Rose Bowl team. Emanuel and the Beck boys were from the powerhouse Harrisburg Tech. Alvin "Doggie" Julian was a bright young man out of nearby Reading by way of Bucknell University. In later years he coached football at Muhlenberg College and then became one of the nation's foremost basketball coaches at Dartmouth and Holy Cross, where he directed the 1947 national champions and had such stars as Bob Cousy and Tommy Heinsohn.

Wilbur Henry, called "Pete" or "Fats," was built like a bartender. He was 5-foot-11 and 250 pounds and outrageously potbellied, but he was one of football's greatest linemen and an early member of the Hall of Fame. A native of Mansfield, Ohio, he was All-American tackle three times at Washington and Jefferson College, where later until his death in 1952 he was athletic director. Fats was with the Canton Bulldogs, and when that famed club temporarily broke up he signed with the Maroons. In a critical game against the coal-region rival, the Coaldale Big Greens, Fats popped a 55-yard field goal for a 3–0 victory.

The 1925 Maroons lost Henry, Julian and Emanuel, as well as Carl Beck, but they were an even stronger team with Jack Ernst, quarterback from Lafayette; Walter French, halfback from Army and an outfielder for Connie Mack; Charley Berry, who was Mack's catcher and had been an All-American end from Lafayette; Hoot Flanagan, a young dentist who was a halfback from Pitt; Howard "Fungy" Lebengood, a local Pottsville boy; Tony Latone, of Edwardsville who averaged 5.5 yards per carry; Barney Wentz; the Stein brothers from Niles, Ohio, and Clarence Beck, who had been a great tackle at Penn State. Russ Stein, the other Maroons tackle, had been an All-American at W & J, the successor to Fats Henry, while brother Herb Stein won All-American honors at center for Pitt. Another tough Maroons lineman was Frank H. Bucher, of Rochester, N.Y., who eventually became the executive vice president of A & P Food Stores.

The handsome Richard H. Rauch was the coach. A lineman with Clarence Beck on the 1920 undefeated Nittany Lions, Rauch had come out of Harrisburg Tech. He was an unusual man, obsessed with football but also an amateur poet and an ornithologist of some skill. He and Penn State's Dick Harlow were bird-watchers and some of the rare eggs they found were entered in the Smithsonian Institution collection. After his football days, Rauch became the keeper of the Harrisburg Zoo.

Dr. John G. Striegel, a prominent Pottsville physician, was the owner of the team.

The 1925 Maroons whipped through a 10–2 season, including a devastating 49–0 win over the Frankford Yellow Jackets before 9000 fans at Minersville. Flanagan scored four touchdowns, two of them on gallops of 90 and 55 yards. Ernst completed 10 out of 15 passes, hitting French for two scores. Berry caught a touchdown pass and kicked a 20-yard field goal. The rival Yellow Jackets were not exactly pushovers, either. In 1924 they finished third in the league with an 11–2–1 record and in 1925 had a 12–7 season, including an earlier 20–0 win over Pottsville.

On Dec. 6, 1925, the Maroons traveled to Chicago's Comiskey Park to meet the big Cardinals, starring one of football's finest heroes, Paddy Driscoll. The Cards were heavily favored in the 18-degree cold. Russ Stein was back in Pittsburgh on a pickup team facing the touring Red Grange, so on Chicago's frozen turf the Maroons had to make a critical line-up change. The Cards were rugged, fracturing Flanagan's shoulder and breaking French's nose, but the Maroons clearly won the game, 21–7. Wentz tallied twice, and French scored on a 30-yard sprint.

The following Saturday, the Maroons were at Shibe Park to defeat the old Four Horsemen of Notre Dame and their newly organized touring pro team. Before a crowd of 15,000, Latone plunged for a score and Berry kicked a 15-yard field goal, and the Maroons had the game, 9–7. The next week they completed their official season by beating a pro team in Atlantic City, 6–0. But meanwhile, it was protested that the Maroons had violated the Yellow Jackets' Philadelphia territorial rights by playing at Shibe Park.

The NFL hurriedly scheduled two extra games for the Cardinals. At Milwaukee, the Cards beat a team, 59–0, which had four high school players. "It wasn't a football game, it was a practice," commented the

Chicago *Tribune*. "Certainly a weird game to base a championship on." And then the Cards made their record 11–2–1 by defeating a similarly inept team in Hammond, Ind. "A pretty scurvy trick," said the Philadelphia *Inquirer*.

The official 1925 season ended with Chicago's having a .846 year to Pottsville's .833. Detroit was in third place in the 20-team league with 8–2–2 and the New York Giants in fourth place, 8–4.

The Maroons came back in 1926 with another excellent team, good enough to have a 10–2–1 record, but they finished third and were knocked out of their title bid by a 9–7 defeat to the Chicago Bears. Undoubtedly their greatest win was over the Giants, 3–0. The two teams met at Wilkes-Barre on Johnny Mitchell Day, the miners' holiday of October 29. Steve Owen played tackle and H. L. "Hinkey" Haines, of Red Lion and the 1919–20 Nittany Lions, was at quarterback for the New Yorkers. The rugged Maroons got a 32-yard field goal in the second quarter to win. In 13 games that season, the Maroons blanked the opposition nine times.

That was really the end. The 1927 Maroons were eighth in the NFL among 12 clubs with a 5–8 record and in 1928, eighth among 10 clubs with a 2–8 mark. Overall, their official NFL record for four seasons was 27–20–1.

The Pottsville franchise was moved to Boston in 1929, where the team had a 4–4 record. For old-time sake, Boston played an exhibition game in Pottsville, the last appearance of the Maroons. In 1937 the franchise went from Boston to Washington, where the Redskins, acting like the old Maroons, won the NFL title in their first year, beating a Chicago team no less, the Bears, and doing it in Chicago, too, but their championship laurels were not stripped from them.

The Frankford Yellow Jackets had a longer go of it than the Maroons in the NFL, from 1924 to 1931. Their overall record was 68–46–14, and five of their eight years they were in the first division. They won the 1926 championship with a 14–1–1 mark and finished second in 1928. By 1931 they were dead last at 1–6–1, and ready for Bert Bell to buy them for $2,500 and transform them into the Philadelphia Eagles in 1933—named for the New Deal's eagle symbol of economic recovery. Unfortunately, the new Eagles did not do much in the way of recovering football glory. In their first 10 years, they finished last five times and next to last, five times. It was not until the wartime year of 1943 when the Eagles and Steelers combined that Philadelphia, as well as Pittsburgh, had a team win more games than it lost.

The days when the Maroons sought glory will never come again. A league membership could be had for $500. Playing fields were rented at

$300 or less. Ticket prices were 50 cents to $1. Players signed on for $100 or less a game. The Maroons, in fact, became an excellent team because its management insisted that the players reside in town and hold daily practice. Many of their rivals were little better than pickup teams.

Vic Emanuel and Carl Beck, both of Harrisburg Tech, were typical players of the era, though Beck unquestionably was one of the greatest runners ever produced in Pennsylvania while Emanuel, at 6–foot-1 and 180 pounds, was slightly bigger and stronger than the average pro of 50 years ago. Emanuel played for Tech in 1912–15 and captained the 1920 Gettysburg College team. Beck scored 34 touchdowns for the 1919 Tech eleven—five years after his brother Clarence, then a back, had scored a legendary 105–yard TD against Steelton. As collegians, Emanuel played pro under the alias "French," while Carl Beck used "Andy Smith." Beck played for the Maroons and Yellow Jackets after college ball at West Virginia and Vermont. Emanuel, an end, played for Massillon, Pottsville, Lancaster, Atlantic City, Holmesburg and the U.S. Ambulance Club from 1917–29. In 1917 he played with Massillon on a team with Knute Rockne and Penn State's Eugene "Shorty" Miller against Jim Thorpe's Canton Bulldogs. He remembered watching a Sunday pro game composed of Notre Dame and Illinois players under assumed names who the previous day had used their real names in playing college ball against each other. In later life Emanuel became a high school coach, while Carl Beck was a beer distributor. Carl and Clarence Beck to this day are regarded as the greatest athletes Harrisburg ever produced. They died within eight months of each other in 1962–63. Carl, who played football with Thorpe, once tried all of Jim's Olympic events and outdid him in the broad jump, shot put, discus and all running races, but was behind the great man's marks in the javelin and high jump. Yet Carl insisted Thorpe was the greatest athlete who ever lived.

In Pennsylvania the early, rough professional game had thousands of fans, sponsors like Doc Striegel and, most importantly, an abundance of hardnosed players. Pioneering sports historians, such as Dr. Henry March of 40 years ago, already were calling the Commonwealth, especially Western Pennsylvania, the "birthplace" and "cradle" of pro ball.

There is an argument over when and where pro football did begin. The accepted date is Sept. 3, 1895, at Latrobe, when the Latrobe YMCA defeated the Jeannettee Athletic Club, 12–0. An earlier date is Nov. 12, 1892, when the Allegheny Athletic Association supposedly paid Yale's three-time All-American running guard, the immortal William "Pudge" Heffelfinger, $500 for his services.

Pittsburgh was very big in early professional sports. It had minor-league baseball in 1876 and a National League team in 1887, when Exposition Park opened. The Allegheny AA was founded in the 1880s, and the University of Pittsburgh had student football teams in 1890. The Allegheny AA beat the Frankfords in football, 4 goals to 0, on Oct. 22, 1892, and then the Homesteaders, 11–1. On Thanksgiving Day of 1892, the Allegheny AA beat Cleveland, 4–0, while the Pittsburgh Athletic Club was losing to a team called Lehigh, 21–0, at the same time the nation's first international rugby match was going on at Expo Park with Toronto defeating Pittsburgh, 7–2.

The Allegheny AA and Pittsburgh AC slugged out a 6–6 deadlock early in the 1892 season. For the November 12 rematch, the Allegheny AA went out and got Heffelfinger, the biggest name in American football at the time. It worked. From his left guard position, Pudge jarred a PAC ballcarrier, scooped up the fumble and ran 25 yards for the only score of the game. Allegheny won, 4–0, as touchdowns counted for only four points. The club netted $621 for the game, after payoffs to Heffelfinger, Ben "Sport" Donnelly and perhaps another player or two. The following year, both teams signed players to contracts, so pro ball was underway.

Greensburg claims it had the first pro team in 1894 when it paid Lawson Fiscus $20 a week. Fiscus was a 186-pound halfback from Princeton. By 1895 Greensburg had Richard Laird, the Grove City College quarterback, and in 1896 it had Fiscus and two of his brothers, plus Adam M. Wyant. At 6-foot, 196 pounds, Wyant was one of the game's first big men. He played four seasons at Bucknell and two at the University of Chicago, and then became a Greensburg lawyer. From 1921 to 1933 he represented the district in Congress.

What makes this history confusing is the plain disorderliness and under-the-table tactics of slipping $10 sawbucks to players. Amateurism was highly respected, especially since YMCAs, athletic clubs and other non-profit organizations were sponsoring football teams. The YMCA, with its high standards, had been a major backer of sports in Pennsylvania for years. The Pittsburgh, Lancaster and Harrisburg Y's were organized in 1854, the year of the first YMCA convention, and the York and Philadelphia Y's were started the following year. The YMCAs gave trophies to winning athletes, but they frowned upon paying expense money. With the development of football teams, the trophies became hockable at the nearest pawnshop and opponents of the YMCA teams were paying expense money that often was double what the true expenses were. It was, frankly, more honest to put a man under contract, but nobody wanted to admit this.

For the Latrobe-Jeannette game, Johnny Brallier was slipped $10 to come from Indiana Normal School. Though only 18 and just 5-foot-6 and 125 pounds, he was signed by Latrobe newspaper owner David J. Berry and YMCA secretary Russ Aukerman because they could not secure the quarterback they wanted from the University of Pennsylvania.

Latrobe, population 3600, that Sept. 3, 1895, was having a Civil War veterans reunion. Berry had been a football player until his jaw was broken. For the game with Jeannette, he rounded up steel puddlers and coal miners. Aukerman, formerly of Mercersburg Academy and Gettysburg College, played halfback and scored both touchdowns, while Brallier dropkicked the extra points. Brallier later played for W & J, became a dentist and had his practice in Latrobe until his death in 1960.

Much of the credit for Latrobe's being acknowledged first in pro ball belongs to Berry's brother, Vernon, a noted football historian, and to Brallier himself, who simply outlived his colleagues from the early days. Interestingly, the old Pittsburgh *Post* thought the Latrobe game worth only one short paragraph, but in 1946 the NFL considered locating its Pro Football Hall of Fame in Latrobe.

This early Pennsylvania football was really semi-professional. Greensburg, however, got so emotional that its football club's financial committee signed up the entire Lafayette College backfield of Bray, Barclay, Best and Walbridge, or "the three Bs and a W." To keep up with Greensburg, the Latrobe supporters intercepted Thomas "Doggie" Trenchard at the railroad station, offered him $75 a game and stole him from their arch-rivals. Trenchard had been a great All-American end for Princeton and was coaching at West Virginia University. He played three seasons for Latrobe and was a good scorer. Marcus Saxman, of Swarthmore College, was another top-notch recruit on the Latrobe team. Saxman, nearly bald, is in the annals of football because he was the first to wear a helmet.

The great Bucknell star, Christy Mathewson, played briefly with the Duquesne Country and Athletic Club, another of the semi-pro teams. The Homestead Library and Athletic Club was a powerhouse with such players as Arthur Poe of Princeton, George H. Brooke of Penn and the Indian brothers Bemus and Hawley Pierce of Carlisle. Sponsored by the Carnegie Steel Company, Homestead was undefeated in 1901.

The pro game perhaps received its first big recognition in 1902 with the Pittsburgh Professionals and the Philadelphia Athletics. Dave Berry ran the Pittsburgh club, while Connie Mack and Ben Shibe used their baseball money to sponsor the A's. Both claimed to be the champion.

The Pros had unofficial wins over Bucknell, Pitt, West Virginia, the Pittsburgh YMCA and the Pennsylvania Railroad. Mack's team defeated everyone it played, though the records are skimpy on all this.

On Nov. 8, 1902, the A's beat the Pros in Philadelphia, 11–10, when Hawley Pierce, the Seneca Indian, started the rally by recovering a fumbled punt. Then on November 22, again in Philadelphia, there were apparently two different Pittsburgh and Philadelphia teams—or at least having different names in their line-ups—and this time the club called the Phillies won, 11–0, with Penn's Charley Gelbert the star end. Finally on Thanksgiving Day, November 27, in Pittsburgh, the A's and the Pros (sometimes called the Stars), met for what they considered the championship.

The Pros had Arthur Poe, who had played previously for Homestead. The A's had Earl E. Hewitt, Curly Davidson from Penn and Edgar "Blondy" Wallace, the Penn tackle who later played for the Canton Bulldogs after being Mack's team captain. Hewitt, who had been Penn State's star quarterback, later was a state legislator for 20 years from Indiana County.

The big game almost didn't get started. Mack, always close with the dollar, demanded his $3,000 guarantee in his hands. A gentleman on the sidelines accommodated him, writing out a check. "Who are you anyhow?" asked Mack. "I'm William E. Corey, if that means anything to you," the man said. The 36-year-old native of Braddock was president of Carnegie Steel and wanted to see the game.

The A's and the Pros played in mud and rain before 4000 fans. It ended 0–0, with the ball on Pittsburgh's 3-yard line. Immediately, Mack and Berry scheduled a replay for two days later, a Saturday. From this point, history gets confusing again. Various records, including Hewitt's testimony, claim that Philadelphia won, 12–6, with Davidson's scoring after Poe had let Cornell's Twister Steinberg get by him for a 45-yard play. The Pittsburgh *Post*, however, covered the game, noting that it was 0–0 with five minutes left and then the Pros' fullback bucked over, more points were scored and the game ended 11–0 for the home team.

Whoever was champion, Philadelphia or Pittsburgh, both teams broke up following that game. Mack and Shibe lost $4,000 in football, and they did not think they could afford more of that.

In 1903 the little town of Franklin in Venango County, population 7300, picked up the best of the A's and Pros' players and had a great year. On December 15 and 17, Franklin climaxed the season with victories over the Orange Athletic Club and the Watertown Reds and Blacks in Madison Square Garden. This was promoter Tex O'Rourke's

"World Series," and Franklin copped it with twin 12–0 triumphs. The New York *Herald* acclaimed Franklin's play as the best football it had ever seen, while the Wall Street *News* observed on how the Western Pennsylvania fans bet on their teams: "On account of so much money being taken out of the city by the Franklin contingent, a financial stringency is expected. We may have to look to Franklin for help."

Players from Franklin migrated to Canton and Massillon in Ohio for the 1904 season. Meanwhile, little Latrobe kept its professional team until 1906. The previous season Latrobe beat Canton, 6–0, but then in 1906 it was clobbered and that finished its venture in pro ball. Furthermore, the YMCA objected to Sunday football, and Pennsylvania's Blue Laws until the mid-1930s banned that anyway.

All this pro football fervor from Latrobe to Pottsville was just part of a larger Pennsylvania scene.

Tremendous enthusiasm for the game had developed even earlier at the college and high school level. The vigor, exhilaration and especially the violence of football had an almost universal and instant appeal in Pennsylvania. With the possible exception of Ohio, no state suddenly had so much football. The result is evident in Pennsylvania newspapers, where a column or two had been devoted to baseball and then an entire page was given over to sports coverage, and increasingly that of football.

After football's first intercollegiate game, Princeton v. Rutgers in 1869, it did not take Pennsylvania long to get active. Penn had its first three games in 1876. The *Pennsylvania College Monthly* of March, 1877, noted: "It was very exciting—that game was. There were 21 men and two boys playing, and two of the lot were unhurt. The remainder nursed cracked shins and sore bruises. Six were on one leg, and three 'on their ear.' They were playing football. . . . When one man hurt another the latter always blamed the man who didn't do it. When the ball got past a certain line, varying according to circumstances, the outsiders would say 'ottobonds,' and then some fellow would throw it over his head to another of the same opinion with himself, as regards the direction the ball wanted to take, and the latter would become excited and shove it in the opposite direction. . . . We watched it all in breathless suspense, and would have joined in it, but didn't want to tear our breeches like the other fellows did. One-half of those fellows wouldn't work half that hard to saw wood for their mothers; so we thought."

Haverford had organized football in 1879, the same year Swarthmore students ignored a faculty injunction and played an unauthorized game with Pennsylvania Military Academy. Lafayette started in 1882, and its famed rivalry with Lehigh began two years later. Penn State and Bucknell had home and away games, almost of a club nature, in 1881, though Bucknell claims it did not begin football until 1883 and Penn State really did not organize a team until 1887. Pitt started in 1890 with a victory over the Geneva College Covenanters and a defeat to Washington and Jefferson. The Generals gave an example of what strength there was in Western Pennsylvania by stepping into football with 20 consecutive winning seasons and, in all, had only two losing years between 1890 and 1932.

Some other dates for Pennsylvania college football are: Dickinson, 1885; Allegheny, 1888; Franklin and Marshall, 1889; Gettysburg, 1890; Grove City, Westminster and Thiel, all 1892; Duquesne and the Carlisle Indians, 1893; California State, 1899, and Muhlenberg, 1900.

Quality players poured into and out of the Pennsylvania colleges. W and J was famous. Geneva excelled in 1900–03, and Lafayette had top teams in 1899–1911 and 1919–28. Pitt had a record of 37–2 for 1914–18. Penn had its greatest years, an 87–6–2 mark for 1894–1900 and a 38–3–4 mark for 1907–10, filling 21 All-American positions alone in the 1890s.

Almost immediately there was a problem about pure amateurism. Little Westminster College as early as 1896 gave four scholarships for baseball and football. Dr. Saul Sack, of Penn, the foremost scholar on the history of Pennsylvania higher education, discovered in the minutes of the Pitt trustees in 1897 this commentary: "I may say that we have succeeded in so far that only students in regular standing have been permitted to play in match games and no allowance whatever in fees or tuition has been given. The result has not been satisfactory from the fact that professionalism seems to be too deeply rooted in college circles and among the so-called amateur clubs. A large number of our own students have been, to use plain English, 'hired' to play elsewhere, and have in fact told us that as the university does not offer any financial inducements, they must play where they are paid. I am continually approached by students who offer to matriculate here, and to play on our athletic teams, provided they may be given their tuition or other valuable considerations. In many cases these students are not equal to the work of the classes in which they seek to matriculate." That idealism lasted exactly a year, or until the Pitt chancellor requested the trustees to give him the authority to grant financial assistance to needy athletes.

The colleges started football in Pennsylvania. The professionals borrowed from them, as the pros always have. Meanwhile, the secondary schools quickly became a supplier of footballers. For almost 90 years

Pennsylvania's high schools have had a reputation for winning football and outstanding talent.

In Philadelphia, the private academies, such as Episcopal and Penn Charter, began football before 1887, because that is when the Inter-academic League started, as researched by historian-statistician Roger Saylor of Penn State Capitol Campus at Middletown. Central High in 1890 was the first Philadelphia public school to compete in football, and through 1892 Central was recognized as the Commonwealth's mythical high school champ. The Philadelphia Public League started in 1909 with Central, Northeast, Southern and other schools. Meanwhile, Roman Catholic in 1896 became the first Pennsylvania parochial school with football. The suburban rivalry between Lower Merion and Radnor began in 1897.

Some of the Eastern schools with football in the 1890s were Chester, West Chester, Norristown, Coatesville, Lancaster, Reading, Sunbury, Shamokin, Allentown, Mahanoy City and Pottsville.

Out in Western Pennsylvania, the bigger high schools all had or-ganized football by 1900, and so did some of the smaller schools like Oil City, Titusville, Warren and Bradford. The Pittsburgh City League started in 1913 and the Western Pennsylvania Interscholastic Athletic League in 1914–17, growing so large in the Pittsburgh region that it had to split into classifications in 1928.

Central Pennsylvania was in on the birth of schoolboy football, too. The Harrisburg Academy had a team as far back as 1883. Old Harris-burg Central High School started football in 1887 and was state champs 1893–95 and 1898–1900. In its 31-year existence, Harrisburg Central had a record of 137–91–18, according to statistics gathered by the late Clarence W. "Bus" Funk, one of Harrisburg's top sports writers. Cen-tral admitted only girls after 1918, but its rival, Harrisburg Tech, in its lifetime, 1904–25, outdid even Central with a record of 131–53–11. Tech in 1918 had a 9–0 season, scoring 597 points to its opponents' 10. In 1919 the Tech Maroons may have had the greatest season ever recorded in Pennsylvania schoolboy annals, a perfect 12–0 with 701 points scored and only 12 scored against them. Tech's lifetime mark would have been better if Greensburg had not defeated the Maroons seven times in 11 encounters. Tough Greensburg was state champs in 1914, 1916, 1920 and 1921.

Williamsport started off in 1891 and was state champs in 1896–97 and 1904–05. The Millionaires possibly had even greater years, 1927–33, under Coach Sol Wolf. Previously at Lock Haven, Wolf had teams that were runner-up state champs in 1922–23, the state champs in 1924 and the acclaimed national champs in 1925 with a victory over Englewood High in Illinois.

York was state champs in 1901; Easton, 1902; Lebanon, 1903; Johnstown, 1906, and Shamokin, 1907.

Tiny Steelton began football in 1894 and by 1957, when it entered a jointure with Highspire, had won 67 percent of its games, or only two points less than bigger Williamsport. In 63 seasons the Steamrollers had only 11 losing years. Its male enrollment was seldom more than 200, but Steelton had such great eras as 1924–28, a 44–5–2 mark; 1933–37, a 44–9–5 mark, and 1946–50, a 41–5–3 mark. Led by halfback Warren Heller, later the Pitt All-American and Steelers star, Steelton was the state champion in 1926.

Reading, beginning in 1892, did not do so well, winning only 49 percent of its games through 1966. Its greatest year was 1951 when Lenny Moore ran the Red Knights to a 9–1 season, toppled only by a 21–16 loss to Williamsport. Carlisle's Thundering Herd, starting in 1915, won 68 percent, and Middletown during 1921–66 won 58 percent.

John Harris High School in 1926 succeeded Harrisburg Central and Tech in the Hill section of the capital city. In its lifetime, 1926–70, it won 73 percent of its games. Probably no Pennsylvania team was comparable to the Pioneers in the 1960s when its record was an awesome 105–8–3 and it sent such fine players as Jimmy Jones, Jan White and Ed Beverly on to college stardom and the pros.

To this day, the wealth of football talent in Pennsylvania seems inexhaustible. No major college recruiter or pro scout has done his job if he does not spend a few autumn weekends in Pennsylvania.

Master Coaches

... *Brainpower Went with Manpower*

If "God is always on the side which has the best football coach," as Heywood Broun maintained, then maybe that is why Pennsylvania's football for almost 100 years has been so good. The Keystone State's coaching ranks, certainly in its collegiate circles, have long had a national reputation.

The most recent headlines acclaim Penn State's Joe Paterno, Pittsburgh's Johnny Majors and Temple's Wayne Hardin.

The Nittany Lions are old-hat. They have not had a losing season since 1936. Paterno's 1966–74 mark of 80–14, plus a bowl record of 5–1–1, makes him the nation's winningest coach in big-time college football. Majors and Hardin turned their college teams around, out of the losers' circle and into the winners'. In the case of Pitt, it had lost consistently from 1964 through a disastrous 1–10 season in 1972, and then All-American Johnny arrived. With the encouragement of Chancellor Wesley W. Posvar, the 1956 Tennessee star halfback started a heavy recruiting program. Majors took 11 trips to Aliquippa, beat out 100 other recruiters, and landed Tony Dorsett, potentially one of the finest running backs ever.

The Pennsylvania recruiting wars rival the action down on the field in intensity. Jimmy Cefalo came from Charley Trippi's hometown of Pittston. In three years as a running back he scored 64 touchdowns and gained 4427 yards. Fourteen Pennsylvania colleges and 70 others came after Cefalo, who was named to the Pennsylvania Big 33 team. He rejected Notre Dame, Ohio State, Stanford and Harvard. He listened to offers from Pitt and Temple, and then took Penn State. Meanwhile, Steve Joachim, another high school All-American out of Haverford, went to Penn State for a season and transferred to Temple. In two years as the Owls' quarterback, he led them to a 17–3 record and won the 1974 Maxwell Award.

Gridiron talent like this has been part of the Pennsylvania scene for decades. The home-grown manpower is a basic reason why the greatest coaches have been attracted to this state. Nobody rivals Pennsylvania for its list of illustrious, innovative and popular coaches—figures like Pop Warner, Jock Sutherland, George Washington Woodruff, John W. Heisman, Richard Cresson Harlow, Edward "Hooks" Mylin, Carl G. Snavely, George A. Munger, Charles "Rip" Engle, Alfred Earle "Greasy" Neale, and many others. Some, like Warner, Sutherland, Mylan and Neale, skippered two or more Pennsylvania teams, because they recognized that this is a state where football is taken seriously.

The modern wizards like Paterno, Majors and Hardin follow in a long tradition.

George Woodruff at the University of Pennsylvania devised, or at least was among the first, to employ backs in motion, an unbalanced offensive line, the quick kick, the coffin-corner kick, the direct snap from center to the kicker, in-tight and rushing defensive ends, the line-backer, an inner shift with a guard pulling out to carry the ball (now illegal), and "guards back" to form a wedge for blocking. Techniques like these not only advanced the game from rugby's bloody push-and-shove, but enabled Woodruff to produce a 124–15–2 record at Penn. In addition, he had a 10–4 record in 1905 as the advising coach to the Carlisle Indians, and that season he beat both Penn State and Washington and Jefferson by 11–0 scores.

Woodruff was born Feb. 22, 1864, at Dimock. He played guard at Yale under the immortal Walter Camp, won his "Y" in three sports and was Phi Beta Kappa. More importantly, he learned that running interference is the most vital aspect of offensive football. He became a lawyer, taught at the Hill School and Penn Charter, and then was Penn's third coach, incorporating blocking tactics that others had never seen.

Penn started football in 1876 and had 20 winning seasons in its first 21 years. In the 1890s the Quakers filled 21 All-American positions.

It was a rough game that Woodruff played, and he made it even rougher by 1893 when he introduced the flying wedge. Men in that era played without helmets. They would start letting their hair grow in June so that by football season they would have additional protection. The field usually was 110 yards long. There were three downs to make a first down. With few substitutions, sometimes none at all, the teams played 45-minute halves. One of Woodruff's great kickers and twice All-American was George H. Brooke, later the Penn coach from 1913–15. Covering football for the Philadelphia *North American*, Brooke noted that 1902 had been a fairly clean year for the game. No player had been deliberately knocked out with a punch to the jaw, as had happened frequently in past seasons. Brooke observed that dirty play had succeeded the simply rough play in 1893, when one already injured Ivy Leaguer had his collarbone broken when another player intentionally jumped feet first upon him when he was prone.

Coach Woodruff did not seek mayhem, just victory. He coached from 1892 through 1901 and produced some magnificent teams and players. In 1894–97, his Quakers won 55 of 56 games, losing only to a sharp Lafayette team, 6–4. After that loss, Penn turned in a 31-game winning streak.

The most famous of Woodruff's stars was T. Truxton Hare, four-time All-American guard, 1897–1900. Hare is "a devastating berserker on the gridiron," a New York *Sun* sportswriter wrote. With Thorpean versatility, Hare made the 1900 Olympic team and in later life became an expert archer. He died at 77 in 1956, after a career as a utility lawyer and author. Charley Gelbert, three-time All-American end and the father of the big-league shortstop of the same name, was another of Woodruff's heroes.

Woodruff left football when he was at his peak. He became part of Teddy Roosevelt's "Tennis Cabinet" as the law officer for the U.S. Forest Service. In 1907 he was acting Secretary of the Interior, and later a judge in Hawaii. He and Gifford Pinchot had played football together at Yale, so in 1923 Pinchot as governor made Woodruff his attorney general. Woodruff was a Pennsylvania utility commissioner when he died in Harrisburg in 1934.

The incredible Glenn Scobey Warner followed Woodruff on the Pennsylvania scene. He was born at Springville, N.Y., on April 5, 1871, and was All-American at Cornell in 1894. It was in Pennsylvania, however, that Warner had his days of glory—13 years at the Carlisle Indian School, nine years at Pitt, and six years at Temple University.

It is a toss-up if Pop Warner or Knute Rockne is the most legendary coaching figure in American football. Pop—his Indian players gave him that name—was a non-practicing lawyer, a landscape painter, a tinkerer who loved to strip down automobiles, an excellent sportswriter, and such an inveterate itch that he whittled golf clubs out of bedposts.

Warner's immense contribution was to take football out of the hands of the brutes and make it a game of speed and deception. He was a "master strategist," in the words of Jock Sutherland who played two years under him at Pitt. Warner helped devise the single-wing and double wingback systems. To open up play, he was a pioneer in the use of the forward pass. Frank Mt. Pleasant might have thrown the first spiral pass to defeat Penn in 1907 for Pop's Indian team. Warner also had his Indians put spiral spins on their punts to get greater distance.

For his quick, wide attack, Warner adopted the Indian-style rolling body block, or the "Indian block." Among the greatest of innovators,

(Pop Warner Little Scholars)

Glenn Scobey Warner

Pop was forever applying his fertile mind to a new strategy or method for playing the game. He was one of the first to design protective equipment for his players.

Pop was a gruff, yet warm-hearted individualist who seemed to inspire loyalty from the poorest Indian boy who played for him to the richest lad on his Stanford teams. "His big, powerful beaming countenance, his quiet, slow, soft-spoken voice, always reassuring and encouraging," was the way Sutherland described Warner. Players were eager for Pop's next idea, such as the time in 1903 when he had his Indians use the hidden-ball trick against Harvard. Actually, Warner had used the same play in 1897 for Cornell to defeat Penn State.

It was in Pennsylvania that Pop Warner was at his best, though he also coached at Georgia, Cornell and Stanford, where his teams played in three Rose Bowls.

Warner's Indians in 13 years faced the nation's toughest teams, but had only two losing seasons and an overall record of 109–44–8. In the nine years Carlisle had football without Warner, it had but one winning season.

Pop then moved on to Pitt, and from 1915–23 was just as brilliant, with a 59–12–4 record. The Panthers were a powerhouse. In fact, from 1913–39, or from before Warner until well after him, Pitt had 27 consecutive winning seasons. With stars like Claude "Tiny" Thornhill, Bob Peck, Pat Herron, Red Carlson, George McLaren and Sutherland, the Pitt teams of 1915, 1916, 1917 and 1918 were undefeated. In those four years, Pop's offensive-minded Panthers scored 872 points and gave up only 81. They registered 21 shutouts.

After nine years at Stanford, where Warner had a 71–17–8 record, he made a surprising move to Temple. The Owls had begun football in 1925 and never had a losing season when Pop joined them in 1933. He kept that mark going through 1937, but in his last year, 1938, fell behind with a 3–6–1 season. In all, Warner at Temple produced a respectable 24–15–9 figure, including a Sugar Bowl appearance in 1935 when Tulane beat the Owls in the final quarter, 20–14.

Pop Warner ended his full-time coaching career at Temple. He had started in 1895. There is an argument whether he won 313 or 316 games, because his contemporary, Amos Alonzo Stagg, in 57 years won either 311 or 314 games. Warner died in 1954 at 83. So famous has he remained that many sports fans even today can recall his middle name of "Scobey."

Stagg, incidentally, coached briefly in Pennsylvania. When he was 81 in 1943 he became assistant coach under his son, Amos Alonzo Jr., at Susquehanna University. The grand old man, who had been on Camp's first All-American team in 1889, worked with the Susquehanna players for 10 years, mainly on offensive strategy. He used his wife as a scout. One Saturday night she reported back from Dickinson College, "You can pass on their left halfback. He's slow." Amos Alonzo Sr. relayed that information to Amos Alonzo Jr., and Susquehanna defeated Dickinson with a pass late in the game over the head of the tardy left halfback.

Pitt followed the lovable Pop Warner in 1924 with its own boy, the dour giant of the gridiron, Dr. John Bain Sutherland. The Panthers responded to Jock by winning their first three games by shutouts, but the rest of the season was more difficult and they ended up 5–3–1. Jock stayed 15 years and never had a losing season. His Pitt record of 111–20–12 remains the mark that every Panther coach through Johnny Majors has aimed to duplicate, but none has.

Sutherland was born March 21, 1889, in the backward village of Coupar Angus, Scotland. At 18 the "Silent Scot" came to America, first making river barges at Ambridge and then being a policeman in Sewickley. At 6-foot-1 and 220 pounds, he looked like an athlete. Studying nights at the YMCA, he also looked like a student. And so with financial assistance, he was enrolled in the Pitt Dental School in 1914. His coach was Joe Duff, the former All-American guard at Princeton and the older brother of Gov. James H. Duff. Joe, who died in World War I, put Jock at the guard position. That line, with Tiny Thornhill from Beaver and Bob Peck from Lock Haven, became virtually impassible.

In four years on the Pitt varsity, Sutherland played in 33 winning games and only one losing game, a 13–10 loss in 1914 to Washington and Jefferson. Pitt outscored the opposition, 939 to 106, and shut out 14 opponents. Jock really did not know what it was like to lose until he played a professional game with the Massillon Tigers in 1919 against the Canton Bulldogs. He, Thornhill, McLaren and Herron were on the Tigers. The Bulldogs had Jim Thorpe, Lou Little, Joe Guyon, Pete Calac, Eugene "Shorty" Miller, Tuss McLaughry from Westminster and later a great coach, and Bob Peck. In what must have been a monumental contest, the Bulldogs won by 3–0.

Sutherland became a dentist, and for 12 years was in the crown and bridge department at Pitt. But he loved pulling out guards for interference more than pulling out teeth.

Jock started his coaching career with Lafayette in 1919, and in five years had a 33–8–2 record, including an undefeated season in 1921. Lafayette, like W & J, had a reputation in those years as one of the nation's top teams, even though it was a small college. It had started football in 1882 and two years later began its Lehigh series with a

(Pro-Football Hall of Fame)

Dr. John Bain Sutherland

50–0 win. Lehigh in 1974 won the 110th game of the series—some years they had played two games—with a crushing 57–7 victory, but the overall series mark of Lafayette 62 wins, Lehigh 43 and five ties indicates how good the Easton college has been. Sutherland's team never lost to the Engineers. They split four games with Pitt and four with Penn. Amazingly enough, Lafayette in the Sutherland era never gave up more than 47 points in any entire season.

A bachelor and a stern technician, Sutherland believed that on the football field there is "no place for the weakling, the coward, the whiner or the half-hearted." The words "admiration" and "respect" were the most important in his vocabulary. Grinding out victories with a mixture of speed and pulverization was his style.

Jock became, in his determined way, a Pittsburgh legend. Players vowed that he was the inspiration of their lives. He was asked to run for mayor and for lieutenant governor. He churned out 22 All-Americans and an unbelievable 79 shutouts. Jock's first undefeated Pitt season was in 1927. In 1929 he had another, still another in 1932 and finally his fourth in 1937. He had six years with only one loss a season. Only in Sutherland's first season did the Panthers lose as many as three games. Jock's single-wing purred to such perfection that from 1931–38, the Panthers averaged better than five shutouts a season. In 1933 they gave up a mere 13 points and in 1928, just 15. Unfortunately, the success did not rub off in the Rose Bowl. Jock took them to Pasadena four times, but won only on his last outing in 1936, a 21–0 victory over Washington.

Sutherland entered the professional ranks to coach the Brooklyn Dodgers for two years and then the Steelers, where he had a 13–9–1 record. Art Rooney Sr. signed him for $15,000 a year on a five-year contract that gave him an additional 25 percent of the profits for increased attendance. In Jock's final year with the Steelers, he was ready to cop the division title but lost a crucial play-off to the Philadelphia Eagles, 21–0. That was his last game, but Rooney credited him with saving the Steelers for Pittsburgh. On a winter scouting trip, Sutherland suffered a complete collapse and was found walking dazed along a road near Cairo, Ill. He died back in Pittsburgh on April 11, 1948, of a brain tumor. The big man was 59.

The grim, kindly and intelligent Sutherland left behind a career coaching mark of 172–44–15—or 80 percent of the games Jock coached, he won.

John W. Heisman played guard at Penn and later coached the Quakers, 1920–22. He was an early advocate of the forward pass at Georgia Tech, where he turned in a fine 100–29–6 record. He also coached at Clemson, Auburn, Rice, Oberlin and Akron. He was the prototype of that breed of sideline generalissimos. "The coach shall be masterful and commanding, even dictatorial," he said. "He has not the time to say 'please' or 'mister.' He must be severe, arbitrary and little short of a czar." Heisman made the record book at Georgia Tech for running up a 222–0 score against Cumberland College. The Heisman Trophy was named in his honor in 1935, the year before his death.

Two Pennsylvania coaches, William M. Hollenback and William W. Roper, in their later years became Philadelphia councilmen. Penn's Hollenback, at 6-foot-3 and 200 pounds, was one of the game's first big fullbacks. He coached Penn State to a 20–11–2 mark and also coached briefly at Missouri and Syracuse. Roper, a native of German-town, played end on the 1899 Princeton team, and, after coaching at Penn Charter, spent 18 years at Princeton with an 89–28–16 mark. He is remembered as one of the most inspirational coaches of his day, and also as an independent politician who wanted to do away with Prohibition.

The famed Alvin "Bo" McMillin coached briefly at Geneva College. Bo brought along 6-foot-5, 250-pound tackle and fullback Cal Hubbard as a player, getting him a side job at the Beaver Falls cork factory. Hubbard then helped McMillin's team upset Harvard. Earlier as the Centre College quarterback, Bo had defeated Harvard, too. Late in his career, McMillin returned to Pennsylvania to coach the Philadelphia Eagles.

Dick Harlow came out of Philadelphia's Episcopal Academy to be a tackle, baseball player and boxer at Penn State. He coached the Nittany Lions' line for Bill Hollenback and as head coach himself had three winning seasons, 1915–17. He went on to Colgate, Western Maryland and then Harvard, where he became one of the most admired men in the game. A real student of football, Harlow said that Warner, Hollen-bach and Sutherland were the masters he studied most. An unusual man, Harlow earned his master's degree at Penn State and was recog-nized as a fine botanist and ornithologist. He also was curator of zool-ogy at the Harvard Museum of Comparative Zoology, a strange moonlighting assignment for a football coach.

George A. Munger, a native of Elkins Park and another Episcopal Academy athlete, became Penn's coach in 1938 and set a record for the Quakers by lasting until 1953. Like Sutherland, he fancied the single-wing. With players such as Chuck Bednarik, Skippy Minisi and George Savitsky, the single-wing often worked well, and in 16 years Munger was 82–42–10.

Carl N. Snavely was born in Omaha, Neb., but starred in football for Lebanon Valley College. He coached at Kiski Prep, Vandergrift High School and the Bellefonte Academy before going to Bucknell in 1927. With the Bisons, he had a 42–15–8 record, and a 1931 undefeated season when Clark Hinkle ran the ball for him. A serious man who favored mousetrap plays and end-around sprints, Snavely went on to Cornell and North Carolina. Like Munger, he will be remembered as one of the great gentlemen in football. So will one of his successors at Cornell, George K. "Lefty" James, a noted end from New Cumberland and Bucknell who went on to coach the Big Red at Ithaca for 13 seasons.

Hooks Mylin was entered in the National Football Foundation's Hall of Fame in 1974. A quarterback out of Franklin and Marshall College, he took Bucknell to the Orange Bowl in 1935 and beat Miami, and in 1937 and 1940 had undefeated teams at Lafayette. He was Coach of the Year in 1937, and his 1939 and 1940 Lafayette teams bumped off Penn State and Army. Mylin, now retired, lives in Lancaster.

Rip Engle was a mule driver in the Elk Lick coal mine at 14. Then he was a mine superviser at 19, but took off to become an outstanding end for Dick Harlow at Western Maryland College. Engle began his coaching at Waynesboro High School. In eight of his 11 years, he won conference titles, three of them with undefeated teams, and his overall record was 86–17–5. He then coached Brown University for six years, with a 28–20–4 record, developing the wing-T offense that soon became popular nationwide. Rip took over at Penn State in 1950 with a respectable 5–3–1 season. He stayed at the helm for 16 years, turning in a 101–47–4 mark, plus a 3–1 record in bowl games. Engle's prize season was 1962, when he had a 9–1 year with such future pro stars as Roger Kochman, Pete Liske, Glenn Ressler, Ralph Baker and Dave Robinson.

Duffy Daugherty was born near Barnesboro in 1915 and worked his way through Syracuse University, where he captained the team though he was only a mediocre player. For 19 years, ending in 1972, he coached Michigan State University, producing a brilliant 109–65–5 record in Big Ten football. Twice his Spartans captured national titles and went to the Rose Bowl. One of his All-American guards was Frank Kush, a miner's son out of Windber. Kush became coach at Arizona State in 1958, and currently is second only to Joe Paterno as the winningest big-time collegiate mentor.

Daugherty was able to remain a taskmaster yet witty at the same time. In 1954 when his Michigan State team received notoriety because one player was out on bail on a charge of rape, another had knocked some teeth out of a teammate, a third had assaulted a fellow student, and one of the stars had been in a sorority house brawl, Daugherty calmly assessed the situation and remarked, "Our squad's behavior is as good as any in the country." What hurt most was that the season turned out to be the Spartans' first losing one in 14 years. One of his best off-the-cuff comments was before the fame tie game with Notre Dame in 1966. "Playing for the national championship isn't a life-or-death matter," Duffy said. "It's much more important than that."

Among the possible future collegiate greats is George Chaump, an assistant to Woody Hayes at Ohio State. Chaump, from West Pittston, played guard at Bloomsburg State, coached at Shamokin and then skippered John Harris High School in Harrisburg, 1962–67. He won six straight Central Pennsylvania titles with a 58–4 record, and had a 35-game winning streak when he left for Ohio State.

Greasy Neale has been Pennsylvania's most notable resident professional coach—unless the Steelers' Chuck Noll goes on winning. As a kid in Parkersburg, W.Va., he called another boy "Dirty," so he was tagged with "Greasy" in return. The nickname stuck, even through his years as assistant coach at Yale.

A tremendous athlete, Greasy played the outfield for the Cincinnati Reds and the Phillies from 1916 through 1924, with a lifetime average of .259. He hit .359 in the 1919 World Series. At the same time he coached football in the fall at W & J, where in three seasons, 1921–23, he had a record of 23–4–3. Neale directed one of the greatest surprises in the annals of football, the 0–0 deadlock between W & J and California in the 1922 Rose Bowl. The Generals actually scored on a wet field with a 35-yard play but it was called back for off-sides. The great Russ Stein missed field goals of 45 and 39 yards. And W & J led the highly favored Golden Bears in first downs, seven to two. It was the one game in Greasy's career that he certainly deserved to win but didn't.

He coached the Eagles, 1941–50, with a 66–45–5 record. In 1947 he won the division title, but Charley Trippi scored two long touchdowns and the Chicago Cardinals took the championship from the Eagles, 28–21. The Eagles with Steve Van Buren came back to win in 1948, with a 7–0 triumph over the Cards. They won again in 1949 with a 14–0 victory over the Los Angeles Rams. Neale died in 1973 at 81, recognized as the strategist who devised pro football's man-for-man defense and the nine-man line, among other things.

Chuck Knox, of the Rams, is the one native Pennsylvanian in the pro ranks today. Knox was born in Sewickley in 1932, played tackle at little Juniata College and then became an assistant coach there. In Knox's senior year, 1953, the Juniata Indians were undefeated and in his year as assistant coach they also were undefeated. Actually between 1953 and 1959, Juniata was one of the nation's top small-college teams with a 50–2–2 record.

Knox moved on to be line coach at Tyrone High School and then head coach at Ellwood City, 1956–58. He graduated to the college ranks as an assistant at Wake Forest and Kentucky and then put 10 years on the coaching staffs of the New York Jets and Detroit Lions. Los Angeles signed him on for its top job in 1973, and in his first two years Knox led pro football with the best regular-season mark of 22–6.

Penn State Wizard

... *Paterno Is the Thinking Man's Coach*

Joseph Vincent Paterno is a challenge for the critics who like to ridicule contemporary football coaches as Jockstrap Einsteins or Junior-grade Pattons. The Penn Stater is something different in collegiate football.

He is the nation's winningest gridiron coach with a 1966–74 record of 80–14, plus 5–1–1 in bowl games. He is the one the New England Patriots tried to buy in 1973 for $1 million. Earlier, Art Rooney Sr. got a refusal from him on the Pittsburgh Steelers job. "I just feel Penn State's too good a place to leave" was his simple explanation.

Paterno is an absolute phenomenon—so far, or at least as long as he keeps winning. He is at the top in college football, and roared there without a great deal of difficulty, yet Penn State is the only head coaching job he has ever held.

His 1971 biographers, Mervin D. Hyman of *Sports Illustrated* and Gordon S. White Jr. of the New York *Times*, summed him up in exaggerative fashion: "This, then, is Joe Paterno. Football coach, intellectual maverick, philosopher, social worker, leader, gambler, idealist, Romanticist, humanist, activist."

73

By the nature of his success, Paterno is repeatedly in the headlines, but he retains a mysterious quality unintentionally. There is a bit of the intellectual in him. Penn State seldom has commencement speakers, but it broke with tradition in 1973 to put Paterno on the platform. With aplomb, he quoted Walter Lippmann, W. H. Auden and Gunnar Mydral and instructed the graduates not to be content with materialism. But in his specific profession, Paterno is not conspicuously disparate from the conventionally good coaches.

He can be shy in some instances and convivial in others. He is outspoken on matters that he feels deeply about, such as undergraduate education, yet he is never preachy. As a full professor, he is respected, even by most of his academic colleagues.

He does not even look like an athlete. Someone said that with his glasses, prominent nose and one-of-the-boys appearance, he looks like the saxophone player at an Italian wedding. On the street, even on the sidelines, he looks like the neighborhood friendly insurance man. Outwardly, he does not come across as the perceptive, analytical man that he is. It is a hallmark of Joe Paterno that he is not a stereotype of anything.

There is a refreshing lack of pretense or role-playing about Paterno. His basic level-headedness was shown in 1974 when he was asked about Ara Parseghian's resigning from Notre Dame. "You have to tell yourself not to worry about anything but your squad and your family. And you don't worry about whether you win or lose. It's tough," Paterno said. Then questioned about the demands of the job and whether it did not take too much time away from his wife, Suzanne, and their five young children, Paterno quipped that occasionally he did dream of liberating himself from football, usually after losing a game.

Unlike the Warners, Sutherlands and Neales, Paterno is a great coach who was not a great athlete. His skill was good enough to get him halfway up the pyramid of football glory, however. Born Dec. 21, 1926, the son of a New York City clerk of courts, Paterno went to Brooklyn Prep and starred on an 8–1 winning team. He was quarterback and his younger brother George, now head coach at the Merchant Marine Academy, was halfback. Both made the New York City All-Metropolitan Team. Interestingly enough, Prep's only loss was to St. Cecilia's of Englewood, N.J., a team coached by the late Vince Lombardi.

After military service, the Paterno boys went to Brown University, where the football coach was Rip Engle. Joe, like Brooks Robinson of the Baltimore Orioles, is left-handed in everything he does but throwing. At 5-foot-11 and 180 pounds, he was not physically endowed for

(Pennsylvania State University)

Joe Paterno

big-time football, but led Rip's team in the 1948–49 seasons to a 15–3 record. "I couldn't throw well, but I was a pretty good defensive back," he said. "A mediocre player who can't do things naturally must study everything. He concerns himself more with technique." Joe also played varsity guard in basketball, but once again was not exceptional. In football, nobody got him confused with the nation's leaders of his time, both Pennsylvania boys, Arnold Galiffa and Babe Parilli, but so well did Paterno learn the game that Engle took him on as an assistant after graduation. Paterno made the critical choice of his life by deciding not to enter law school.

When Engle came to Penn State in 1950, he brought along Paterno. Joe worked with the quarterbacks and produced a succession of fine ones—Tony Rados, Milt Plum, Richie Lucas, Dick Hoak, Galen Hall and Pete Liske. Later as head coach, Paterno had some pretty good quarterbacks too, such as Tom Sherman, Chuck Burkhart, John Hufnagel and Tom Shuman. The Nittany Lions never favored passing over their traditionally strong running game, but few schools can match it in the quarterback department.

Engle stepped down after a 5–5 year, and Paterno followed him with a 5–5 year in 1966. But that was the last time the Nittany Lions ever lost more than three regular-season games. Paterno started chalking them up: 1967, 8–2; 1968, 10–0; 1969, 10–0; 1970, 7–3; 1971, 10–1; 1972, 10–1; 1973, 11–0, and 1974, 9–2. There was a 31-game winning streak, and then thrills like the 15–14 win over Kansas in the 1969 Orange Bowl and the 41–20 romp over Baylor in the 1975 Cotton Bowl. Penn State fans had never seen anything like it before.

There are a multiple of reasons for Paterno's success.

The first is that he is the totally modern coach. He is neither the rah-rah type nor the hard-boiled despot. He does not have Knute Rockne's gift for the inspirational, Pop Warner's innovative talents, nor Vince Lombardi's absolute control. Rather, Paterno is part-manager, part-counselor, and a full-time football scholar. He can be exciting because he will gamble against his own knowledge of the odds. In his second season at the Gator Bowl, he had a 17–0 lead over Florida State, but with fourth down on his own 15-yard line with one yard to go, he failed in a high-risk bid for ball control and did not punt. Florida State bounced back for a 17–17 tie.

He is respected as an individual who has ideas beyond how to lug a football. He repeatedly insists that football is only a game, not a mark of manhood or 60 minutes of war. He has opposed Little League over-competitive sports. He has recommended a return to one-platoon football as a way to save costs, but perhaps be costly to his own football record. He has suggested that college athletics be bossed by the college presidents and faculty, that paying players a monthly wage might be an alternative to under-the-table sponsorship, and that without institutional responsibility big-time college football is headed toward a debacle. Talk like this separates Paterno from the routine football coach.

The Penn State typical Eastern schedule enhances its won-loss record. It embarrasses Paterno that in 1968 and 1969, when the Lions were undefeated, or in the 1971–73 span when they lost only two games, they never were named the nation's mythical champions, though he once was Coach of the Year. As Penn State's schedule toughens, the Paterno record will slip—but that is an exchange he welcomes.

Lastly, there is Penn State's material, which is both exceptionally good and made to look good by Paterno's skills. He is "very conscious of the big play, and very conscious of special teams and doing little things correctly," linebacker Jack Ham has said of Paterno. In 1974 the pros had 27 Penn Staters on their rosters, or two more than Southern California, seven more than Notre Dame and nine more than Nebraska. Great linebackers came up under Paterno, such as Ham, John Skorupan, Doug Allen, Jim Laslavic, Ed O'Neil, John Ebersole and Bruce Bannon. There have been fine running backs like Franco Harris, Lydell Mitchell and John Cappelletti, as well as other stars like defensive tackle Mike Reid and tight end Ted Kwalick.

In Paterno's approach to the game, especially in his thoroughness at planning and practicing, Ham compares him to the Steelers' Chuck Noll, while Cappelletti compares him to the Rams' Chuck Know. Paterno recruits well, drills well and handles his material well. His old Brooklyn Prep Coach, Sev Graham, once remarked, "Even then, he was a thinking man's football player." And he is a thinking man's football coach.

A measure of the man is revealed in the story Cappelletti told at the New York Hilton when he received the 1973 Heisman Trophy. Cappelletti, of Upper Darby, had been a high school star, and recruiting coaches beat a path to his door. "When he came to my house," said Cappy, "I think that besides recruiting he was after a good Italian meal. My brother Joe was lying on the couch. He was sick then, sicker than usual. Coach Paterno showed more concern for him than he did in recruiting me." Cappy signed with Paterno, and went on to dedicate his Heisman to little Joe, a victim of leukemia, in one of the most moving presentations in the annals of football.

The Original Steeler

... Art Rooney Won a Title After 42 Years

Arthur Joseph Rooney Sr. came dressed to the Super Bowl in a white shirt, a flowered tie, a yellow sweater, a dark baggy suit, a grey herringbone overcoat and a checkered cap. He had his thick eyeglasses, a cigar in his mouth, and a smile of cordiality on his face. He looked like a convivial Irish character out of a Frank O'Connor short story.

Someone asked him if he had prayed to win the big one. "You don't place that kind of request on God. He knows what He's doing," replied Rooney.

After the Pittsburgh Steelers defeated the Minnesota Vikings, 16–6, team captain Andy Russell presented the game ball to Rooney. "This one's for the chief," said Russell. "It's a long time coming," said Rooney.

It had been a long time coming—42 years. Rooney's club was the last of the National Football League's early franchises to win a league championship, just as it had been the last to draw big crowds and the last to abandon the single-wing formation. If Pittsburghers hadn't loved Art Rooney so dearly, they would have thrown him out of town decades

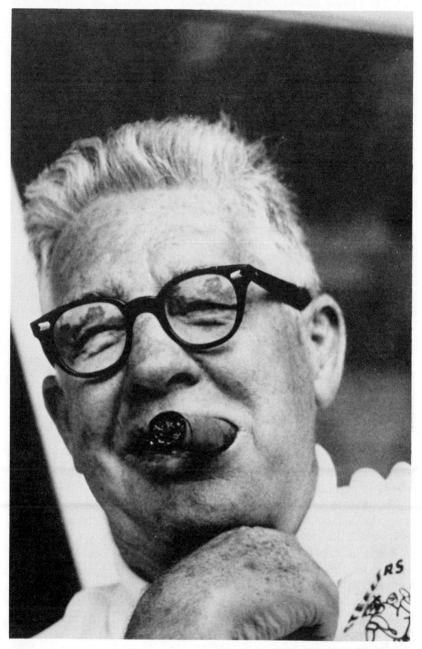

Art Rooney

(Pittsburgh Steelers)

ago. Some of his Steeler teams in the early and middle years of the NFL were enough to make grown men weep, and they did.

Until recent years, culminating in the 1975 Super Bowl two weeks before Rooney's 74th birthday, the Steelers outdid every other pro team in producing so little in so long.

Rooney is a lovable, bullshooting, charitable and unpretentious guy, kindly and aglow with good humor and politeness. He has needed all those qualities. He started NFL ball in Pittsburgh in 1933, and did not have a winning season until 1942. In fact, in his first 36 years, he had only seven winning seasons. Seldom were his teams even in contention for a title. In his first eight years, the Steelers were shutout 23 times. All told, they had been blanked 36 times—an unusual mark in high-scoring professional football, though it must be acknowledged that since 1964 they have not been zapped.

"I never root when I'm watching a game," Rooney once said. "I never say a word. No one would know I had anything to do with it."

Rooney's overall regular season record from 1933 through 1974 is 200 wins, 294 losses and 21 ties, or a percentage of .405. "It used to be we were made to feel we were dumb losers and that the winners were smart," said Rooney. "It sounded like we were too stupid to come in out of the rain. But you know, just because you lose, it doesn't mean you don't have any brains."

Sportswriter Jerry Izenberg called the old Steelers "Destiny's stepchildren . . . the Little Match Girl in shoulder pads."

Pittsburgh is a winner's town. Losers in professional basketball and hockey did not last long. The Pirates for 70 years have been one of baseball's most consistent winners because of a deep appreciation in the executive office of the acute sensitivities of Western Pennsylvanians about victory. Only Art Rooney was able to have 11 winning years, 26 losing ones and five tie seasons, and still not be dumped into an open hearth.

The glorious 1974 season obliterated the horrible memories of times past. The Steelers rolled through a 10–3–1 season and knocked off the Buffalo Bills handily in the first playoff game. In Oakland for the critical league championship, they were the underdogs but held the Raiders' running to a mere 29 yards and won, 24–13. Then it was on to the Super Bowl, where the Vikings could gain only 21 yards on the ground. It was fantastic, and the universal hero was the pink, pudgy-faced, sudsy Art Rooney. Telegrams and letters poured in. "Congratulations," wrote John Dockery, "it couldn't happen to a finer man." Dockery was the defensive cornerback from Harvard cut from the Steelers' squad before the season opened.

(Marty Wolfson/Pro-Football Hall of Fame)

John Unitas as a Pittsburgh Steeler

Reporters suddenly found that hidden in Pittsburgh all these years was an exceptional man. The Rooney demeanor charmed them; what warmth and genuineness. In the locker room after the victory over the Raiders, Rooney saw his big defense tackle, Joe Greene. "Congratulations, Joe," he said. "Congratulations to you," Greene replied. "Thank you a lot, Joe," said Rooney. Solid stuff, no exclamation points needed.

The Steelers were a joke to everybody for years, but not to Rooney. "I was supposed to be the guy who just walked away from his defeats without so much as a second thought," he said. "That's a bunch of nonsense. Every loss in those days got me right here and I took it home with me and it stayed here until the next week when I went back for another dose of the same. I had this standing rule in my house when our five boys were growing up—nobody was allowed to mention the Steelers for two days after we'd lose. That's how much it bothered me. I didn't want to read about it, I didn't want to see the films, I didn't want to have anybody tell me we gave it a good try. Losing to me will always be losing. After many years of this, I've learned one thing: it doesn't get any easier. No sir, no easier at all."

The Rooney record on letting great quarterbacks go is legendary. The Steelers traded off the rights to Sid Luckman. They had Johnny Unitas, Earl Morrall, Len Dawson, Jackie Kemp and Bill Nelsen, but neglected to use their talents.

At the neighborhood saloons, puddlers double or triple their "Boiler-makers" when they think about some of those early Steeler draft picks. In 1974 when the "Pittsburgh Man" was found at Avella in Washington County, it was dated as the oldest human artifact in Eastern United States, somewhere back in the Ice Age of 13,000 B.C. "Looks like they uncovered another of Art Rooney's first-round draft picks," a fan said.

In the 11 critical years between 1958 and 1968, for example, the Steelers signed just 10 players capable of professional football. Only one was a first-round pick. Most were names grabbed out of the pot at the end of the day. The greatest of them, Andy Russell, the tremendous linebacker, came on a 16th pick as if he were a Steelers' afterthought.

The prime reason why the Steelers won in 1974 is that they became serious about the football draft. The high selections of Mean Joe Greene, Terry Bradshaw, Ron Shanklin, Mel Blount, Frank Lewis, Jack Ham, Franco Harris, Lynn Swann and Jack Lambert provided the horsepower. The 1972, 1973 and 1974 seasons were the best in the annals of the Steelers. Of course, the new Rooneymen were not perfect. In 1969 they had eight rounds to get Schenley High's great running back Larry Brown, but he ended up with Vince Lombardi's Washington Redskins.

The inside tip on Art Rooney is that he is as much Pittsburgh as its soot and its steel. That is why the fans forgave him for years like 1969, 1941 and 1939, when the Steelers won only once in the season, or 1944 when they failed to win at all.

"You are the best influence in Pittsburgh," a priest once wrote to Rooney. Considering Rooney's association with saloons, horses, boxers, politicians and other distractions, it takes some doing to canonize him immediately, however.

Yet there is nobody in sports who knows Rooney who does not like him. "Art is truly a great man and a great owner who grew up and lived with his players," said the late Bullet Bill Dudley, the fabulous triple threat of the 1940s. And from the United States Supreme Court spoke Justice Byron White: "Art is the finest person I've ever met. He's the same man every day, win or lose, and I think you have to admire that quality in a person." Rooney broke the NFL's low-pay barrier in 1938 by signing White out of Colorado for $15,800, and the Whizzer went on to be the league's rookie-of-the-year halfback on a team which won just two games.

Almost everybody in sports has a story about Rooney.

Art Jr. told sportswriter Ray Didinger: "My father is a unique person. He could come into the office at midnight and find one of his employees carrying the safe out on his back, and Dad would say to him, 'Hey, working kinda late, aren't you? Tell me, how's the wife and kids?' "

Writer Roy Blount Jr. of *Sports Illustrated* has one about the time Rooney went to see his sons Tim, John and Pat play sandlot baseball. Tim singled and at first base ran off the foul line. "You're supposed to turn toward second," shouted Rooney. Tim, then about 12, shouted back, "That's the way you old guys did it." In a huff, Rooney hollered, "Give me those balls and bats. I don't want people to know you're a Rooney." Then Rooney told Blount, "I never watched them play ball again. You'll have to ask them about their athletic abilities. For this reason: I never thought much of 'em."

The Rooney clan is a big one. He has 34 grandchildren, at last count. The best athletes of the gang remain Art Sr. and his brothers. Dan, the oldest son who handles the Steelers for his father, did make second-string quarterback on Pittsburgh's 1949 All-Catholic team. He played for North Catholic. "Some of my teammates told me I was better than that quarterback from St. Justin's who was chosen first string on the all-star team," said Dan. "I took a look at him and knew he was better— Johnny Unitas." With typical Rooney charm, Dan admitted that he was puzzled about how the selectors made their choices, because he was a senior and Unitas only a junior. Meanwhile, the story goes on with the usual Steeler script. Unitas played for $6 a game for the semi-pro Bloomfield Rams in Pittsburgh, but he couldn't make the Steelers. He was drafted ninth by the Steelers from the University of Louisville in 1955, but never saw combat. A telephone call from the Baltimore Colts started him on to football immortality.

Rooney was born Jan. 27, 1901, in Coulterville, a mining town outside Pittsburgh. His father, Dan, was a coal miner and steel puddler who became a saloonkeeper and Republican ward leader when he opened Rooney's Saloon in Pittsburgh's old First Ward on the North Side. The saloon was within a block of Exposition Park and was on what is now the Three Rivers Stadium's parking lot.

"Whenever somebody spit, the Allegheny started to flood," said Rooney. "So one day when the water was high, I was in a canoe with Squawker Mullen and my brother Dan. Squawker was a kid who later did a little boxing around town for me. Anyway, Squawker stands up, the canoe tips over, and I'm in right field of old Expo Park with boots and an overcoat and trying to swim to make the grandstand. Squawker and Dan didn't have coats or boots, so they made it easily, but I just got to the left-field stands. I never stand here in the stadium and not remember that time 60 years ago when I had to swim for dear life."

Art was the oldest of six boys and two girls. Art, Dan and Jim were top amateur boxers as young men. Art, only 5-foot-8, represented the United States as a welterweight. Dan and Jim were good heavyweights. Art and Dan did the carnival circuit, taking challenges and knocking the midway champions flat. In an amateur tournament in Boston, Art had seven three-round fights in one evening, conserving his stamina by knocking out some opponents in the first and second rounds. Dan turned down a New York Yankees' bonus to be a catcher and became a Franciscan priest in New York State, China and Boston. Jim went on to be a running back and punter for the University of Pittsburgh. John and Tom were in World War II. John was wounded and Tom was killed at Guam. The sixth brother, Vincent, is still part of the Rooney clan.

Rooney's Saloon with its nickel beer was a gathering spot for athletes and the local "Galway Irish," or poor Irish. Art grew up knowing everybody. Better yet, he liked everybody. He went to the nearby St. Peter's parochial school, and ever since has lived in the neighborhood, a five-minute walk from Three Rivers Stadium. He and his wife Kathleen, another neighborhood girl, own a three-story Victorian house on North Lincoln St. that they bought for $5,000 during the Depression. The tough old ward is pretty desolate these days, but the Rooneys are proud to live there.

Nobody in American sports has deeper community roots than Rooney. He knows some families back for four generations. Undoubtedly no Pittsburgher has gone to as many funerals and wakes. When the mother of a sports bar owner in Homestead died, Rooney was there. He has so many prayer cards that he uses them for bookmarks. One day in 1974 at the stadium, as he was puffing on a big cigar, he was approached by a young man who sought a recommendation for St. Vincent College. Chatting about the boy's father and grandfathers, Rooney signed the paper immediately and then said, "I know you must be a good student. If you need any more help, let me know and I'll be glad. An education is important."

Rooney himself bounced through a few colleges, eventually winning a degree in business at Duquesne University in 1923. While at Indiana University of Pennsylvania, he went out for track. He was in one meet, running 100 yards at Penn State, except that he never finished. He jumped the gun, pulled back, gave up twice, and ended by trailing the pack.

He played football, but was more interested in boxing and baseball. As a fast outfielder with the professional Wheeling Stogies in the Middle Atlantic League in 1925, he hit .369 and stole 58 bases. His brother Dan on the same club hit .359 and stole eight bases. Art signed contracts with both the Boston Red Sox and Chicago Cubs, one for $250 a month, but a sore arm ruined his chances of ever getting in a big-league game. The best Rooney can do is see the Pirates play virtually all their home games.

When Rooney got involved in sports promotion in the mid-1920s, the costs of staging an event or fielding a team were minimal. He always liked athletes—to this day, he cannot remember one he didn't like. "The prices were so low in those days that you couldn't make much or lose much. It was that type of thing," he said. "Sports were my life. When you love something, you don't just walk away from it for some other business."

In the 1940s he did think of politics. Though a friend of the late Mayor and Governor David L. Lawrence, Rooney remained a Republican. He was a follower of James J. Coyne, the last GOP boss of Pittsburgh who served 10 years in the Pennsylvania Senate. Coyne put him up for the county row office of Register of Wills. Rooney made a speech in which he said he did not know where the office was located or what its duties were, but that if elected he would hire a good man who did. The candid statement made the papers and national news magazines, and the voters wisely let Rooney stay in the sports business.

When Rooney got going in paid football in 1923, Western Pennsylvania was a hotbed of semi-pro teams. The world's first professional football game had been played in Latrobe on Sept. 3, 1895. Independent teams sprung up, like the McKeesport Olympics, the Pitcairn Quakers, and the Bradley Eagles in McKees Rocks. Rooney had various teams with such strange names as "Majestic Radios," "James P. Rooney" and "Hope-Harvey," the latter club named after the fire engine company in the ward and the doctor who was the free team physician. Rooney not only was the Hope-Harvey owner, but coach and halfback. Against Jim Thorpe's Canton Bulldogs, he tried a field goal. It was blocked, and Thorpe ran it back for a touchdown, the margin of Hope-Harvey's 6–0 loss.

Bert Bell and others organized the NFL in 1933, and Rooney put up $2,500 for a franchise. Part of the legend is that Rooney won the money at the track the day before. In any case, Rooney could never refuse a request from his dear friend, Bert Bell. Bell, who died in 1959 at 65, was another original like Rooney, except that he came from the Philadelphia plutocracy. His given name was deBonneville Bell and he was the son of Pennsylvania's attorney general and the brother of its future chief justice. Once the 5-foot-8, 155-pound quarterback for the University of Pennsylvania, Bell headed the syndicate that bought the Frankford Yellow Jackets for a similar $2,500 and made them into the Philadelphia Eagles. He became full owner after the Eagles lost $80,000 in their first three years and he was able to buy the club at auction for $4,500. He was coach, business manager, publicity man and ticket-seller, or Philadelphia's version of Pittsburgh's Art Rooney. In 1940, Bell and Rooney actually became partners in Philadelphia, as Rooney temporarily sold his Pittsburgh interests. Bell briefly became the Steelers' coach for a disastrous season, and during the war the Eagles and the Steelers merged for a year. From 1946 until his death 13 years later, Bell was the commissioner of the NFL. It was Bert Bell who devised the collegiate draft system in 1935, which as much as anything added balance and excitement to pro football.

Rooney called his team the Pirates from 1933 to 1940, when they were renamed the Steelers. They won their first game in 1933 against Cincinnati, 17–0. They drew 3500 fans, while the powerful undergraduates, the Pitt Panthers, drew 35,000 or more to their games. Pitt, one of the great football universities in the nation, had been undefeated in 1932, only to be knocked off in the Rose Bowl by Stanford, 7–0. It had outstanding players like Warren Heller, of Steelton, Isadore Weinstock of Wilkes-Barre, and Joe Skladany of Larksville, all of whom moved on to Rooney's team.

This early football, as it had been with the semi-pros, was "all pushing, shoving and pile-up football," in Rooney's words, but it was tough and had an appeal for the workingman who could afford a $1 ticket or less. Rooney's payroll was $75 to $100 a game per player, and he did not lose enough money to discourage him. His first season's record was 3–6–2, but the next year it got worse, 2–10. Appropriately enough, Rooney started out in pro football in last place, right below the Philadelphia Eagles in 1933 and 1934.

Charmed by unusual people, Rooney invariably had a collection of characters on his club. In 1937 he signed John Victor McNally, the grandson of a Philadelphia saloon owner, to be player-coach. This was Johnny Blood, for 15 years an NFL great. Johnny, however, was unpredictable. He once went to Chicago to see the Green Bay Packers play, forgetting that his Steelers had a game with the Eagles the same day. In his three years as the Steeler mentor, everybody had fun, but the team won only 7 of 33 games.

More reliable coaches came along, such as Walt Kiesling, Jock Sutherland, Johnny Michelosen, Joe Bach, Buddy Parker and Bill Austin, but it was not until Chuck Noll took over that the Steelers began to soar. Noll's first season of 1969 started splendidly with a 16–13 win over the Detroit Lions. Then the Steelers lost 13 consecutive games. They lost three straight in 1970, and finally got winning. In 1972 they won the American Football Conference play-off with a thrilling 13–7, last-second victory over Oakland, the game in which the Terry Bradshaw pass bounced off a Raiders' hands and into the arms of Franco Harris for a desperation score.

The 1972 loss to the Miami Dolphins in the AFC championship game, 21–17, was a disappointment, but not as bad as some previous defeats. The Eagles and Steelers tied in 1947 seasonal play, but the Eagles took the division title in a 21–0 play-off game. In 1963 the Steelers would have won the NFL Eastern Conference had they repeated their earlier 31–0 triumph over the New York Giants, but in the critical game the Giants' Y. A. Tittle and Frank Gifford took them easily, 33–17.

Rooney lived through many disappointments, but never would he sell the team for big money or take it to New Orleans, Houston, Baltimore or other cities for what looked to be better franchise possibilities. "I couldn't leave Pittsburgh," he said. "I wouldn't leave Pittsburgh. My home's here."

The Rooneys raised a family of five boys and a niece. Dan handles the Steelers, while Art Jr. is in charge of scouting. Tim does Yonkers Raceway and the family's Palm Beach Kennel Club for dog races. John is president of the William Penn Racing Association in Philadelphia, and his twin brother Pat presides over the Rooney racing establishment in Vermont. The family also has a major horse breeding farm in Sykesville, Md.

Not content with promoting football, baseball and soccer teams, boxing matches and even the stock market as an investor, Art Rooney for 50 years has loved the sport of kings. In the days before parimutuel machines, Rooney did his trade with bookies. Some regarded him as the greatest horseplayer in America. One weekend in 1936 at two different New York tracks, Rooney started with $300, played long shots and is said to have won between $250,000 and $400,000 from the bookies. Even more astounding is the way the Rooney family has borrowed at least $60 million to invest in sports, and come out ahead.

Pittsburgh has been remarkable for its colorful millionaires—such as Andrew Carnegie, Henry Clay Frick, H. J. Heinz and the Mellon clan. Include the name of Art Rooney as the most improbable of them all.

TOP 100 PENNSYLVANIANS IN FOOTBALL
Old-Timers

(Position, name, hometown, college, and teams)

E. Albert Exendine (Carlisle Indians)
E. Laughing Larry Kelley (Williamsport), Yale
T. Bemus Pierce (Carlisle Indians), Homestead AC, Oorang Indians
T. Claude "Tiny" Thornhill (Beaver), Pitt, Massillon Tigers
G. T. Truxton Hare (Phila), Penn
G. Frank "Dutch" Schwab (Madera), Lafayette
C. Bob Peck (Lock Haven), Pitt, Canton Bulldogs
QB. Frank Mt. Pleasant (Carlisle Indians)
HB. Joe Guyon (Carlisle Indians), Geo.Tech., Oorang Indians, Giants
HB. George McLaren (Pgh), Pitt, Massillon Tigers
FB. Jim Thorpe (Carlisle Indians), Canton Bulldogs, Oorang Indians
K. Christy Mathewson (Factoryville), Bucknell, Pgh Pros

Modern Offense

E. Fred Biletnikoff (Erie), Fla.St., Raiders
E. Mike Ditka (Aliquippa), Pitt, Bears, Cowboys
T. Stew Barber (Bradford), Penn St., Bills
T. Stan Jones (Lemoyne), Md., Bears
G. Chuck Drulis (Girardville), Temple, Bears
G. Glenn Ressler (Dornsife), Penn St., Colts
C. Chuck Bednarik (Bethlehem), Penn, Eagles
QB. Joe Namath (Beaver Falls), Ala., Jets
QB. Johnny Unitas (Pgh), Louisville Un., Colts
HB. Lenny Moore (Reading), Penn St., Colts
HB. Charley Trippi (Pittston), Ga., Cardinals
FB. Larry Brown (Pgh), Kan.St., Redskins
K. George Blanda (Youngwood), Ky., Bears, Oilers, Raiders

Modern Defense

E. Jim Katcavage (Phila), Dayton, Giants
E. Joe "Muggsy" Skladany (Larksville), Pitt, Steelers
T. Dick Modzelewski (West Natrona), Md., Giants, Browns
T. Mike Reid (Altoona), Penn St., Bengals
L. Jack Ham (Johnstown), Penn St., Steelers
L. Walt Michaels (Swoyersville), W & L, Packers, Browns
L. Joe Schmidt (Pgh), Pitt, Lions
B. Herb Adderley (Phila), Mich.St., Packers, Cowboys
B. Johnny Lujack (Connellsville), ND, Bears

B. Emlen Tunnell (Garrett Hill), Iowa, Giants, Packers
B. Clyde Washington (Carlisle), Purdue, Patriots, Jets
P. Joe Muha (Presston), VMI, Eagles

Quarterbacks—Arnold Galiffa (Donora), Army. John Hufnagel (Coraopolis), Penn St., Broncos. Jimmie Johnson (Carlisle Indians). Eugene "Shorty" Miller (Harrisburg), Penn St., Canton Bulldogs. Babe Parilli (Rochester), Ky., Packers, Patriots. Dick Shiner (Lebanon), Md., Redskins, Steelers, Falcons. George Welsh (Coaldale), Navy. Gus Welsh (Carlisle Indians).

(Oakland Raiders)

Fred Biletnikoff

(Nate Fine/Washington Redskins)

Larry Brown

Backs—Carl Beck (Harrisburg), W.Va. Un., Maroons, Yellow Jackets.
John Cappelletti (Upper Darby), Penn St., Rams. Ernie Davis
(Uniontown), Syracuse Un. Chester "Cookie" Gilchrist (Bracken-
ridge), Bills, Broncos. Warren Heller (Steelton), Pitt, Steelers. Bill
Hollenbach (Blue Ball), Penn. Dick Hoak (Jeannette), Penn St.,
Steelers. Leroy Kelly (Phila), Morgan St., Browns. Glenn Killinger
(Harrisburg), Penn St., Yellow Jackets. Mercury Morris (Pgh),
W.Tex.St., Dolphins. Jim Nance (Indiana), Syracuse, Patriots. Dea-
con Dan Towler (Donora), W & J, Rams.

Ends—Gary Collins (Williamstown), Md., Browns. Leon Hart (Turtle Creek), ND, Lions. Ted Kwalick (McKees Rocks), Penn St., 49ers. Bill McPeak (New Castle), Pitt, Steelers. Jim Mutscheller (Beaver Falls), ND, Colts. Ed Rutkowski (Kingston), ND, Bills. Bob Tucker (Hazleton), Bloomsburg St., Giants. Joe Walton (Beaver Falls), Pitt, Giants.

Tackles—Doug Crusan (Monessen), Indiana, Dolphins. Gus Dorizas

(Baltimore Colts)

Lenny Moore

(Phila), Penn. Harry Schuh (Neshaminy), Memphis St., Raiders, Rams.

Guards—Joe Bedenk (Williamsport), Penn St. William O. Hickok III (Harrisburg), Yale. Tony Liscio (Pgh), Tulsa Un., Cowboys. Duke Maronic (Steelton), Eagles. Rich Saul (Butler), Mich.St., Rams.

Center—Chuck Cherundolo (Old Forge), Penn St., Steelers.

Defensive Ends—Pete Duranko (Johnstown), ND, Broncos. Mike Mc-Coy (Erie), ND, Packers. Lou Michaels (Swoyersville), Ky., Steelers, Colts. John Paluck (Swoyersville), Pitt, Redskins. Ron Kastelnik (Ebensburg), Cincinnati Un., Packers, Colts.

Defensive Tackles—Bucko Kilroy (Phila), Temple, Eagles. Chuck Walker (Allison Park), Duke, Cardinals, Falcons.

Linebackers—Al Atkinson (Phila), Villanova, Jets. Ralph Baker (Lewistown), Penn St., Jets. Doug Buffone (Yatesboro), Louisville Un., Bears. Ralph Cindrich (Avella), Pitt, Patriots, Oilers. Dan Conners (St.Mary's), Miami Un., Raiders. Chuck Drazenovich (Brownsville), Penn St., Redskins. John Ebersole (Altoona), Penn St., Jets. Bill Koman (Hopewell), N.Car., Eagles, Cardinals. Mike Lucci (Ambridge), Tenn. Un., Lions. Ed O'Neill (Warren), Penn St., Lions. Dennis Onkotz (Northampton), Penn St., Jets. Myron Pottios (Charleroi), ND, Steelers, Rams, Redskins.

Defensive Backs—Ross Fichtner (McKeesport), Purdue, Browns. Richie McCabe (Pgh), Pitt, Steelers. Ken Reaves (Braddock), Norfolk St., Falcons, Cardinals. Ed Sharockman (St. Clair), Pitt, Vikings.

Kickers—Fred Cox (Monogahela), Pitt, Vikings. Bert Rechichar (Rostraver Twp.), Tenn. Un., Colts. Larry Seiple (Allentown), Ky., Dolphins.

Honorary Pennsylvanians—Charley Berry, Maroons end, born Phillipsburg, N.J. W. T. "Mother" Dunn, immortal Penn St. guard, born Youngstown, Ohio. Red Grange, famed runner, born Forksville, Pa., but raised in Wheaton, Ill. Franco Harris, Penn St. and Steelers back, born Fort Dix, N.J. Wilbur "Fats" Henry, great W & J and Maroons tackle, born Mansfield, Ohio. Bob Higgins, Penn St. end and coach, born Canton, Ohio. Lydell Mitchell, Penn St. and Colts halfback, born Salem, N.J.

50 GREATEST PITTSBURGH STEELERS

Offense	Defense

Offense

E. Ray Mathews, 1951–59
E. Gary Ballman, 1962–66
T. Frank Varrichione, 1955–60
T. Jon Kolb, 1969–75
G. John Nisby, 1957–61
G. Bruce Van Dyke, 1967–73
C. Chuck Cherundolo, 1941–48
QB. Bobby Layne, 1958–62
B. Lynn Chandnois, 1950–56
B. Bullet Bill Dudley, 1942–46
B. Franco Harris, 1972–75
K. Roy Gerela, 1971–75

Defense

E. Lou Michaels, 1961–63
E. L.C. Greenwood, 1969–75
T. Ernie Stautner, 1950–63
T. Mean Joe Greene, 1969–75
L. Andy Russell, 1963–75
L. Dale Dodril, 1951–59
L. Jack Ham, 1971–75
B. Jerry Shipkey, 1948–52
B. Jack Butler, 1951–59
B. Marv Woodson, 1964–69
B. Mel Blount, 1970–74
P. Bobby Walden, 1968–74

OE. Buddy Dial, Roy Jefferson, Bill McPeak, Elbie Nickel, Ron Shanklin. OT. Charley Bradshaw, Mike Sandusky, OG. Gerry Mullins. C. Bill Walsh. QB. Terry Bradshaw, Jim Finks. B. Johnny Blood, Johnny Clement, Joe Geri, Dick Hoak, John Henry Johnson, Franny Rogel, Byron "Whizzer" White.

DE. Ben McGee, Dwight White. DT. Ernie Holmes. LB. Myron Pottios, John Reger. B. Glen Edwards, Brady Keys, Mike Wagner.

50 GREATEST PHILADELPHIA EAGLES

Offense	Defense
E. Pete Pihos, 1947–55	E. Norm Willey, 1950–57
E. Pete Retzlaff, 1956–66	E. Tom Scott, 1953–58
T. Al Wistert, 1943–51	T. Mike Jarmoluk, 1949–55
T. Bob Brown, 1964–68	T. Floyd Peters, 1964–69
G. Vic Sears, 1941–53	L. Chuck Bednarik, 1949–62
G. Bucko Kilroy, 1943–55	L. Maxie Baughan, 1960–65
C. Vic Lindskog, 1944–51	L. Bill Bergey, 1974–75
QB. Tommy Thompson, 1941–50	B. Russ Craft, 1946–53
B. Tommy McDonald, 1957–63	B. Tom Brookshier, 1953–61
B. Timmy Brown, 1960–67	B. Don Burroughs, 1960–64
B. Steve Van Buren, 1944–51	B. Bill Bradley, 1969–75
K. Bobby Walston, 1951–62	P. Joe Muha, 1946–50

OE. Harold Carmichael, Jack Ferrante, Bud Grant, Bill Hewitt, Harold Jackson, Charley Young. OT. Jerry Sisemore, Lum Snyder. OG. Duke Maronic, Mark Nordquist. C. Alex Wojciechowicz. QB. Adrian Burk, Sonny Jurgensen, Davey O'Brien, Bobby Thomason, Norm Van Brocklin. B. Bosh Pritchard, Tom Woodeshick.

DE. John Green, Ed Khayat. DT. Marion Campbell, Jess Richardson, LB. Wayne Robinson. B. Jerry Norton, Jerry Williams, Roy Zimmerman.

The Legendary Carlisle Indians

... They Did Lose, But Not Often

"They didn't want to say a damn grammar school beat us, so they just called us a college," explained Joe Guyon, one of the great running backs of the Carlisle Indian Industrial School.

It was particularly embarrassing for the universities and established colleges, for from 1898 through 1913 this tiny Indian School had winning football seasons, taking on many of the top teams in the nation and usually defeating them.

Today the Carlisle Indian School is a legend. It lasted only from 1879 through 1918 and played football from 1893 through 1917, but it made a lasting mark in the annals of sports.

Jim Thorpe and Joe Guyon were just a few of its stars. Among the others were Gus Welch, Isaac Seneca, Albert Exendine, Bemus Pierce, Frank Mt. Pleasant, Pete Hauser, Frank Hudson, Joe Bergie and Jimmie Johnson. The supporting cast included such colorful names as American Horse, White Thunder, Shinbone, Little Old Man, Silverheels, Tomahawk, Afraid of Bear, Wounded Eye, Asa Sweetcorn and Bull Frog. In baseball, there was Charles Albert "Chief" Bender, the

Chippewa whom Connie Mack proclaimed the greatest money pitcher of all time. And in track, Louis Tewanima, the little Hopi, won the Olympic silver medal for the 10,000 meters.

Beyond even the expectations of its most famous coach and athletic director, Glenn Scobey "Pop" Warner, the Indian School in the Pennsylvania country town won immortality.

It was founded by Capt. Richard Henry Pratt, a 39-year-old Civil War veteran. Pratt had commanded a Negro regiment after the war and then fought against the Cheyenne, Comanche and Kiowa. In charge of Indian prisoners in Florida, he became interested in the challenge of educating them. "He believed that the solution of the Indian problem did not lie in any attempt to preserve and develop a distinctly Indian culture but lay rather in teaching the individual Indian to make a place for himself in the white man's world," wrote John Bakeless. The son of the head of instruction at Carlisle, Bakeless was the only white boy to grow up in the school and he later became a prominent expert and writer on the American Indians.

The government turned the old military post, dating back to 1757, over to Pratt. Later when the school disbanded, the installation became the Army War College.

The first Indians, 82 Sioux in tribal costumes, arrived at the 311-acre school on Oct. 6, 1879. By the turn of the century, when the school was in its prime, there were 1200 Indian students from 79 tribes. Prof. Oscar H. Bakeless deliberately had Cheyenne room with Sioux, and Seneca with Chippewa. In promoting the white culture, the school sought to destroy the Indian tribal culture, especially the language ties. That point is important, because one of the reasons for the emphasis on music and football was that these were the interests of white America.

Pratt stayed until 1904, when he retired as a brigadier general. He died in San Francisco in 1924. He planned his curriculum to accentuate vocational training, with a smattering of academic instruction. Jim Thorpe, for example, was trained to be a tailor. The faculty apparently was quite capable. Pulitzer Prize poet Marianne Moore was a young teacher of rapid calculation from 1911 to 1915. She lived in Carlisle with her widowed school teacher mother, returning from Bryn Mawr College to be with her. Each morning Miss Moore would bicycle out to the school to teach, and, incidentally, she became a lifelong sports fan. Once before her death, she was asked if she ever had Jim Thorpe in her class. "Yes," she said. "I always called him James."

Pop Warner, already a famous All-American quarterback and coach at Cornell and Georgia, turned down the University of Minnesota to accept the Indian School job for $1,200 a year. He came in 1899 and stayed for 13 years, with a break to go back to Cornell in 1904–06.

The Indians loved him and gave him the nickname "Pop." He had only two losing seasons at Carlisle. In fact, the nine years the Indians played without Pop as coach, they had eight losing years. The glory of Carlisle football is almost as much Pop Warner's story as it is the Indian boys themselves.

Just how boyish many of the Indians were and just how small the school was are controversial issues. Thorpe was 24 and had four years of college football by his final season in 1912 under Warner. "None of my boys is more than 16 or 17," Warner once told sportswriter Gene Fowler. "Yes, Pop," replied Fowler, "they may have been kids when they started playing for you, but they were old men when they stopped."

Warner similarly wrote that his little school for 15 years faced the big universities which had as many as 5000 students, but few schools in those days were that big. Warner said he had his pick from only 250 lads of football age, but the Indian agents did some recruiting for him. He did keep his football squad to 15 men. On his track team, he seldom had that many. Warner's trackmen showed up in Eastern in 1909 with Thorpe, Tewanima and three other Indians and defeated the 46-man Lafayette College team, 71–31—a story as colorful as any that ever came out of Carlisle. Of course, Thorpe won five events and finished second in the 100-yard dash. Later at Syracuse, Warner used an eight-man team to win by a point, with Thorpe scoring five firsts, a second and two third places.

It was "more like a home than an institution," wrote Warner in later years. His players were awakened at 6 a.m. by bugler James Garvie, a Sioux who was a student there 1912–15. The boys drilled for an hour, went to breakfast and then had studies the rest of the day until 4 p.m. Then Pop got in two hours' football practice while the other students, such as Garvie, went to band rehearsal. The music program, incidentally, was fabulous. From Theodore Roosevelt's day on, the Indians played at the inaugurations. Garvie became a professional musician, directing the Lebanon American Legion Drum and Bugle Corps and the VFW Girls Corps to state championships.

The Indian boys, as Warner pointed out, were not experienced football players. They had natural speed, alertness, perseverance and skill in using both hands and feet. Most could kick. A few liked body contact, but all of them preferred the art of deception—and that was the game Pop Warner loved anyway. So versatile were they that most played more than one position.

"There wasn't an Indian of the lot who didn't love to win and hate to lose," wrote Warner, "but to a man they were modest in victory and resolute in defeat. They never gloated, they never whined, and no matter how bitter the contest, they played cheerfully, squarely and cleanly."

Added Pop, "There were better teams than the Indians, but none more colorful and fascinating with their tricks, speed, fearlessness and skill."

Up against all-white teams, mainly the sons of the Eastern elite, the Indians used football, said Warner, "to show the palefaces what they could do when the odds were even."

The Indians began their football in 1893 by winning two games by a total score of 60–0. The following season Vance McCormick came as the volunteer coach. McCormick had just graduated as the All-American quarterback at Yale. He was of the wealthy Cameron-McCormick clan of Harrisburg and later was its mayor and newspaper publisher. He rejected numerous colleges and prep schools and took the unpaid coaching job at Carlisle. In two years his rookie teams won 5 and lost 12. He was succeeded by William O. Hickok, another Harrisburg scion and volunteer. "Wild Bill" Hickok, two-time All-American guard at Yale, got the Indians winning with a 6–4 season. That Dec. 19, 1896, he took them against Wisconsin under the lights at Chicago. Some 15,000 fans saw the Red and Old Gold of Carlisle win 18–8 in football's first big night game.

With Warner in 1899 came the glorious days. Losing only to Harvard and Princeton, the team was 9–2, including a 16–5 victory over Penn and a 2–0 triumph in San Francisco over California, a game where Warner showed up with a 14-man squad. Halfback Isaac Seneca, a Seneca Indian who played five years at the school, was on that team and was Carlisle's first All-American.

By the time the Indians were done with football in 1917, they had an amazing 169–87–13 record, and 24 of those defeats came in the school's final four years when the institution was being phased out.

Often the Indians were simply brilliant. They shut out Lebanon Valley College for 13 straight years. Their record against Penn State was 4–1–1, against Pitt, 4–4–1, against Bucknell, 6–4–1 and against Dickinson, 12–0–1. Harvard took them, 2–12 and Penn, 6–13–2, but these were the greatest years ever for these Ivy League schools. Carlisle was the only team to score a touchdown against Penn in 1908, holding the undefeated Quakers to a 6–6 tie. In their 1903 Harvard game, the Indians worked the hidden ball trick, with Jimmie Johnson taking the kick-off and tucking the ball under guard Charlie Dillon's jersey. Dillon did 100 yards in 10 seconds, but Carlisle lost the game, 12–11. Only Princeton held a whammy over the Indians. In six games, the Indians scored but a total of 6 points and lost every contest.

The Indians never had an undefeated season. Their greatest years were 1907, 1911 and 1912, the Thorpe teams incidentally, but always they would let down for one game. When they ripped Penn 26–5 and Harvard 23–15, Warner claimed the 1907 club was second only to his

1916 Pitt Panthers as the greatest team he ever coached. His 1911 Indians were 11–1, with only a 12–11 loss to Syracuse. That year the Welch-Thorpe team scored 298 points to their opponents' 49. But in 1912 they scored 504 points to 114, a year when no other college scored above 400 points. The Indians were 12–1–1, with a 34–26 loss to Penn and a 0–0 tie with Washington and Jefferson. Big Jim Thorpe, All-American for a second season, tallied 25 of the Indians' 66 touchdowns.

The Indians did not like playing on wet fields, naturally enough because of their speed and their lack of size. They loved tackling, forward passing and kicking. Warner claimed that Frank Hudson, a 5-foot-4, 133-pound Pueblo, was the greatest drop-kicker the game has ever known. Though clean players, the Indians suffered repeated penalties—many of them suspicious, as referees might not have wanted the big universities to be embarrassed on the scoreboard.

Privately, the Indian boys had their quirks. Thaddeus Redwater slept under the bed at Princeton's Nassau Inn. Asa Sweetcorn held up the Carlisle railroad station to get a train ticket. Nikifer Shouchuk, the quiet but outstanding center, seemed out of place in the group until his teammates explained that he was an Eskimo.

Perhaps some of their talents were exaggerated, but their records seem to prove otherwise. Thorpe undoubtedly remains football's greatest star. Joe Guyon, a 5-foot-10, 178-pound Chippewa, played tackle and then halfback, went on to All-American honors at Georgia Tech and was with the New York Giants at age 35. Mt. Pleasant, a 140-pound Tuscarorra, was one of football's first great passers. Albert Exendine, a 166-pound Arapahoe, played end as well as any man Warner saw in almost 50 years of football. Exendine became a lawyer. Gus Welch, a Chippewa and another good student, was superb for five varsity years and later graduated from both Dickinson College and the Dickinson Law School. Bemus and Hawley Pierce, Elmer Busch, Pete Calac and others went into professional football.

From a crowded roster of stars, Warner once listed his All-Indian team: E. Exendine and Ed Rogers. T. Emil Wauseka Hauser and Hawley Pierce. G. Martin Wheelock and Bemus Pierce. C. Lone Wolf Hunt. QB. Jimmie Johnson. HB. Thorpe and Guyon. FB. Pete Hauser. The substitutes would be Gus Welch, Mt. Pleasant, Hudson, Calac, Seneca and Little Boy.

Only a handful of Carlisle Indian graduates remain today. What is left are a few memories and some faded photographs of Indian teams with their deadly serious-looking players staring straight ahead. And then there are the legends of their remarkable exploits. It will be the legends which endure.

The Greatest Athlete in the World

... *"Thanks, King,"* *Said Jim Thorpe*

James Francis Thorpe is accepted as the greatest American athlete of all time. In fact, next to Babe Ruth, he remains the most illustrious figure in the sporting world. Yet many experts question whether this quiet but roughhouse Indian would be a superstar in modern football.

Thorpe himself was never sure if he were the nation's top all-around athlete. He was a modest, realistic man, not skilled at self-promotion. But he was certain he could have played modern football and been good at it.

"When I played at Carlisle," he said in 1941, "I was as fast as any of them, but oddly enough they always stressed my strength more than my speed. I twice ran the 100 in 9.4. I could do it any day in 10 flat. In football togs, I could step off the 100 in 11 flat. Having had speed, the modern game would have been made to order for me, so when I hear someone say Thorpe would have been no great shakes at this kind of football, it kind of gets under my skin. Basically, football is no different from the kind of game we played at Carlisle under old Pop Warner. A lot of new tricks have been added, of course, but the original skeleton is

(Pro-Football Hall of Fame)

Jim Thorpe

there, with perhaps a little new meat. We ran and kicked very much the same as they do today."

Thorpe actually was football's first modern player. He ran with such power that a single tackler who hit him above the knees never could bring him down, seldom even hold on to him. The New York *Times'* Allison Danzig saw most of the greats play, and he rated Thorpe as among the toughest to stop. Joe Guyon, a great halfback himself, played with Thorpe at Carlisle and in the professional ranks. He claimed that while Red Grange was strictly a better runner than Jim, nobody was a better all-around player. Thorpe was an excellent punter, a field-goal kicker, blocker and even passer. He was a devastating tackler, usually throwing his entire body at a runner and bowling him over. With his speed, hands and amazing jumping ability, he would have been a superb pass receiver had football in his day used backs to break up a zone defense.

He had tremendous stamina and an exceptional body for absorbing punishment. "Who in hell can get hurt playing football?" he once asked. "I never needed to call time out during any college game."

Perhaps the nearest modern-day equivalent to Jim Thorpe was Cleveland's Jimmy Brown, who in his prime was a perennial All-Pro.

Thorpe at 6-foot-1 and 185 pounds was not a big man by today's standards. He and Jack Dempsey were about the same size, but both hit with the force of men 25 and 30 pounds heavier. With today's nutrition and training, Thorpe certainly would have been a muscular 200 pounds or more.

So remarkable an athlete was Thorpe that, unlike all others in sports history, people wanted to know what he did not excel at. His poorest sports, frankly, were baseball, tennis and billiards, yet with more practice and motivation even in these games he might have become spectacular.

He joined the Harrisburg Indians baseball team in the International League in 1915, just three years after being the greatest Olympic hero the world has ever known. Thorpe was not an outstanding baseball player, but in his first day in a Harrisburg uniform against Providence, the switch-hitting Thorpe batted three for nine, one a tremendous home run over the centerfield fence. The crowd of 5822 that July 25 was astounded. No records were ever kept at old Island Park, but it is believed that the three longest blasts ever made there were by Jim Thorpe, Babe Ruth and Willie Mays.

Thorpe was a skillful dancer. He hit in the low 80s in golf and bowled over 200. He was proficient at hockey, lacrosse, swimming, rifle shooting, archery, squash, handball, hunting, wrestling and horsemanship. He could box, ice skate, handle a canoe and play a good game of basketball.

In track and field, his accepted marks are: 100-yard dash, 10 seconds; the 220, 21.8; the 440, 50.8; the mile, 4:35; the 120 high hurdles, 15; the 220 low hurdles, 23.8; the broad jump, 23 feet 6 inches; the high jump, 6 feet 5; the pole vault, 11 feet; the shot put, 47 feet 9; the discus, 136 feet, and the javelin, 163 feet. And track was only a sideline for him.

In baseball, where he was at his greatest disadvantage, his lifetime mark for 289 major league games was .252, or above average for a big leaguer, especially in his day. In his last season in 1919, he hit a respectable .327 for the New York Giants and Boston Braves.

"Sir," said King Gustav V of Sweden at the 1912 Olympic Games, "you are the greatest athlete in the world." "Thanks, King," Jim replied.

When the Associated Press asked sportswriters to name the greatest athlete of the 1900–1950 era, the results for first-place votes were: Thorpe, 252; Babe Ruth, 86; Jack Dempsey, 19; Ty Cobb, 11; Joe Louis, 5; Lou Gehrig, 4; Red Grange, 3; Jackie Robinson and Bobby Jones, each 2, and Bronko Nagurski, Walter Johnson and Cornelius Warmerdam, each 1.

Like Ruth, with whom he is always compared, Thorpe's athletic achievement is only part of the legend. The man behind the records remains more fascinating than his exploits in sports.

Thorpe was the orphaned Indian kid who could never quite adjust to the white man's ways and commercialism. Not a stupid man, but as honest as Will Rogers, he was a culturally misplaced person. He rose to the top and then sunk to being a pitiful figure. Even after his death, his admiring public is trying to decide what to do about Jim Thorpe.

He was born May 28, 1888, near Prague in the Oklahoma Territory. He was a big boy at birth, 10 pounds, and was a twin. His great-grandfather was Black Hawk, the Sac and Fox chief. His father, Hiram, was half-Irish, and his mother, Charlotte View Thorpe, was part-French. His Indian name was Wa-Tho-Huck, meaning "Bright Path." Jim regarded himself as an Indian, but actually he was five-eighth Indian.

A series of tragedies befell Thorpe early in life. His twin brother Charlie died at 8. His mother died when he was 12, and his father when he was 15.

In 1904, just before his father's death, young Jim was entered in the Carlisle Indian Industrial School. He was 5-foot, 115 pounds, and the schoolmasters thought he would make a good tailor. He was never much good at mathematics and, like Babe Ruth, found academic studies more of a bore than a challenge.

Pop Warner put him on the football team in 1907 when he was 19, but he rode the bench until the Penn game at Franklin Field. The first time Thorpe got the ball, he lost five yards. The second time he got it, he went 75 yards for a touchdown. The Indians defeated the Quakers, 26–6, and Warner said it was his greatest Carlisle team.

Thorpe turned in many long scores. Against Army and a halfback named Dwight D. Eisenhower, Jim had to run almost 200 yards for a TD, because his first field-length gallop was called back for a penalty. Thorpe had an interesting incentive for breaking through the defense line and streaking for the end zone. He instinctively disliked being tackled. It hurt his pride when even three men gang-tackled him. He was absolutely insulted if one person tripped him up.

In 1908 Thorpe made Walter Camp's third-string All-American team. He was out of school in 1909 and 1910, and then Warner got him back in 1911 to prepare for the Olympics. In 1911 and 1912 he was on the first team All-American. Quite possibly in 1912, when he made 25 touchdowns and scored 198 points, he had the greatest season any collegiate players ever has had. In all, he played four years for Carlisle, and the Indians had a 43–5–2 record.

Pop Warner also used Thorpe for track, starting in 1908. Had there been an All-American team for this sport, Jim would have been an unanimous selection. He typically would win five events, plus a few seconds, in any track meet. Lazy when it came to practicing and always more intent upon achieving the proper mental attitude, Thorpe invariably won a race by a few inches, not streaking away. He played football the same way. Warner complained that Thorpe never gave 60 minutes' worth, but saved some game time for resting up and not provoking the opposition.

The 1912 Olympics were the highlight of his career. At Stockholm he won four of the five Pentathlon events and scored 8412 of a possible 10,000 points in the Decathlon. It was the most brilliant one-man performance in sports history. He came home with $50,000 worth of Olympic trophies and to parades in Carlisle, Philadelphia and New York. Then a 28-year-old reporter, Roy Ruggles Johnson, on the Worcester *Telegram*, revealed on Jan. 22, 1913, that Thorpe had violated his amateur standing by playing professional baseball with Rocky Mount in the Eastern Carolina League in the summers of 1909 and 1910. The Amateur Athletic Union took the trophies and first-place finishes away from Thorpe. The AAU's decision has never been reversed, and it remains one of the great controversies in the sporting world. Later the same thing happened to Paavo Nurmi, the Finn, and

Karl Schranz, the Austrian, but their cases have never received the attention that Thorpe's has.

In early 1913, following his straight-forward admission that he had played pro ball, Jim signed a long-term contract for $5,000 a year with the baseball Giants. It was another of his many mistakes. With any other team than John J. McGraw's, Thorpe would have been given a chance. McGraw put him on the bench, criticized him unmercifully, and for the first time in sports Jim Thorpe lost confidence in himself. He played big-league ball from 1913 through 1919, but only appeared in 289 games. His most memorable feat was with the Cincinnati Reds in 1917 when his infield chop scored a run from third and broke up the scoreless double no-hitter with the Chicago Cubs.

The book on Thorpe was that he could not hit curveballs. Possibly so. In 698 times at bat in the majors, he got 176 hits but struck out 122 times. He hit 20 doubles, 18 triples and seven home runs and had 29 stolen bases and 82 runs batted in.

He was farmed out to Milwaukee, Jersey City, Harrisburg, Akron, Toledo, Portland, Ore., and Hartford. He played with the Harrisburg Indians from July 25 to Aug. 29, 1915. They were in fourth place in the International League when he was unaccountably dismissed with a .298 batting average and 21 stolen bases. They fell to sixth place without him. He had two weaknesses in Harrisburg—clumsy fielding and off-field hijinks with pitcher Al Schacht, later the clown-prince of baseball. But he was a drawing card in Harrisburg, as well as in Buffalo, Montreal, Rochester, Richmond and around the league.

Thorpe meanwhile returned to his real love, football, and was in the pro game from 1915 to 1929. He played with the Canton Bulldogs, the Rock Island Independents, the New York Giants and with teams in Cleveland, Hammond, St. Petersburg and Portsmouth, Ohio. His last game, at age 41, was with the Chicago Cardinals in a 34–0 losing effort against Red Grange's Chicago Bears. Thorpe also had his own team, the Oorang Indians, and in 1920 was the figurehead president of the American Professional Football Association. He could earn $15,000 a year in football, and was the biggest name until Grange came along.

His private life was a mess. He married Iva Margaret Miller at Carlisle's St. Patrick's Catholic Church in 1913, with Joe Guyon as his best man. Their oldest child, Jim Jr., died of polio in 1917, the year Muggsy McGraw wouldn't play Thorpe in the World Series. Jim had three daughters with Iva and then was divorced. In 1926 he married Frieda Kirkpatrick, by whom he had four sons. Again he was divorced, and in 1945 he married Patricia Askew, who survived him.

Sweets and alcohol were his weaknesses. Even before he quit football, his weight shot up to 235 pounds. The liking for liquor went back to his Carlisle days. One story is that after the famous 6–6 tie with undefeated Penn in 1908, the great Penn fullback Bill Hollenback and Thorpe each spent a week in the hospital. Hollenback was recovering from injuries. Thorpe, it is said, was recovering from his post-game celebration. His drinking problem was cited in his divorces.

Thorpe went from one job to another. He was an able-bodied seaman, a guard at a Ford Motor plant, a bouncer, a bartender, a $4-a-day ditch digger in Los Angeles, a traveling lecturer and an extra in the movies. For the film on his life, *Jim Thorpe, All-American*, he received $25,000 for coaching Burt Lancaster in the title role.

Thorpe suffered his first heart attack in 1943 and another in 1952. He underwent a lip operation for cancer in 1951 as a charity patient at a Philadelphia hospital. He was living in an auto trailer near Los Angeles when on March 28, 1953, at age 64 he suffered his third heart attack and died. He left this world as he had entered—penniless.

Even in death, the Thorpe story wasn't over. He was buried dressed in buckskin and moccasins, and thousands viewed his body. Temporarily laid to rest at Shawnee, Okla., his remains were removed to Tulsa and finally to Mauch Chunk. To the best of knowledge, this old Molly Maguire town had never seen the live Jim Thorpe, but its citizens voted to change the name and to raise $17,000 for a mausoleum a month after his death. On Feb. 8, 1954, the body of Jim was brought there. The mausoleum has never been a tourist attraction. Jim Thorpe, Pa., remains more famous for its jail where four Mollies were hanged and for the "curse mark" in Cell 17 that ringleader Aleck Campbell angrily placed there. But the town has rejected attempts to revert the community's name back to Mauch Chunk.

The legend of the man has been embellished by passing time. President Nixon made April 16, 1973, "Jim Thorpe Day." The Olympic medals have never been returned to a Thorpe shrine, but in 1974 the United States Treasury struck off a commemorating medal, some priced as high as $5,000, in his honor. An official of the Jim Thorpe Memorial Committee said, "We finally got the U.S. government to recognize that Thorpe was an honest man." That was a strange comment. Nobody ever asserted that Jim Thorpe was not America's greatest athlete or that he was dishonest.

Quarterback Country

... *Pennsylvania Specializes in QB Production*

Quarterback is the most celebrated and glamorous position in modern American team sports, and Pennsylvania has dominated it. With remarkable frequency, the biggest collegiate and professional names at quarterback have been Pennsylvania boys.

It is the most skilled position in football, the glory spot watched by every fan. Few teams can win without at least an average quarterback. Consistent winners require great quarterbacks. For the men who excel at the position, especially in the pro ranks, it is the culmination of years of training, study and experience. Great quarterbacks must love the game, and they reflect their own individuality in the way they call plays, create offensive momentum, throw passes and give an image to their teams.

In a state obsessed with football for so long, it is only natural that it almost mass-produces quality quarterbacks. Some start throwing footballs as early as 6 years of age, as Joe Namath did on the vacant lots of Beaver Falls. By the time many are 16, their passes are accurate within 40 yards, they know the fundamentals of the game, and they are thinking ahead for careers in college and possibly the pros.

107

The nurturing of quarterbacks goes on in Pennsylvania, community after community. It is an effective developmental program, almost as foolproof and natural as nine generations of 400 related musicians named Bach in an earlier German culture. When Pennsylvania stops turning out great quarterbacks, it has stopped caring about football. Nobody foresees that.

The assembling of quarterbacks is so proficient that on the All-American teams of 1946–74, Pennsylvanians made first-string quarterback seven times and runner-up, five times. On the All-Pro teams of 1948–74, Pennsylvanians were on the first team ten times and on the second team, seven times.

Certainly the most technically expert quarterback of all time was Johnny Unitas, the intense, long-faced kid out of Pittsburgh. Wearing high shoes for 18 pro seasons (1956–73), Unitas passed for a record 23 miles with a record 2830 completions, hitting for a National Football League high of 290 touchdowns, all but three of the TDs for his famed Baltimore Colts. He won five league championships for the Colts and one Super Bowl. Three times he was the NFL's most valuable player. In one stretch of 47 games, Unitas connected on a touchdown pass in every contest. Old No. 19 was so good that he threw 37 more TDs than interceptions. The defense had to key on him so much that Unitas fumbled 95 times, the NFL career record.

On any dream team, if the crew-cut Unitas weren't the choice for quarterback, the long-haired Joe Willie Namath would be. In ten seasons with the New York Jets (1965–74), Namath passed for 13½ miles and made 151 touchdown passes. Occasionally interception prone and not quite the obvious flawless technician like Unitas, Sid Luckman, Otto Graham or Bart Starr, the flashy Namath has an arm the equal of Sammy Baugh and unmatched predatory instincts for picking apart defenses and moving his own offense. Three times his teammates chose him the most valuable Jet, contradicting the prima donna image he has. No other football player was ever quite like Namath, and he achieved a super-stardom all his own.

Sportswriter Dick Schaap is right when he claims that Broadway Joe is in an illustrious circle with Babe Ruth, Jim Thorpe and Arnold Palmer as a celebrity even to the non-sportsminded public. Political columnist James Reston in 1970 went so far as to call him the "New Anti-Hero."

"One of the most interesting symbols of America today is Joe Namath, the quarterback of the New York football Jets," wrote Reston in the New York *Times*. "Joe is not only in tune with the rebellious attitude of the young, but he doubles it. He defies both the people who hate play-boys and the people who hate bully-boys. He is something special: a long-haired hard-hat, the anti-hero of the sports world." Reston saw the Namath values as showmanship, personal and financial aggrandizement, and the pragmatic faith in that whatever succeeds is right.

Little of the Namath personality would amount to anything if he could not "wait until the uttermost split-second, while his receivers were driving and faking for that extra step on the defenders, and then throw with geometric accuracy, long or short, bullet or lob, to the primary or secondary target, just before he was buried by the charging front four of the opposition," in Reston's words. Besides remarkable ability, observed Reston, what Namath had was, "Hemingway's definition of courage: grace under pressure."

James Reston concluded with a hesitant admiration for Joe Namath, and some Presidents and Secretaries of State are not accorded that much.

By 1974, Namath, the son of an immigrant steelworker, was classed with Wilt Chamberlain and Arnie Palmer, also Pennsylvanians, as the three richest American athletes. The U.S. Postal Service in 1973 rated him fourth, behind Hank Aaron, Dinah Shore and Johnny Carson, in the volume of fan mail. A market research poll placed him second to Willie Mays among sports figures for being well-known, but true to his anti-hero image, he was 124th for being admired, 143rd for being well-liked as a person and 156th for being trusted for endorsements.

George Blanda and Johnny Lujack were only a shade behind Unitas and Namath in ability as super quarterbacks.

Blanda, the durable Slovak from Youngwood, was the Pro Football Hall of Fame's 1974 Man of the Year. At age 47, Blanda was semi-retired as a quarterback, though he did throw one of his career's 236 touchdown passes in 1974. As a kicker for the Oakland Raiders, he put 77 points up on the board, running his all-time NFL scoring record to 1919 points or more than 500 points ahead of the number-two man, Lou Groza. Blanda also holds the career field-goal mark of 322.

Blanda started at the University of Kentucky and in 1949 signed with the Chicago Bears for $6,000 in salary and $600 in bonus. He moved to the Houston Oilers in 1960 and to the Raiders in 1967. As football's Methuselah, Blanda in 1972 surpassed Ben Agajanian as the oldest man to ever play the pro game. A living landmark, Blanda in 1975 will be donning his football togs for his 26th professional season, adding to his record 328 pro games that has made him football's equivalent to baseball's Lou Gehrig.

In Blanda's first pro game as a quarterback, he substituted for Lujack. The 6-foot-2, 218-pound Blanda, handsome in the John Wayne masculine fashion, could throw a football. In his career, he passed for more than 15 miles. He is tied for the pro record of seven TD passes in a game. He holds the season record of 36 TD passes with Houston in 1961, and against Buffalo in 1964 he set another mark of 37 completions in a contest.

He has had many great games, but none finer than in 1970 against Pittsburgh. The Steelers knocked starter Daryle Lamonica out with a back injury. On the field trotted old George. He had just turned 43, but obviously arthritis hadn't set in yet. He fired three touchdown passes, kicked three extra points and added a field goal, and the Steelers were beaten, 31–14. He earned his year's salary of $40,000 in that game alone.

Johnny Lujack started in Connellsville and probably was the most versatile Pennsylvania footballer in the skilled positions since Jim Thorpe. Though not brawny at 6-foot and 180 pounds, Lujack could call plays, throw passes, run, kick and tackle. He was two-time All-American at Notre Dame, 1946–47, and All-Pro with the Bears in 1950.

Lujack's finest hour was in the great 0–0 standoff between Frank Leahy's Fighting Irish and Earl Blaik's Black Knights of West Point. It was Nov. 9, 1946, before 74,100 fans at Yankee Stadium. Notre Dame had a 5–0 record; Army, a 7–0 mark. Previously as a sophomore, Lujack had beaten Army, 26–0, and had turned in a memorable play when his pass was intercepted by Glenn Davis and he knocked down two blockers and then tripped up Davis in open field to prevent a runback touchdown. Now in 1946, he came up again with a great game. He averaged 40 yards on eight punts, one a booming 55-yarder. Of 17 pass attempts, he completed only six and he threw three interceptions— all nabbed by Army quarterback Arnold Tucker. But Lujack, No. 32, made two key tackles. His shoe-string grab stopped Tucker from making a score on a keeper play. And then in his most sensational play, Lujack brought down Doc Blanchard head-on to save the day for Notre Dame.

The Pennsylvania factory list of top quarterbacks just begins with Unitas, Namath, Blanda and Lujack. There are at least 30 others:

John Brallier (Latrobe), the first recognized pro player in 1895. Chuck Burkhart (McKees Rocks), the winningest quarterback Penn State ever had. Tom Clements (McKees Rocks), one of the five Pennsylvanians, to star at quarterback for Notre Dame. Arnold Galiffa (Donora), 1949 All-American at Army. Terry Hanratty (Butler), the

1968 All-American who surpassed George Gipp's offense record at Notre Dame.

Sam Havrilak (Monessen), Bucknell ace who became a fine flanker for Unitas' Colts. Earl Hewitt (Penfield), a great with Penn State in 1899, then with Connie Mack's football Athletics and finally a state legislator for 20 years. John Hufnagel (Coraopolis), a tall, rawboned, exceptionally accurate passer for Penn State who received 1973 all-American citations. Steve Joachim (King of Prussia), the 1974 Temple wizard who won the Maxwell Trophy. Jimmy Johnson (Carlisle Indians), 1903 All-American and Pop Warner said he was the game's best at his position.

Jimmy Jones (Harrisburg), schoolboy phenom, Southern California star and whiz with the Canadian League's Alouettes. Richie Lucas (Glassport), took 1959 All-American honors at Penn State for his sizzling style. Ted Marchibroda (Franklin), a star at St. Bonaventure, a top Steelers' draft pick and now the Colts' coach. Johnny Mazur

(Chicago Bears)

Johnny Lujack

(Plymouth), the throwing half of Notre Dame's Mazur to Jim Mut-scheller combination, and later a pro coach. Vance McCormick (Harrisburg), Pennsylvania's first All-American quarterback, at Yale in 1892, and the first coach of the Carlisle Indians.

Kim McQuilken (Allentown), passed for almost four miles at Lehigh and then played for the Atlanta Falcons. Eugene "Shorty" Miller (Harrisburg), a 1911–12 Penn State southpaw who was one of football's greatest 5-foot-5, 140 pounders. Frank Mt. Pleasant (Carlisle Indians), diminutive magician who probably threw football's first spiral pass. Babe Parilli (Rochester), with 23 TD passes led Kentucky in 1950 to a 10–1 season and then stopped Oklahoma's 31-game streak in the Sugar Bowl, later All-Pro quarterback. Tony Rados (Steelton), the first Penn State T-formation quarterback and the rifle-arm who got the ball to Jesse Arnelle.

Johnny Rauch (Yeadon), second-team All-American at Georgia in 1948 and a pro coach. Gil Reich (Steelton), superb high school and Kansas play-caller. Ed Rutkowski (Kingston), big at Notre Dame and super as a pro flanker with Buffalo. Corny Salvaterra (Wilkes-Barre), brainy Pitt quarterback and all-around star. Dick Shiner (Lebanon), a standout at Maryland and in the pros 11 years.

Tom Shuman (Pottstown), underrated at Penn State until his brilliance in the 1975 Cotton Bowl against Baylor. Sandy Stephens (Uniontown), first nationally noted black quarterback and a second-team All-American at Minnesota. Gus Welch (Carlisle Indians), for five years a star for Pop Warner and the one who called the plays for Thorpe. George Welsh (Coaldale), led Navy and the nation in total offense and passing in 1955 and a second-string All-American, later assistant coach at Penn State and then head coach at Navy. Tom Yewic (Conemaugh), great at Michigan State and a fine pro punter.

To this list should be added Albert L. Howard, a native of Waynesburg, who in 1939 completed a pass for little Waynesburg College against Fordham. It went for 80 yards and a touchdown, and was the world's first pass ever seen on television.

The TV long-bomb that the late Al Howard introduced reached its zenith in the Unitas-Namath duels. They were two of the most thrilling football games in history.

The first was Super Bowl III at Miami, where the Jets upset the Colts, 16–7. Unitas' club had lost merely two games in two years and was favored by 17 points. The 6-foot-1, 205-pound Unitas was 35 and in his 14th season, but he had a sore elbow most of 1968 and Earl Morrall started the Super Bowl contest. Namath was 26 and in his fourth season. Back in Beaver Falls as a kid, he so idolized Unitas that he wore

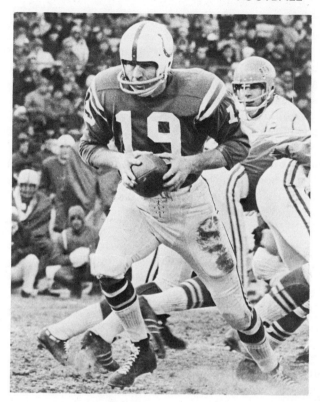

(Baltimore Colts)

Johnny Unitas

his No. 19. Now wearing No. 12, he brashly predicted three days before the game that he would win the American Football League's first Super Bowl. That he did, hitting on 17 of 28 passes for 206 yards. With Unitas-like precision, Broadway Joe picked apart the famed Colts' defense, negating linebacker blitzes and finding holes in zone coverage. A sullen Unitas got into the game with only 3½ minutes to go, but he marched his team down the field, hit on 11 of 24 passes for 110 yards, and at least put the Colts on the scoreboard. Namath later said that on any other day, his Jets would have beaten the Colts worse. But on any other day, Swoyersville's Lou Michaels would not have missed two early field goals and Morrall before the half ended would have seen flanker Jimmy Orr standing all by himself in the end zone.

What Namath did in Super Bowl III was not annihilate the Baltimore Colts, but establish the AFL as a league worthy of merging equally with the senior NFL. That is Joe Namath's lasting historic importance.

Early in the 1972 season, Unitas and Namath met again. They were weary warriors. Unitas in his final season with the Colts had an arm that no longer could bullet a ball 60 yards. More a loner than ever, John was making it on his tremendous courage and experience. Namath, meanwhile, was the golden cripple. He was in that period between 1967 and 1974 when he did not have 20 touchdown passes a year. His right knee had been messed up in his senior year at Alabama. In 1970 he broke a wrist. In a 1971 exhibition game, Detroit linebacker Mike Lucci, a contemporary from Beaver County, picked up a fumble and Namath tore his right-knee ligaments trying to tackle him. "I read in the papers how stupid it was for me to try to tackle Lucci, but I believe a man should always play to the ultimate when he's on the field," explained Namath.

Now in 1972, Broadway Joe was going for an injury-free season—or, more correctly, no additional injuries. "I have a pair of legs that only an orthopedic surgeon could love," he said. "I'm planning to give them to science, if my lawyers can figure out a tax deduction. I can't run, and when the weather's cold and damp, walking's a real adventure. My way of life is to avoid body contact—on the football field."

What always remained in top condition was the Namath body above the legs. He has never been out of shape, never overweight, and never sore-armed. But because of the encased right knee, he would lunge backwards with his weight on his left leg while spotting receivers. He always had the quickest release in football, setting up and unloading faster than the best-legged men the game ever saw.

Old-old pro Unitas and old-pro Namath met this time in Baltimore in September of 1972. Again the Jets won, 44–34, after an NFL passing mark of 872 yards was established. Unitas hit for 376 yards, two touchdowns and no interceptions. Namath hit for 496 yards and six TD's—four of them 65 yards or longer. In a two-minute exchange, Namath connected on a 67-yard bomb, and the Colts came back with a 93-yard kickoff return touchdown, then Namath hit on successive 42-yard and 28-yard plays for a score, and finally Unitas fumbled and Namath put it by the flags a third time on a 10-yard pass. As the greatest two-minute quarterback football has ever known, Unitas closed the gap with a 22-yard strike to Tom Matte, only to stand on the sidelines and see Namath slap an 80-yard retaliatory touchdown.

It was Unitas v. Namath in electrifying football—two superstars of opposite temperaments but of stellar, well-trained ability. And they played the game so skillfully and yet so nonchalantly that it was as if they were still kids warming up back on the sandlots of Western Pennsylvania.

Ferocious Linebackers

... Take a Boy from a
Small Pennsylvania Town

Chuck Bednarik once explained his linebacking method to stop the opposition's ground game: "On a run, you just go up and knock the guy on his can."

George Woodruff, the great University of Pennsylvania coach, devised the position of linebacker sometime in the mid-1890s. Little did he realize that 50 years later perhaps the greatest defensive player of all time, Charles Bednarik, would be backing up the line with absolute ruthlessness, first for the Penn Quakers and then for the Philadelphia Eagles.

Linebackers are the steel and coal of defensive football. And just as Pennsylvania produces an abundance of quality quarterbacks for offensive football, it forges linebackers for defense.

The numbers count is astounding. In the 25 years of professional football from 1950 through 1974, nine Pennsylvanians won 36 linebacker slots on All-Pro teams. In that quarter-century, in fact, there were only four years when a Pennsylvania linebacker was not an All-Pro. In 1974, there were 15 Pennsylvanians playing linebacker in the National Football League and one in the Canadian League. Penn State

115

in 1974 alone had 10 of its graduates, seven of them native Pennsylvanians, gainfully employed as NFL linebackers.

Jack Ham, of Johnstown, made second team All-Pro in his sophomore year with the Pittsburgh Steelers and followed that in 1974 with an unanimous selection on the first team. He said Western Pennsylvanians have a deep understanding of his position. "Pittsburgh is a blue-collar town that has never gone much for guys wearing clean uniforms," he said. "New York is a quarterback town. Pittsburgh is a fullback and linebacker town."

There is a definite Pennsylvania appeal in the hardnosed, predacious style that a good linebacker must have. "They hit like tackles and they run like halfbacks and they're agile as monkeys," Johnny Unitas said respectfully of the linebackers who swarmed over him.

Many Pennsylvania kids who want to be where the action is, end up linebacking.

"Our linebackers have to be strong enough to stop the run and quick enough to cover passes in the secondary," said Jerry Sandusky, the expert linebacking coach at Penn State. "The people we select have to have the speed of a defensive back and yet be bigger and stronger." With few exceptions, Sandusky, a former Washington High School and Penn State defenseman, finds a Pennsylvania boy, usually from a small town, who is 6-foot-2 or 3, about 230 pounds and who can run 40 yards in 4.8 seconds or less. Then if this boy has an obsession for popping ballcarriers and can react quickly to the fast-moving, complex defensive patterns of the Nittany Lions, he has a job and perhaps the ticket for future professional employment.

Until the millennium comes, Chuck Bednarik is likely to be regarded as the greatest linebacker who ever lived. The son of a steel-mill laborer, he was a skinny, 185-pound, all-around athlete at Bethlehem's Liberty High School. Then he grew to be 6-foot-3 and 235 pounds and as tough as Lehigh County cement. Incidentally, he retired in 1962, lives in Abington, has five daughters and no sons, plays 7-handicap golf, and is in the cement business.

Bednarik was the last of football's 60-minute players. Even near the end of his 14 seasons with the Eagles, he would be alone on the field, usually in a mud-caked uniform, as the offensive and defensive teams switched. At age 35 in the 1960 championship game, he played 58 minutes. Even more remarkable, at that advanced age he was All-Pro in one of the most punishing positions in all sports. Bednarik was a great center, but an even finer linebacker. He is the only defenseman enshrined in both the college and pro Halls of Fame. The other two players are Jim Thorpe and Don Hutson.

Chuck Bednarik

(Philadelphia Eagles)

He was All-American in 1947–48 at Penn under Coach George Munger. It was then that he got the nickname "Clutch," supposedly after he missed a tackle—something that he probably never did again in his career. He was the first draft choice of the Eagles for 1949, and signed for $10,000 in salary and $5,000 in bonus. Only the great Steve Van Buren was higher paid on the Eagles at the time.

The man was almost indestructible. He missed only three of 161 pro games. From 1950–57 he was either first or second team All-Pro, and in 1960 he was "All-Everything."

There are two memorable Bednarik incidents, both happening in 1960. The Eagles were playing the Giants in New York and had a seven-point lead late in the fourth quarter. Halfback Frank Gifford, deceptively middle-size looking for a man 6-foot-1 and 198 pounds, took a pass and Bednarik tackled him from the blind side. Gifford was groggy for 36 hours, and he was out of pro football for the rest of 1960 and all of 1961. He took an early retirement after 1964 and became a broadcaster. Though Bednarik was much criticized for his hard tackling of Gifford, it was perfectly legal. The play resulted in a fumble recovery for the Eagles, and Bednarik would have been remiss if that had not been his intention. Gifford never blamed Bednarik.

That December, the Eagles met the Green Bay Packers in the NFL championship. The Eagles were ahead, 17–13, with 20 seconds remaining. On the Eagles' 27-yard line, quarterback Bart Starr passed to fullback Jim Taylor, and Bednarik smacked the pile-driving Taylor at the 10-yard line. Then the national television audience saw what was the equivalent to boxing's long count. Old No. 60, Bednarik, was half-sitting and half-pinning the squirming Taylor to the turf. Taylor tried to free himself to get back to scrimmage so that the Packers could call another play. Bednarik held on. The clock ticked off. "It went down to no time. I stopped squeezing," Bednarik said.

Bednarik once explained the aches and pains of linebacking as, "Monday is not a good day for linebackers." But for him, Saturdays and Sundays were magnificent.

Pittsburgh's Joe Schmidt was Western Pennsylvania's version of Chuck Bednarik. At only 6-foot and 220 pounds, Schmidt lacked Bednarik's size. In fact, Schmidt was petite for a pro linebacker. He actually started off at fullback at Pitt, but injuries made him too slow for that position. Yet without size and speed, he was devastating. "You can express yourself as a tackler," he once said.

Schmidt was All-Pro for the Detroit Lions from 1957–63. He belted the biggest men in the game, Jimmy Brown, Jim Taylor, John David Crow and the rest. No linebacker was ever more astute at reading plays.

Joe Schmidt

(Detroit Lions)

After only three years as a pro, he was the Lions' defensive captain. In 1956 he made twice as many tackles as any other member of the Lions' championship team. In later years he was the Lions' coach and a Hall of Famer. The saddest story is that the floundering Steelers of that era neglected to draft this hometown boy. He would have made a difference.

Joe Namath once said of Walt Michaels, "For him, football is a life-and-death proposition. He bleeds every time the defense gives up a

(Philadelphia Eagles)

Walt Michaels

Ralph Baker

(New York Jets)

(New York Jets)

John Ebersole

yard." Michaels, now an Eagles defense coach, backed up the line for ten of Paul Brown's clubs in Cleveland. He was one of seven sons of a coal miner in Swoyersville. Lou Michaels, the fine defensive end and place-kicker, is a younger brother. Walt was a fullback and linebacker at Washington and Lee University, then played a year with the Packers before moving to Cleveland, where he was on two NFL championship teams and was cited for All-Pro honors from 1957–61. Just ruggedness personified, Michaels' play was described as being that of "relentless fury."

Chuck Drazonovich came out of Brownville as a single-wing blocker and passer. He and Johnny Lujack were opponents in the memorable 13–13 standoff between Brownsville and Connellsville. At Penn State, Drazonovich and his brother Joe were on the 1948 Cotton Bowl team. Chuck then headed for the Washington Redskins, where he had All-Pro mentions from 1954–58. He was heavyweight boxing champ at Penn State, and a very tough character.

Bill Koman, out of Hopewell and the University of North Carolina, was one of the first blitzing linebackers when he won All-Pro citations in 1963–64 for the St. Louis Cardinals. Myron Pottios, of Charleroi, captained Notre Dame and appeared to have a bright future in the NFL when he was All-Pro in 1963 for the Steelers. At 6-foot-2 and 232 pounds, Pottios was big and fast. Injuries, however, curbed his career as a varsity player, but he remained good enough in 1974 to play for the Washington Redskins as a utility linebacker at age 35.

Mike Lucci was the successor to Joe Schmidt at Detroit. Lucci, of Ambridge and the Tennessee Volunteers, was 6-foot-2 and 230 pounds. He got All-Pro mention in 1969 and 1971 and from 1969–71 was the Lions' most valuable defenseman. Liking Western Pennsylvania products, Detroit then drafted Ed O'Neil of Warren and Jim Laslavic of Pittsburgh, both Penn Staters. O'Neil is 6-foot-3 and 245 pounds, and Laslavic is 6-foot-2 and 230 pounds.

Dan Conners of Clearfield has long been one of the unsung stars of the NFL. For 11 years he has backed up the line for the Oakland Raiders. At middle linebacker and the mainstay of the Raiders' famed defense, Conners did receive All-Pro mentions from 1967–69. At 6-foot-1 and 230 pounds, he played his college football at Miami. Doug Buffone of Yatesboro has played nine years with the Chicago Bears, usually in the shadow of Dick Butkus and invariably on losing teams. He went to Louisville University and is 6-foot-2 and 225 pounds, noted for being an exceptionally hard hitter.

The New York Jets found three excellent linebackers in Pennsylvania. Ralph Baker, of Lewistown and Penn State, has been with the Jets

(Oakland Raiders)

Dan Conners

for 11 years; Al Atkinson, of Philadelphia and Villanova, has been with them 10 years, and John Ebersole, of Altoona and Penn State, goes into his sixth season in 1975. Baker is renown for his lack of speed, but he is the same guy who made a critical interception in the Super Bowl win over the Baltimore Colts. In the Jets' final game of 1974, Atkinson popped O. J. Simpson on a pass play. Baker scooped up the Simpson fumble and lumbered 67 "very slow yards" for a touchdown, as the Philadelphia *Inquirer's* Bill Lyon put it. "The crowd was cheering him for running out the clock," Ebersole quipped about Baker.

Some past Pennsylvania linebackers of note have been the late Emil Karas, of Swissvale, who was a regular with the San Diego Chargers in 1960–64; Denny Onkotz, of Northampton, a Penn State All-American who was injured before he could show his great speed for the Jets; Chuck Weber, of Abington, a collegiate wrestler at West Chester State and a fine pro with the Eagles, Cards and Browns, and, finally, the late Joe "Muggsy" Skladany. One of six football-playing Slovak brothers from Larksville—next door to the Michaels' Swoyersville—Muggsy was one of Jock Sutherland's greatest players at Pitt. He made the 1934 All-American team and later played with the Steelers. Technically, Skladany was an offensive and defensive end, and at 6-foot and 180 pounds he was the belligerent, battling type that Sutherland loved. In the football of today, Muggsy would have been a linebacker, and All-Pro at that.

Some contemporary Pennsylvania linebackers are Jim Romaniszyn, of Titusville and Edinboro State and now with the Browns; John Skorupan, of Beaver, an All-American at Penn State and now with the Buffalo Bills; Ralph Cindrich, of Avella, a standout with Pitt and now with the Houston Oilers; Steve Smear, of Johnston, a great at Penn State and now with the Toronto Argonauts; Tom Hull, of Uniontown, a Penn Stater who was a surprise choice of the San Francisco 49ers; John Pergine, of Norristown, a fine schoolboy basketball player, a star at Notre Dame and now with the Redskins, and Mark Gefert, out of North Braddock and Purdue who played the Steelers' suicide squad in his 1974 rookie year.

Jack Ham is the prize native son in today's pro football. Cherubic-faced, he appears neither to be as big as he is, 6-foot-1 and 225 pounds, nor as intimidating. He made the Big 33 team out of Johnstown's Bishop McCort High School, the same school that produced Smear and defensive end Pete Duranko. Ham was the last player in 1967 selected for a scholarship by Penn State, however. "I think I went there on a grant they had left over from wrestling," he said. Once at State College, he developed quickly. He was All-American in 1970 and was grabbed immediately by the Steelers. He was a utility player in 1972, second-term All-Pro in 1973, and everybody's All-Pro in 1974. In the critical playoff game against Oakland in 1974, it was Ham who came up with two interceptions. In both that game and the Super Bowl, it was Ham all over the place, as the Steelers held both Oakland and Minnesota to under 30 yards rushing. With the Penn State package of Franco Harris for offensive and Jack Ham for defense, the Steelers look set for a long time.

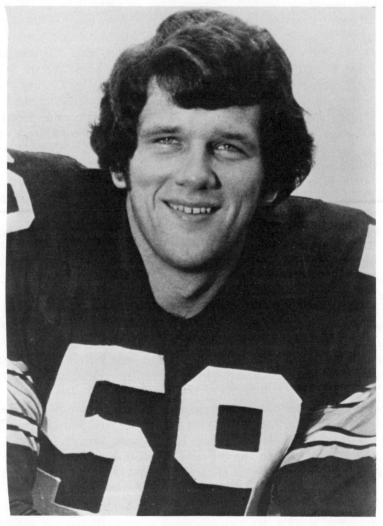

(Pittsburgh Steelers)

Jack Ham

Don't Knock the Rock

... Slippery Rock Isn't Funny

In the absence of a real Podunk University, the name Slippery Rock State College has been the favorite of those who giggle when they hear football scores announced for funny-named institutions.

The Rock's name is resounded nationwide. Some of her rivals, with conventional tags such as Edinboro, Clarion or Lock Haven, must be envious that Slippery Rock is the most well-known state college in Pennsylvania and, for that matter, one of the most popular small institutions of higher learning anywhere. "Slippery Rock is probably the 'unofficial alma mater' of more football fans than any school in the nation. Maybe even more than Notre Dame's famed 'subway alumni,' *The Sporting News* said in 1974.

If a humorous title were all that is needed, then Aroostook State, Eureka, Tougaloo or Ursinus would be household names too, but what Slippery Rock has going for it is an historical gimmick and winning football.

Slippery Rock is in the sports belt, 50 miles north of Pittsburgh and 35 miles east of Youngstown, Ohio. With 5000 students, it actually is larger than Dartmouth, Holy Cross, Lehigh, Tulane or Wake Forest. It has played football since 1900, or 11 years after its founding. Furthermore, it has played winning football, with an overall record of 252–176–32, or .589.

Its great public relations break came in 1936, a 6–3 season for The Rock and otherwise not that spectacular. The Rockets defeated their neighbor, Westminster, 14–0. Theirs was an old rivalry, lasting from 1900 through 1969, but 1936 was the year to topple Westminster. That season Minnesota and Pittsburgh were battling for the mythical national football crown. One wire service made the Gophers number one, and another made the Panthers. An enterprising sportswriter, his name lost to history, proved that Slippery Rock was really the collegiate champ. After all, it had beaten Westminster; who defeated West Virginia Wesleyan, 7–6; who beat Dusquesne, 2–0; who in turn pulled a remarkable upset over Jock Sutherland's Pitt, 7–0; who beat Notre Dame, 26–0; who beat Northwestern, 26-6, who had stunned Minnesota, 6–0. The story was a fabulous spoof of the sporting world's inane obsession with statistical interpolation, and it made the name Slippery Rock famous overnight.

So excited did everyone become about the small Pennsylvania college with the quaint name that Gary Cunningham, a Boston sportswriter, promoted a game between the Rockets and big Boston University. The two faced off in Bean Town at the beginning of the 1937 season, which for Slippery Rock and a record of 3–6 wasn't a good year. Much to everyone's surprise, the Rockets took the opening kickoff and in a series of plays went to the Terriers' five-yard line. Their game ended there. The proper Bostonians won, 20–0, but Slippery Rock had had its fun.

In subsequent years, Slippery Rock played an occasional game in distant lands. It has an odd record of never winning a major away game—strange, because the losses have not tarnished its image. In 1963 it got bombed at the All-Sports Bowl at Oklahoma City, 59–12. In 1964 in regular season play, Los Angeles State roared over it at Pasadena, 62–6. In 1972 it lost a game in New Orleans and then Bridgeport University took it, 27–22, in the Knute Rockne Bowl. In 1973 it lost again at Tacoma, Wash. And finally in 1974 at the NCAA divisional playoff at Ithaca, N.Y., the New Yorkers stopped Slippery Rock from going to the Amos Alonzo Stagg Bowl, 27–14.

What Slippery Rock does best is play in Pennsylvania. Through 1974, it was undefeated in 31 straight games on home-state sod.

Small-college Pennsylvania football can be very good, or it can be recreational. In the past, Washington and Jefferson, Lafayette, Geneva, Duquesne, Gettysburg, Juniata, Bucknell and Wilkes, to cite a few,

Coach Bob DiSpirito of Slippery Rock

have had powerhouse teams. In the Pennsyslvania Conference of state colleges, West Chester, East Stroudsburg, Bloomsburg and Clarion usually are tough.

Yale undergraduates in the postwar years included the football scores of Bloomsburg State in the student newspaper because they thought the name humorous, something akin to ladies' bloomers. Bob Tucker, the 6-foot-3, 230-pound tight end of the New York Giants, came out of Bloomsburg. "I'd run into players and coaches who would ask me where I was from," said the native of Hazleton. "I'd tell them and they would say something like 'Bloom what?'" When Tucker made All-Pro in 1972, urban folks stopped thinking the Pennsylvania Conference was crumb-bum.

Slippery Rock in the 1971–74 era played some of the nation's top small-college football, with seasons totaling 32–5–1. Coach Bob DiSpirito won a record three straight Pennsylvania Conference crowns, dumping the West Chester Rams three times, each by larger margins.

DiSpirito, a native of Rhode Island and former Bucknell assistant coach, came to Slippery Rock in 1967. His 1974 team was the best he fielded. Larry Giusti, first cousin to Pirates pitcher Dave Giusti, was quarterback. Don Romaniszyn, of Titusville, was a running back. His brother Jim played for Edinboro State and became a Cleveland Browns linebacker. The big name was Ed O'Reilly, a 5-foot-9 tailback from Hicksville, N.Y., and a Little All-American nominee. The idea of someone's going from Hicksville to Slippery Rock excited sportswriters no end.

For the 1974 Pennsylvania Conference championship, 11,000 fans jammed Slippery Rock's 10,000-seat stadium. Ranked 11th nationally among small colleges, the Rockets surged into a 14–0 lead with touchdowns by Romaniszyn and O'Reilly, and defeated West Chester easily, 20–7.

Winning at Slippery Rock is common enough. Since 1969 it has had winning football teams. In its 13-sport male program, The Rock had a 381–171–6 mark, or .690, for the 1971–73 school years. It was 31–2 in indoor track, 43–5 in golf, 38–6 in wrestling, 22–5 in cross country and 55–22 in basketball. The girls basketball team had an 11–1 record for the winter of 1974, contributing to the overall 52–11 mark produced in the six women's varsity sports. During the 1973–74 school year, Slippery Rock had 19 varsity teams, and only judo had a losing season. All this success just didn't happen fortuitously, however. In 1975 Pennsylvania's Auditor General, Robert P. Casey, reported that the college practised questionable recruiting tactics.

Without its winning sports, Slippery Rock would be just another small American liberal arts college. Its name is folksy, but hardly funny. It comes from the creek in which, according to legend, a clumsy Indian slipped while chasing palefaces.

The school does enjoy the attention it receives. "It takes me an hour and a half to make phone calls after a game," said sports information director John Carpenter. "I make at least a dozen out-of-state calls. We've got a fan club in Sacramento. We've always been big in Ann Arbor. And there's a club in Arlington, Texas." Coach DiSpirito added, "We get telephone calls from Joe's Bar in Wichita wanting to know the score for their football pool. We're the 'Snoopy' of football. Everybody loves us, but, in the meantime, we're playing some pretty good football."

3

GOLF

The Palmer Magic

. . . Arnie Is America's
Most Successful Athlete

Latrobe is a small borough of 11,750 persons in West-moreland County, 50 miles east of Pittsburgh in the Laurel Highlands on the foothills of the Alleghenies. It once produced soft coal and timber, as well as firebrick and paper. Since World War I, it has turned out specialty steel for springs and cutting tools.

The Latrobe Country Club was founded because its steel executives and businessmen were avid golfers. The Greensburg Club ten miles away was not close enough, even though Latrobe really could not afford a country club of its own. But the 1921 Recession came along, labor was cheap, and the executives had the time to design their own club and course. Not even an architect was hired.

Milfred J. Palmer, known as "Deke," was one of the first laborers signed to work on the course. He carried water, dug ditches and even drove the mules that dragged the scoops to make the course. When the club opened in 1923, Deke was hired on as the greenskeeper. His previous experience had been sweeping sawdust at the papermill and working in the steel-spring shop and the brick yard. Sometimes he

131

repaired motors at the nearby coal mine. For extra nickels, Deke hustled at pool-shooting.

The Latrobe Country Club struggled to remain solvent, but finally during the Depression it was taken over by a holding company. Meanwhile, its first two golf pros quit, and so to save money the board of directors made Deke Palmer the pro. He had never had a formal golf lesson, but he was an accomplished amateur player.

Deke and his wife Doris lived across the road from the club. The Palmer family is of Pennsylvania German stock from Lebanon County. Adam Palmer fought two hitches in the Revolution. Michael Palmer was in the Civil War in a Westmoreland County unit. The Palmers down through the years were poor farmers, house painters and honest workingmen.

Deke and Doris raised a family of two sons and two daughters. The oldest, born Sept. 10, 1929, was named Arnold Daniel Palmer. At the age of five he was out on his father's golf course with a sawed-off club hitting balls. As he got older, the balls went farther. "We all knew him, of course," said Harry S. Saxman, a steel executive and club president. "A nice kid from a great family. And he could hit a golf ball, but none of us thought any more about it."

Just keeping the Latrobe Country Club functioning preoccupied everyone involved with it. The club never had more than 100 members. Its budget was always tight. In fact, until Arnold Palmer himself bought the club in 1971, it was just another of many in Pennsylvania which existed more on love than money.

To men like Harry Saxman, golf was important. He was club champion in 1934, 1937, 1940 and 1944 and runner-up six times. "Had this club never been saved, and I mean by the hard work of Deke Palmer and others," said Saxman, "nobody might ever have heard of Arnold Palmer. He would have played golf, but he would have had to go over to Greensburg, and he couldn't have afforded that. Besides, he would have never gotten all that practice as a kid, and that's what makes a champion."

And there is another thing that made Arnold Palmer. The course his Pap—as he calls him—helped lay out is a typical Scotsman's tough course. When a ball isn't hit straight, the golfer pays in strokes. Accuracy is everything. When the course went to 18 holes in 1963, the same principle was kept. Visiting golfers do a lot of complaining. In 1969 Arnold Palmer set the course record of 60—his all-time low score anywhere, incidentally. The nearest anybody else at Latrobe has ever come to that is 67.

The Latrobe course is considered a good amateur course. Pennsyl-

(The National Foundation, March of Dimes)
Arnold and Deke Palmer

vania's finest professional courses are the Oakmont Country Club, north of Pittsburgh, and the Merion Cricket Club, at Ardmore. Oakmont was built in 1904 by steel magnate Henry C. Fownes, and it is so sacred that it has been virtually unaltered since. Merion was build in 1912 by Philadelphian Hugh Wilson, and with Oakmont is rated among the top ten American courses. Listed with the nation's other fine courses are Laurel Valley at Ligonier, Lancaster Country Club, Saucon Valley at Bethlehem, Aronimink Country Club at Newton Square, Moselem Springs Country Club at Fleetwood, and the Hershey Country Club.

Pennsylvania's obsession with the game goes back at least to Andrew Carnegie, the steel magnate who said "Dr. Golf" is "an indispensable adjunct of high civilization." President Eisenhower was another resident

Pennsylvanian who felt the same way about it. While playing with Palmer at Ardmore in 1964, Ike said to Arnie, "I don't know what I would do without this game. I really love it." To Reading-born novelist John Updike, golf is "an outward projection of an inner self," because of the game's "psychosomatic sensitivity to our interior monologue and the sway of our moods."

Pennsylvania's tradition of great golfing goes back a way too. John McDermott, a Philadelphian, won the 1911 U.S. Open and at 19 was the youngest and first American-born golfer to do so. McDermott would demonstrate his amazing accuracy by spreading a newspaper on a course and driving a ball on it. He won the U.S. Open again in 1912 with a then-record low of 294, but soon after he became mentally ill and remained so until his death in 1971.

Arnold Palmer had the advantage of being the poor son of a poor golf pro with a good course in his backyard in a state with a long tradition for golf. Coupled with the Palmer personality, it was an un-beatable combination.

"I can remember Arnold as a kid throwing a club one time," said Saxman. "Deke chased him right off the course."

"As a boy," said Deke, "Arnold wanted to play golf. He had tremen-dous desire. He wanted the caddie master's job badly. He cut grass on the course and caddied for club members. Then when he became the caddie master, I'd look for him and couldn't find him. He was always out playing golf."

Deke Palmer celebrated his 70th birthday in 1974. "I still bawl out Arnie whenever he needs it," he said. When Arnold bought the club, Deke said, "I think he might be a pretty good boss. I'll probably be telling him what to do."

Arnold Palmer's roots are deep, and he has never really left home. His father and mother live nearby the 6412-yard course. Arnold's fam-ily, his wife Winnie and his daughters Peggy and Amy, live in a modest, white brick, ranch-style house overlooking the third hole, a 442-yard par four which is considered the toughest on the course and is named Palmer Hole.

Deke taught his son that "90 percent of golf is played from the shoulders up." Palmer has always believed that. In his 158-page book on how to play golf, Arnold takes three chapters of 32 pages to con-centrate on the right mental attitude for the game. A player, he says, should have a winning attitude, relaxed concentration and fortitude. Don't be in a mood to get irritated. Approach golf as a friend, not an enemy. Rivals say that Palmer has the "mystical quality" of putting the pressure on his opponents even when he is behind. Palmer, said veteran pro Jerry Barber, "goes right to the throat of a course and shakes it to death."

By the time Arnold was 8, he was in love with what he has called "the greatest game any man was ever privileged to play." By 12, he was breaking a score of 70.

Deke Palmer taught the fundamentals. Ability is of minor importance. The right mental attitude is necessary. A proper grip—"the gearbox for horsepower"—also is a must, and only one out of 50 players have a proper grip on their club.

Arnold once translated what his father taught him into: "Pick up a stick and hit a ball with it, straight and as hard as you can."

But it was a bit more complicated than that. As a high school sophomore, Palmer was third in the Western Pennsylvania Junior Amateur tournament, and then he won it the following two years. To win, he learned, that: "Golf takes more mental energy, more concentration, more determination than any other sport ever invented. . . . If you make a careless move, the course will swallow you up. To win, you have to hit every shot to the maximum of your capabilities, from first drive to final putt. You can't afford a single, lackadaisical swing. You can't afford a mistake."

At 5-foot-11 and 185 pounds for most of his career, he kept himself in excellent shape for the top physical effort required for four-hour, tense professional play. He is very masculine looking, with massive shoulders, wrists like a blacksmith's and a waist as thin as a boxer's. That waistline is the reason he is famous for hitching up his pants as he plays. Someone once counted 345 Palmer pants-hitches in a single round of golf.

The Palmer face with that broad forehead is classic Pennsylvania Dutch. What the camera misses about him are the huge, chestnut brown eyes behind the contact lenses. All this masculinity coupled with Huckleberry Finn exuberance, and it is no wonder that most of the golfing world has had a love affair with Arnie Palmer.

The first time Palmer's name was mentioned nationwide was when he was an eleventh grader and won the national Hearst Junior Championship. To older friends like Harry Saxman, the young Palmer looked good, but that is all. Saxman encouraged him to go to Wake Forest College, where Palmer won three Southern Conference golf titles in four years. He studied business administration, appropriately enough, but joined the Coast Guard one semester short of graduation. He later returned to college briefly, but never completed his degree.

Depressed over the auto death of his college golfing friend, Bud Worsham, Arnold gave up the game for a year. He became a salesman

(Author)

Arnold Palmer's Country Club

in Cleveland, but finally went back to golf. He never lost his ample self-confidence. With some friends he once made a bet. He would get $100 for every stroke he shot under 72, and he would pay $100 for every stroke over 80. Always a money player, he won $400.

Palmer in 1954 at Grosse Pointe, Mich., took the U.S. Amateur title. Shortly afterwards, he was in an amateur tournament at Fred Waring's Shawnee-on-the Delaware. In a week's time he met and was engaged to Winifred Walzer, a 20-year-old business major at Pembroke College and the daughter of a Coopersburg canned foods processor. That was in September. On November 18 he turned pro. In early December, he and Winnie eloped. The Walzers disapproved of their only daughter's dropping out of college to marry someone with no visible means of supporting her.

As for Arnie, back home at Latrobe he had some trouble with Deke Palmer over turning pro. "I told Arnold that I didn't think much of it," said Deke. "I told him there wasn't much money in professional golf and that the crowd he'd be around wasn't that respectable either."

On becoming a pro, Palmer learned the simple lesson that the other 149 men in a tournament can play golf too. In a secondhand trailer on a $600 loan from his father-in-law, Arnie and Winnie started on the tour. In his first outing at the Miami Open, he failed to make the 36-hole cut. He and Winnie survived on the $1,900 he won in unofficial tournaments, and then at the Phoenix Open in February of 1955 he finished eighth—critical for Palmer, because for the first time he knew he could make it as a pro. Later that year he had his first pro win, at the Canadian Open in Vancouver, where he hit a brilliant 64–67–64–70 and won by four strokes.

At the end of Palmer's first full year on the tour, he won $7,958 and ranked 32nd. Most importantly, at the Masters he tied for tenth place.

Palmer advanced to a 19th ranking in 1956 and then a fifth place in 1957. In 1958 he won his initial of four first-place pro rankings. He also won his first of four Masters' titles that year. His Augusta victory alerted the golf world to the exciting Palmer style. In his practice round with Ben Hogan, he hit a miserable 85. Then in the 12th hole of final play, his ball got embedded in mud, yet Palmer kept his cool and won the tournament.

The Palmer glory years were from 1958 through 1963. He led the pros in 1958, 1960, 1962 and 1963, was fifth in 1959 and second in 1961. In 1963 he became the first man to ever win more than $100,000 in official money in a season. He won the Masters in 1958, 1960, 1962 and 1964, was third in 1959 and tied for second in 1961. In the 1959 Masters, he was only two strokes behind winner Art Wall of Mt. Pocono. It was the workmanlike Wall whom Palmer replaced as Pennsylvania's greatest native-born, resident golfer. Wall holds golf's most unique career record—40 holes-in-one in 25 years as a professional.

Palmer won the U.S. Open in 1960 and the British Open in 1961 and 1962. So steady was his golf that four times he won the Vardon Trophy for the best average: 1961, 69.8; 1962, 70.3; 1964, 70.0, and 1967, 70.2. In fact, Palmer's average golf score through 1972 was an amazing 70.73.

"Arnie's Army" started at the 1960 Masters. His adoring fans cheered all the way as Palmer gave them some of the world's greatest and most exciting golf. At the U.S. Open at Denver that year, the pack teed up for the final round and Palmer was seven strokes behind the leader, big Mike Souchak of Berwick. On the first nine, Palmer hit 30. On the second nine, he had 35, and the title. At the 1962 Masters, he ended up in a three-way tie, but his play-off score of 68 took it for him. At the 1962 Palm Springs Desert Classic, he hit five birdies in the final round. At the 1962 Texas Open, he birdied three of the last four holes to win by a stroke. Meanwhile, in the 1961 British Open, which he had lost the previous year by a single stroke, he put a shot through an opening in a bush and won by a stroke.

At the same time, Palmer was never infallible. "Palmer is a slasher and a scrambler who is a favorite because he's frequently hitting trouble shots that the fans recognize from their weekend rounds," said old pro Fred Corcoran. In one West Coast tournament, Palmer used 12 strokes on the 18th hole and failed to qualify. In another match, he hit a duffer's 86. In the 1959 Masters, he needed only par on the final hole to win, but he butchered himself into a double-bogey six.

At age of 33, Palmer had won 42 titles in a mere eight years on the pro circuit. He began to slip, but in 1964 finished second to the new king, Jack Nicklaus, and second only by $81 in prize money. He had winless years in 1968 and 1974, yet with his long drives, his aggressiveness and his knock-kneed putting style, he kept up near the best. By mid-1975, Palmer had 80 titles to his credit and amassed more that $2 million in tournament money—second only to Nicklaus the "Golden Bear," who slipped past him in 1972.

Palmer and Nicklaus have had a keen rivalry. Invariably when they are paired in serious competition, they lose some of their famed inward cool. Nicklaus had a 68 and a 67 in the first two rounds of the 1975 Masters, while Palmer was 69 and 71. In the third round they were together, and Nicklaus shot up to 73 and Palmer to 75. In the fourth frame they were with other partners, and Nicklaus hit 68 to hit his fifth Masters, while Palmer hit 72 to make a respectable tie for 13th place. "Jack wants to beat me real bad and I want to beat Jack, and it affects both of us," said Palmer of that horrible third round.

Palmer rose to fame in the television era with the resurging interest in golf, led by Ike in the White House. Yet there was more to it than Arnold's just happening to be the right athlete in the right sport at the right time.

"He took the gentleness out of the game and made it seem more of a sport," observed young pro Johnny Miller in 1973. "He looks like and is a great athlete. He can relate to the average guy and appeals to everyone—the rich, the poor, even the women. He plays golf like others play football.

Palmer loves golf so much he even enjoys practicing. Yet he was never a perfectionist, such as Ben Hogan who in his early years was the pro at the Hershey Country Club. Palmer, in contrast to Hogan and many famous athletes, has an affinity toward people. "He looks into a crowd, says a few words, and seems to have established a rapport with everyone," said Corcoran in 1971. "Palmer wants to be the best-liked golfer ever. And, as I see it, he is."

His wife Winnie told the New York *Times* in 1970: "He's a mixture of charm, gentleness, ruggedness and wisdom, all the things, except patience. I never cease to be amazed at his patience in public, because it's the one quality he lacks. He's never completely happy unless he's winning a tournament every week." Then she added: "The amazing thing, and the best thing, is that through all the changes in our life, he is exactly the same person I fell in love with. I suppose the fact he hasn't changed is why other people love him, too."

Palmer's winning declined as he reached his mid-40s, but not his

(Arnold Palmer Enterprises)

Arnold Palmer

popularity. The corporate set remains very much a part of "Arnie's Army." In 1973 the Pittsburgh *Press* described a seminar Palmer conducted for 40 top-echelon business executives *Newsweek* flew down to Palmer's Bay Hill Country Club at Orlando, Fla.

"The atmosphere was almost religious as they watched Palmer take the clubs from his golf bag," reported the *Press*. "His words meant little. What was happening was all visual: Palmer, still an awesome physical sight, slamming ball after ball down the practice fairway, straining as his club whipped into the ball, and then hitching up his trousers as he squinted into the distance, following the path of the ball as if he were on the 72nd hole in the Masters. Baseball players may have children who idolize them. With Palmer, it is the country club people, and he is comfortable around them."

At the *Newsweek* affair, a corporate president told the *Press*: "Once I had a chance to play a round with Palmer, and I didn't want to do it. I was afraid I'd blow a lot of shots and embarrass myself by looking so bad. But my son told me, 'Look, Dad, you've got to do it. Palmer'll forget it five seconds afterward, but you'll remember it forever.' And it's true."

In 1971 Palmer and Nicklaus won the national team championship at the Laurel Valley Country Club, not far from Arnie's Latrobe home. Deke Palmer called the story "absolutely ridiculous," but it circulated that a local insurance man of modest means had entered himself and a partner in the pro-am tournament for a fee of $400 in the hope they could play a round with Arnie and Jack. They drew them as partners. Some prankster on the telephone then identified himself as a wealthy coal operator and asked if he could buy the team's place in the draw. "I've already turned down an offer of $1,000," the player said. "Well, how about $12,000?" asked the prankster. There was a pause. "Where can I call you back?"

A legend in his own time, Palmer made the American Golf Hall of Fame in 1969, and the following year was named Athlete of the Decade by the Associated Press. The working president of the Arnold Palmer Golf Company and Arnold Palmer Enterprises, he is worth more than $10 million and is the wealthiest American athlete of all time. A 1973 market research poll found Palmer ranking fourth in believability among sports figures for product endorsements. He ranked fifth—ahead of Howard Cosell—for being well-known.

With the possible exception of Jim Thorpe, he is the most famous Pennsylvania athlete who has ever lived. The kid from Latrobe is more than a superstar. He is beyond that. Nobody has a name for exactly the type of celebrity he is.

4
TENNIS

Blue-Blooded Bill

... Tilden Made Tennis
a National Sport

William Tatem Tilden II came from the Philadelphia gentry with a pedigree name, but he dominated world tennis as no other player ever has. "He was as strange, independent and controversial a figure as ever strutted across the sports scene," Paul Gallico once remarked.

Even as superstars go, Tilden was unusual and colorful.

When the Associated Press polled sportswriters in 1950 for the nation's greatest athletes of the first half of the 20th century, Tilden received 310 of the 393 votes cast in tennis. He was far ahead of his peers in other sports. Babe Ruth, for example, was the king of baseball with 253 votes.

No one matches Tilden in tennis' record books. He was in the big time for 32 years, from his first national title in 1913 until his last in 1945. As an amateur, he won 70 American and international trophies, including 31 U.S. titles.

He was the U.S. singles champ from 1920-25 and again in 1929, and doubles champ in 1918, 1921–23 and 1927. He won the Wimbledon singles cup in 1920–21 and 1930 and the doubles title in 1927. He was the U.S. clay court champ in 1918 and from 1922–27. His match records in Davis Cup play are 17–5 in singles and 4–2 in doubles. And he was the professional champion from 1931–33.

Briefly, he was America's ranking tennis star from 1920 through 1930. Almost until his death at age 60 in 1953, he was considered the equal of any other player, no matter whom, for at least one set of tennis.

It was "Big Bill" Tilden who made amateur tennis a popular spectator sport, taking it off the social pages and putting it in the sport columns. Later he made professional tennis and the touring circuit a popular attraction. Asked why he did not turn pro before age 38, he added a memorable line to American wit, "Why, my dear fellow, I couldn't afford to."

Tilden was extraordinary. With the exception of the marriage listing —he was a bachelor—he made every section of the newspaper.

The sports pages were filled with his victories and his occasional but exciting defeats, such as Rene Lacoste's win over him in the 1926 Davis Cup challenge or Henri Cochet's ending his six-year U.S. championship reign the same year, a time when Big Bill had bad knees and a weak stomach.

The foreign news wire told of the U.S. ambassador to France successfully requesting the U.S. Lawn Tennis Association to restore the wayward Tilden to its ranks so he could play, and beat, Lacoste at Auteuil in 1928.

The medical pages could have a field day with Tilden, whose 6-foot-1, 170-pound frame was seldom free from injuries. He had flat feet and bad knees, and often was hobbled by some ailment. Many matches he played on will power alone. In 1922 he crashed into a court fencing in New Jersey, suffered an infection of the right middle finger of his racquet hand, and had to have the tip amputated.

The book sections reviewed his eight books, most on tennis but some about himself and one a novel. He was a prolific writer, and in his youth was on the reporting staffs of the Philadelphia *Bulletin* and the *Public Ledger*. His syndicated columns, that got him into so much trouble with the Lawn Tennis Association and threatened his amateur ranking, were not ghost written.

The theater pages told of Tilden on stage and of dramas he wrote. He was called the "Barrymore of the tennis court" for more reasons than his exhibitionism. He made his professional stage debut in the early 1920s in Washington in the leading role of "The Kid Himself." The reviews were bad, but that did not stop Tilden from later playing the title role of "Dracula" for 16 weeks with a road company or doing the

Big Bill Tilden

title role of Booth Tarkington's "Clarence." The Hollywood press knew him as a friend and teacher of such celebrities as Greta Garbo, Noel Coward, Lily Pons and Douglas Fairbanks, and he was an occasional movie actor. He gave tennis lessons on the courts of Charlie Chaplin and Joseph Cotton. He wrote poetry, recited Shakespeare, knew classical music, was both erudite and earthy in his speech, played bridge for money stakes, drove fast cars, and wrote some plays, including "New Shoes" in 1948. Oddly enough, he was a confirmed teetotaler, but a chain-smoker.

The business pages described his entrepreneurial talents for grossing in six figures for the pro tennis matches he played in and helped promote. When he turned pro in 1931, he grossed $238,000 for a tour of 76 matches—he won 63 of them—with Karel Kozeluh, the Czech champ. For his pro debut at Madison Square Garden on Feb. 18, 1931, Tilden drew 15,000 fans.

And lastly, and most unfortunately, the police reporters had Tilden in their stories for his arrests late in life for contributing to the delinquency of minors. For two convictions, he served 7½ months and then 10 months in California jails. Tilden had homosexual tendencies.

He led a headlined life, and at his death on June 5, 1953, his obituary made the front page of the New York *Times* and many other newspapers across the nation. "He was the best," wrote Arthur Daley of the *Times*.

Tilden was arrogant, supercilious, unpredictable and a born prima donna. Though petulant and temperamental, he never screamed at himself, threw racquets or challenged hecklers. He did stage sitdown strikes when conditions were not proper. Angered, he would default. Often because of a bad linesman call favoring him, he would give the next point to his opponent. In Davis Cup play of 1923, he gave away an entire set because of a bad call. "Oh, sugar," he would exclaim if he missed an easy shot. When he thought a linesman inaccurate, he would ask, "Would you like to correct your error?" or he would appeal to the spectators, "Ye gods, is there no justice?" And the fans loved him.

Tilden is an "idealist who is more concerned with making a beautiful shot or executing a bit of imaginative strategy than he is in actually winning a point," Franklin P. Adams the columnist noted in 1922. "He is an artist. He is more of an artist than nine-tenths of the artists I know."

He used the all-court technique and played the baselines. His long, thin legs got him across the court in a fluid, majestic style, and his broad shoulders and flailing arms made it possible to get to balls others could not reach and return them for points. Though he had whiplash arms and wrists for the power game, he seldom relied on strength alone. He had tennis' most awesome repertoire of strokes and spins. Constantly moving side to side, he would mix his shots and the speed of the ball. His hallmark was taking a short step just before hitting. Nobody ever got the same shot at the same speed from Tilden, except the great chop-shot artist Wallace Johnson, a fellow Philadelphian and mixed-doubles champion. Tilden whipped Johnson once by just chopping the ball back at him.

Tilden was at his best playing a ground-stroke game. While he had a good overhead, he never had a strong net game. At times his blinding serve was unreturnable, and he usually got 75 percent of his first serves in.

The entire picture of Tilden on a tennis court was that of a master at work, or better, at play. He had a long nose and prominent jaw. His hair was sparse. Gaunt and stoop-shouldered, he had as large an assortment of mannerisms as he had slice shots. In a cable-stitch sweater and deliberately posing casually, he looked every inch the tennis player and the actor.

The trick of Tilden's game was to force the opponent to err. "Never give a player a shot he likes to play," he admonished. Quick-minded with lightning reactions and inexhaustible stamina, often when he was not even in the best of health, Tilden was the ultimate tennis player.

He was born Feb. 10, 1893, the son of a rich and well-known father. Tilden I was a wool merchant, three-time president of the prestigious Union League, a Philadelphia school director, and an advocate of reform politics. The family with five children lived at their estate, "Overleigh," in Germantown. Mrs. Selina Hey Tilden, his mother and a pianist, died while he was a boy. His father died when Tilden was 23, but after Tilden had dumped "Junior," his nickname, and assumed the name Tilden II.

It was an aristocratic family—Tilden is the only scion of the aristocracy to be an American sports legend. The family knew Presidents Theodore Roosevelt and William Howard Taft. Young Bill grew up playing tennis at the Germantown Cricket Club and in the Catskills. When he was 8, he won a tournament for boys 15 and under. The one job he had was that of ballboy at the Germantown Cricket Club.

In 1913 at age 20, Big Bill started winning tournaments. He teamed with Mary K. Browne, the women's singles champ, to take the national mixed doubles two years in a row. In 1916 he lost out in national championship singles, and in 1917 he finished second to William M. Johnston.

During World War I, Tilden served in the Medical Corps in Pittsburgh. The Army rejected him because of flat feet. After the war, he entered the University of Pennsylvania, played varsity tennis, but dropped out of college in his senior year to be a *Public Ledger* reporter covering drama, music and sports.

The Johnston-Tilden rivalry lasted eight years, and was one of the great ones in the annals of American sports. More than anything else, this competition made tennis famous in the United States. "Little Bill" Johnston, two years the junior of Tilden, was 5-foot-8½, 120 pounds. His shoe size was 4½. In 1919 at Forest Hills, the little guy from San Francisco never lost a service against Tilden. More importantly, he noticed Tilden had a weak backhand, and he beat him three straight sets. A chagrined Tilden went to Providence, R.I., became an insurance man, and practiced his backhand until it was almost as good as his renowned forehand. He was self-taught. Tilden never had a formal tennis lesson in his life.

One year later, in 1920, Tilden met Johnston again in the nationals. Big Bill won in four sets and started his domination of American tennis in the 1920s. That match was remarkable. Johnston jumped out to a 6–1 lead, then Tilden won, 6–1. With Little Bill leading 3–1 in the third set, a plane crashed next to Forest Hills and two men were killed. The two kept the set going, and Tilden won, 7–5, and then the fourth set, 6–3.

The rivalry continued through 1925. In 1923 at the Germantown Cricket Club, Little Bill had a lead of two sets over Big Bill, but Tilden rallied—he was one of the greatest come-from-behind players in tennis history.

The drama Tilden wrote was pale in comparison to the drama he enacted on the tennis court.

He and Little Bill each came into the 1922 U.S. championships with two U.S. titles and a third win would give either the cup to keep. Johnston got ahead 2 sets to 1, but then Tilden won six straight games to wrap up the match. Many say it was the greatest tennis Tilden ever played.

In the 1925 Davis Cup challenge in France, Jean Borota had a 2–1 lead in sets and was ahead 6–5 in games in the third set, when the ball actually split on match point. Tilden came on to win. Then Rene Lacosta forged ahead by 2 sets and was 4–0 in games in the third set. Tilden survived four match points—including one where his shot went off Lacosta's shoe—to win. "The monotonous regularity with which that unsmiling, drab, almost dull man returned the best I could hit, often filled me with a wild desire to thrown my racket at him," Tilden remarked two years later when Lacosta of the "Four Musketeers" took the Davis Cup off Tilden's Americans.

Tilden left the amateur ranks after a remarkable win of Wimbledon in 1930 at age 37. Back in 1920 he had been the first American to win on the British courts. Finally he had had it with amateurism. "I must own to a special dislike of amateur sports officials in general," he said in his distinct caustic style.

Tilden's best tennis was behind him when he turned pro in 1931, yet in his first five years he had a record of 340 wins and 147 losses. Once he took Vincent Richards three straight sets, the last game with three ace serves. The youthful Ellsworth Vines defeated him 47 matches to 26. And then when Big Bill was 47, he met Don Budge, only 24, in Edinburgh. Tilden had been in the hospital with a raging fever. "Let's postpone the match, Bill," suggested Budge. "There's no sense in your going out there in your condition and looking bad." "No," Tilden replied, "I'll get the ball back to you." And he did. The old pro took the superb kid in straight sets.

Glory's Net was an interesting title for Tilden to choose for his 1930 novel. It is about a boy named David Cooper who becomes the world's greatest tennis player. He was, as Tilden saw himself, "a definite personality on the court." He was "tall, angular, yet powerfully but awkwardly built . . . his gray steely eyes inclined to be a shade suspicious of strangers, his uneven rugged features pleasant but far from handsome." The boy, so typical of Tilden, "was a student of any game he played. He had to know how and why things were done. He was always willing to experiment."

So true of Big Bill Tilden, it wasn't enough that his fictional hero won at tennis but it had to fit into an acceptable philosophy of life. "Tennis should not be your whole life, but on the other hand it has its place," David's wife Mary explained to him. "You are an artist in your line. Any artist belongs to his country and to the world. The United States needs you in the Davis Cup matches for many years. You must play for your country. You see, David, now you will play as your own master."

No man was ever his own master more in competition than William Tatem Tilden II.

5

BASEBALL

Mr. Mack

... *The Grand Old Man*
Was Nobody's Fool

Connie Mack was an exaggeration of Philadelphia itself in so many ways. A gentleman and a sportsman, the personification of self-discipline and patience, and a proprietor who counted every penny, Mr. Mack had that strange Philadelphia talent for being both exciting and boring to an extreme degree.

"He was tough and warm and wonderful, kind and stubborn and courtly and unreasonable and generous and calculating and naive and gentle and proud and humorous and demanding and unpredictable," wrote sportswriter Red Smith at his death. "Many people loved him and some feared him; everybody respected him and, as far as I know, nobody ever disliked him in the 93 years of his life."

Next to William Penn and Benjamin Franklin, Connie Mack was Mr. Philadelphia. Like them, he wasn't a native, but Philadelphia took him to its heart. Even the Philadelphia patricians liked Connie Mack. He was the first non-scholar and non-scientist to win the town's $10,000 Bok Award, as early as 1930, too, evidence of the esteem he had.

Part of the fascination of the Philadelphia personality is its acceptance, even obsession, with losers. The Grand Old Man of Baseball was a great winner—nine pennants, five World Series, and no major league manager has ever won more ball games. But he also remains the sports world's all-time loser. As much as anyone, this gaunt, dignified gentleman taught Philadelphians how to lose persistently in a fashion that almost relishes defeat. The famed expression of "wait till next year" is credited to the fans of the old Brooklyn Dodgers, but it really started in Philadelphia.

And how Philadelphians endured losing. The old Athletics and Phillies challenged the allegiance of the most diehard. In nine seasons both Philadelphia clubs finished on the bottom of their leagues together. Three times one made it to seventh place while the other was in eighth. Twice both shared seventh-place finishes. The Phillies in 50 years lost 100 or more games 13 seasons, including five straight times. Mr. Mack dropped 100 games ten times. The most horrendous years for Philadelphia baseball lovers must have been 1921, 1936 and 1940, when both clubs lost 100 or more games. No other big-league city in America has been so afflicted with losers. It is no surprise that Philadelphia spectators developed into some of the nation's most raucous hecklers.

For a half-century, Connie Mack programmed winning and losing to reap what benefits he could from each. He was the epitome of honesty, but he also had the soul of a bookkeeper. Certainly he wanted to win—but he was sensible, he didn't want to win at all cost. And, almost until the end, his Poor Richard's instinctive common sense about winning and losing on a profit and loss basis worked for him.

He was manager and an owner of the Philadelphia Athletics from 1901 through 1950, an even 50 years. His teams won 3627 games and lost 3891, for .482 baseball. In both winning and losing, he is baseball's record holder. He also has a record that is sure to remain as long as baseball is played—he managed 19 straight years and didn't win a pennant. Of course, he owned the team, and he was candid enough to admit that was why he wasn't fired.

His real competition was always his National League rival, the Phillies. In Connie Mack's half-century, the Phillies played .438 baseball. The Phillies had 21 managers, while the A's had Mack.

The lifelong trick of Connie Mack was to be just better enough to be profitable. With a competitor for fans like the old Phillies, that wasn't too difficult. The Phillies even rivaled Mack for trading off stars. Connie has the reputation for this trick, but true Philadelphia fans remember that the Phils shipped out such talent as Grover Cleveland Alexander, Bill Killefer, Chuck Klein, Lefty O'Doul, Dick Bartell, Dolph Camilli and Bucky Walters.

Mack was in the second division of the American League for 27 of his 50 years. The Phillies were in the second division for 33 years. From 1918 to 1949, the hapless Phils were in pennant contention past July 4 only twice. What humpty-dumpties they were. Four times (1928, 1939, 1941 and 1945) the Phillies fielded teams that lost more than 70 percent of their games. Dismal as the Athletics could be—and they had streaks of seven and six consecutive years when they never got out of the cellar—Mack had just two teams, in 1916 and 1919, with fewer than 30 percent wins.

The Phillies in Mack's time won two pennants, 1915 and 1950, and were in second place twice, 1916 and 1917. They were dead last 16 times and in seventh place eight times. Mack, in contrast, won nine pennants—second only to Casey Stengel's American League record of 10—and was in second place seven times. His A's also finished seventh three times and eighth a record 17 times.

Mr. Mack faced stiff competition from the Phillies really only twice, in the beginning of his Philadelphia career and at the end.

The Phillies were in Philadelphia first. Connie Mack was the interloper in 1901.

The original Phillies were called the Athletics, and they won the first pennant of the National Association of Professional Base Ball Players in 1871 with a 22–7 record. Founded by ward politicians gathering at McGarrity's Saloon, this was the club that Thomas Eakins, a Philadelphian, probably used for his famous oil painting, "Baseball Players Practicing." In 1876 the organization became the National League of Professional Base Ball Clubs, and that April 22 the A's lost the league's first game to the Boston Red Sox, 6–5, after they committed 11 errors to the Sox's seven. The team folded, and in 1888 Alfred James Reach reestablished it. Sometimes called the Quakers because of the gray, brimmed hats, the team was hopeless on the field, giving Philadelphians a preview of things to come with a 17–81 record, deep in last place. Sid Farrar, the father of opera star Geraldine Farrar, was an infielder.

Al Reach (1840–1928) was an unusual figure. A native of London, he came to Pennsylvania to be an ironworker. A quiet, unobstrusive little man, he became an outstanding left-handed second baseman, and in 1865 was paid $25 a week to play for an early semi-pro Philadelphia team. He thus became baseball's first professional player. He was president of the Phillies from 1883 to 1902 and built Baker Field in 1887. Meanwhile, he became a millionaire sporting goods manufacturer, producing the official ball for the rival American League. Had Reach objected, Mack would have never gotten a foothold in Philadelphia, but Mack's partner was Ben Shibe, who also was Reach's business partner.

Baker Field, or Baker Bowl, was built at Broad and Lehigh Streets. At its best, it held 19,000. Banjo hitters loved it, for its right field was only 280 feet deep. Seldom with many spectators, it lasted until the Phillies moved to Shibe Park in 1938.

Mack's final season of 1950 was woeful. His club turned in a 52–102 record for another cellar position. The Phillies' Whiz Kids, meanwhile, had a 91–63 mark and went to a disastrous World Series with the New York Yankees. As much as anything, the Phillies' success

(National Baseball Hall of Fame)

Connie Mack

did Connie Mack in. He was 88, but still clear enough of mind to recognize that while he had not lost the affection of the fans, he had lost their following. "I am stepping down simply because I feel the fans want me to resign," he announced.

Mack's old star, Jimmy Dykes, a native Philadelphian, became manager for three seasons and then shortstop Eddie Joost for a season. On Nov. 4, 1954, the club was sold to Arnold Johnson, a Chicago real estate man, who promptly moved it to Kansas City, where it stayed until 1968 when Charles O. Finley, the exact opposite character of a Connie Mack, took it on to Oakland.

The Grand Old Man grieved the loss of his ball club until his death on Feb. 8, 1956, at one of his daughters' homes in Germantown.

It often was charged that Connie Mack was not much of a manager. In bad times, he himself joked that he kept the reins simply because he was an owner. Even in the prehistoric days before 1900 when he managed the Pittsburgh Pirates in the old National League and Milwaukee in the Western League, the predecessor of the American League, his combined record was 149 wins and 134 losses, with nothing better than a third-place finish.

Yet top baseball men respected Mack as a manager. Eleven of his players made the Hall of Fame, a mark no other manager approaches. The great catcher Mickey Cochrane said that Mack, by waving his scorecard, had an uncanny ability to spot outfielders correctly. Babe Ruth regarded Mack highly, though the Babe and Christy Mathewson were two of the greatest stars Mack could have signed but didn't.

As an innovator, Mack was one of the first catchers to insist that pitchers throw overhanded and hard. He caught by moving closer to the batter. He helped develop the catcher's mitt from a rubber pad that was used in the 1880s. In a number of ways, he was a founder of the modern game of baseball.

He was a master at handling players. Only he could have controlled the eccentric Rube Waddell, the big left-hander from Bradford who won 131 of his major league 194 wins for Mr. Mack. Hard-drinking Jimmy Foxx and sullen Lefty Grove weren't easy either. Many other managers would have been tempted to change Al Simmons' bucket-step hitting style and ruin a .334 lifetime slugger. With patience and not letting anyone else be boss, Mack made his way into 43 World Series games, second in the American League to Casey Stengel's 63.

In contrast to the fiery, caustic John J. McGraw, the Athletics' chief was a gentleman of remarkable decency. When Max Bishop was thrown out at third base after hitting what should have been an easy triple, Connie said politely, "If you hit another triple, Max, please stop at second base." Once Dykes came to the plate with the bases loaded. "Get them off of there, James," shouted Mack. Dykes hit into a triple play, and Mack said, "Well, James, you got them off there, all right."

The classic Connie Mack story is when Lefty Grove, infuriated as he often was, screamed, "The hell with you, Mr. Mack." And the silken Connie replied, "The hell with you too, Mr. Grove."

The second myth about Connie Mack is that the dollar, not good baseball, came first with him. The truth is that he wanted both the buck and winning baseball to go together.

Nobody could break up ball clubs and sell players like Mack. He wiped out his 1914 team after it won four pennants in five years. First from the "$100,000 Infield" to go was Eddie Collins at second base, to the White Sox for a staggering $50,000—at a time when the young Babe Ruth could have been purchased for $10,000. Then he got rid of Home Run Baker for $37,500 to the Yankees. A trio of other stars went to the Red Sox for $60,000. Mack's Athletics nosedived right into the cellar.

The 1931 club had won three consecutive pennants. Then Mack started selling. Simmons, Dykes and Mule Haas went to the Chicago White Sox for $150,000. The great Cochrane went to the Detroit Tigers for $100,000, and the Red Sox took Grove and two others for $125,000. The sell-off was completed when the Red Sox paid $150,000 for Foxx. There has never been anything like it in the annals of base-ball.

What is overlooked is that Mack sold off the 1914 club fearing an attendance drop because of the approaching World War I and the rivalry for players from the short-lived Federal League. He unloaded the 1931 star players because of the Depression, in which he personally was a big loser in the stock market. Mack had to operate his team close to the vest. The Shibe family controlled the club presidency until 1937, and it was only in 1940 that Mack became the majority stockholder, with another war coming.

Sometimes Mack just made mistakes. Not recognizing the talent of Shamokin's Stanley Coveleski was untypical for Mack. Coveleski went on to win 214 American League games and be named to the Hall of Fame. Trading George Kell and Nellie Fox, of St. Thomas, Pa., after World War II were just bad moves.

Mack was a spender, too, though this fact is usually ignored. He enticed the great Napoleon Lajoie away from Al Reach's Phillies in 1901 by offering Nap a $1,600 boost in salary. He paid $40,000 for a Salt Lake City slugger who never hit big-league pitching. Infielder Benny McCoy cost $45,000 and wasn't worth it. Bob Dillinger, the third sacker, came for $100,000 but his good years were over. In contrast to costly mistakes, Mack shelled out $100,600 to the minor league Baltimore Orioles for Lefty Grove and $50,000 to Portland for Cochrane—the greatest battery the game has ever seen.

Mack had the courage of his convictions. He was an owner of the Athletics because he dared in 1900 to be a partner of Ben Shibe and start the rival Philadelphia team. Connie was a widower then with three young children, but he eagerly accepted the business risk and moved to the city that would make him famous.

In 1902, after Mack won his first American League pennant, he and Shibe formed a professional football team, the Philadelphia Athletics. Rube Waddell was billed as the star, but Edgar "Blondy" Wallace, who had played tackle at Penn, was the team captain. The quarterback was Earl E. Hewitt, the Penn State star and later Republican state legislator from Indiana County. Though Mack's team dropped a critical game to the Pittsburgh Pros, 11–0, Mack claimed the world football championship—thus in 1902 he managed both a baseball and football champion team. The Mack-Shibe 1902 enterprise in pro football, however, ran up a $4,000 deficit, and they disbanded the team.

It was a gamble for Mack and Shibe in 1909 to spend $1 million for the world's first steel and concrete baseball stadium. Better than a record 30,160 showed up for the first game to see Eddie Plank defeat the Red Sox, 8–1. Shibe died in 1922, but Mack refused to let the field be renamed Connie Mack Stadium until 1953. The Phillies became a guest in 1938 and the football Eagles played there from 1940 to 1957. The last baseball game was played Sept. 28, 1969, and Veterans Stadium replaced the old park.

Few baseball men have matched Mack for spotting talent. "For the price of a trip to Gettysburg," as he quipped, Mack signed Eddie Plank and Charles Albert "Chief" Bender. Plank was pitching for Gettysburg College. Bender was on the mound for Dickinson while still a student at the Carlisle Indian School and also making $100 a month for the Harrisburg Athletic Club. Plank shut out Bender, 1–0, and Mack took them both. Bender later admitted that Mack slipped him $1,800, so the price was more than just carfare to Gettysburg. But what great pitchers. Plank with 305 wins remains the most winning left-hander in American League history. He died at 50 in Gettysburg and a college gymnasium was named for him. Bender, half Chippewa, turned in 212 wins and later coached for Mack. "If everything depends on one game, I just use Albert, greatest money pitcher of all time," said Mack.

Mack was the first of baseball's leaders to recognize the talent in the colleges. His signing of Plank and Bender led the way. Later he took

Eddie Collins and Jack Coombs from Columbia and Jack Barry from Holy Cross. A number of his ballplayers later coached in college.

With a few exceptions, he wanted his players young, and then he coached them into stardom. Plank, Bender, Waddell and Grove—what a pitching staff—were the exceptions in that they were polished ballplayers when hardly out of their teens.

Connie Mack was born Cornelius Alexander McGillicuddy on Dec. 23, 1862, in East Brookfield, Mass., the third of seven children in an Irish mill family. Actually, he was always called Connie Mack, because the family itself used the shorter last name. He had a hard childhood, quitting school in the sixth grade to work in the cotton mill and shoe factory. When he was an assistant foreman at 22 in the shoe factory, earning $15 a week, it was shut down. That is when the 6-foot-1, 150-pound Mack turned his avocation as a skinny, brainy catcher into a vocation and began a 76-year baseball career. For a monthly salary of $90, he went behind the plate for Meriden of the Connecticut State League in 1884. He moved on to Hartford and eventually in late 1886 went to the majors with Washington.

In all, he played 736 big-league games with Washington, Buffalo and Pittsburgh, bowing out as a player in 1897 with a lifetime batting average of .249.

At 31 he started managing with Pittsburgh and then with Milwaukee, until Ban Johnson, the founder of the American Legion, sent him to Philadelphia to form the Athletics with Ben Shibe in 1901. Among the players he brought along with him was Harry "Jasper" Davis, the Girard College star who had played with Pittsburgh. First-baseman Davis captained three World Series teams for Mack, led the league in home runs four straight years, and later as a scout discovered Al Simmons. Davis went on in Philadelphia politics to be a city councilman.

Mack was a rarity for his age—a non-smoker, non-drinker, non-swearer, and a careful eater. His stiff collars and high-button shoes belied the peppery character that he was, however.

He had three children by his first marriage. His wife, Margaret, died in 1892, and Connie raised his family by himself while he founded the Athletics. In 1910 he married a second time and had five more children. His three sons, Earle, Roy and Connie Jr., joined him in baseball.

In all, Connie Mack was a manager for 57 years. He was never thrown out of an American League game, but back in 1896 in his third year as skipper in Pittsburgh he was tossed out for disputing a tag at second base. The umpire threatened to call the police to escort the outraged Connie Mack from the field. It was the last time he was ever ungentlemanly.

The Flying Dutchman

... *Honus Wagner Set the Style for Shortstops*

They said Honus Wagner played shortstop for the Pittsburgh Pirates like a truck going over a bumpy road. He was bowlegged, with bear-like paws that hung below his knees. At 5-foot-11 and 200 pounds, he was big and bulky in the shoulders. His stride was a series of long, ungainly bounds. Yet anything slapped near him was gobbled up for a put-out, as he was aggressively quick and had a slingshot arm.

"He had the swiftness of a Phil Rizzuto, the agility of a Rabbit Maranville, the anticipatory sense of a Lou Boudreau, the range of a Marty Marion, the shovel hands of an Eddie Miller and the throwing arm of a Travis Jackson," the late Arthur Daley, sports editor of the New York *Times*, wrote in 1968 in nominating John Peter "Honus" Wagner to baseball's all-time All-Star team. As Daley observed, Wagner and not Ty Cobb nor Babe Ruth was the one unanimous choice for his position—remarkable in itself because shortstop has always attracted the most accomplished ballplayers.

"Cobb was the finest hitter and Ruth the greatest slugger and gate attraction, but Wagner was the best ballplayer," observed Ed Barrow, who discovered Honus and went on to become the famed general manager of the New York Yankees where fine shortstops were common-place. John J. McGraw, the bully leader of the Giants, acclaimed Wagner the greatest because he had the most versatile talents.

The legend of Honus Wagner's fielding ability has outlasted his repu-tation as a hitter and base runner. The game has had few men who could overpower the ball as he did and then leg-out extra bases. "He was the fastest big man who ever played," said baseball historian Fred-erick G. Lieb.

Wagner stole home 11 times in his career. Twice he stole himself around the bases, from first to home, and only Cobb with three such feats exceeds Wagner. He ranks eighth in lifetime steals with 720, and in one five-year stretch averaged 55 steals a season. In baseball gear, the Flying Dutchman could do 100 yards in 10 seconds or less.

His career batting average is a fine .329, top for shortstops. The second shortstop on the list is Pittsburgh's Arky Vaughn at .318. Wagner ranks fifth in hits with 3430, behind Cobb, Stan Musial, Hank Aaron and Tris Speaker. Of the 12 men who have made 3000 hits or more, Wagner was the only shortstop and he leads the other infielders, Eddie Collins, Nap Lajoie and Cap Anson. Wagner is fourth in the all-time rankings in singles and doubles, third in triples, sixth in times at bat, eighth in games played and tenth in total bases.

Wagner played in the era of the dead ball when pitchers had a further advantage of throwing spitballs, shine balls, emery balls and any other pitch they could fit into their repertoire. Wagner's career home run total of 101 does not seem impressive, but he finished up in 1917. Roger Conner then held the lifetime home run mark of 136, a figure Babe Ruth did not surpass until 1921. Had Wagner's 21 big league seasons coincided with the 22 years of Ruth or Hank Aaron, he would have given them a serious challenge for the home run crown.

In his day, old Honus was a brilliant hitter. In 1908 when he made 201 hits for a batting average of .354 to lead the National League, only five men hit more than .300 and the league average was a mere .239. The Dutchman hit over .300 in his first 17 major league years—a record that stood until Ted Williams and his fellow Western Pennsyl-vanian, Stan Musial, tied him. In fact, Wagner batted under .300 only in his last four years in baseball, when he was past 40.

Baseball was a pitcher's game when Wagner played, but the Dutch-man sprayed his hits to all fields and fared well against the titans of the mushy ball. He batted .524 against Amos Rusie, .356 against Nap Rucker, .343 against Cy Young and .324 against Christy Mathewson. The first time Christy faced Honus, he walked him four times. When Honus retired from baseball, Matty remarked, "I have pitched against

Wagner for many years, and though I have been fortunate enough to fool him many times, I always charge those occasions to good luck."

Wagner led the National League in hitting eight times, in doubles seven times, in slugging average six times, in runs batted in and stolen bases five times, in triples three times, and in hits and runs twice. He had no weaknesses and would swing at almost everything near the plate—establishing a particular no-walk Pirate tradition that the late Roberto Clemente and Manny Sanguillen carried on.

Honus played in only two World Series, 1903 and 1909, and his composite average was a lacklustre .269. It was in his 1909 Series, the year the Pirates moved to Forbes Field from Exposition Park near the river, that Wagner had his finest hours in baseball. He hit .333 and stole six bases. The Pirates faced the Detroit Tigers. The first time the competitive Cobb got on base, he cupped his hands and shouted, "Hey, Kraut head, I'm comin' down on the next pitch." Spikes high, Cobb slid in, only to have Wagner slam the ball into his mouth, requiring three stitches to close the wound. "That goddam Dutchman is the only man in the game I can't scare," remarked Cobb. Said Wagner, "I always liked Ty. He was a fighter and he knew it was a fellow's duty to protect himself out there. Lots had trouble with Ty, but I never did."

Wagner's lifetime fielding average of .946 is deceptive. It is not even a Pirate record, as Gene Alley's mark of .979 in 1966 is two points higher than Wagner ever achieved. Wagner, in fact, holds the National League lifetime mark for shortstop errors, 676. His only major league record is an odd one. He and Frank Crosetti are tied for getting no fielding chances at an opening-day game.

There is no way a record book can statistically describe the ground Wagner covered, nor his split-second timing in making plays other shortstops would miss. Playing on the uneven infields of his day and using a lumpy glove with a hole in the center, Honus was famous for making spectacular put-outs and then bobbling easy chances. Even as a risk-taker, Wagner never did worse than successfully handle 92 percent of the balls hit within his reach, and two out of three days he played errorless shortstop.

Until Wagner established a new standard, baseball's premier shortstop was the 5-foot-8, 165-pounder Hugh Ambrose Jennings. He was from Pittston and was four years older than Honus. "E-E-E-Yah-H," as Jennings would shout as captain of McGraw's Baltimore Orioles, played 15 years, including a stretch with the Phillies, and hit .314. The former breaker boy was a picturesque character who one season got on base 47 times by being hit by pitches. He managed the Tigers to three consecutive pennants, was in seven World Series himself, and ended up a lawyer. But only as a manager did Jennings surpass Wagner. Hughie Jennings is in the Hall of Fame too, but it is Wagner who is remembered as Mr. Shortstop.

Honus had a run-in with Jennings and the other tough Orioles in his first big-league game. Wagner came up with Fred Clarke's Louisville club in 1897, then in the National League. In his first time at bat, Wagner hunched over the plate in typical fashion and lunged at the ball, clumsily as his hitting style always appeared. He rapped a single. On his second trip, he belted what should have been a triple. As Honus rounded first base, Jack Doyle gave him the hip and Honus landed almost in right field. Jennings planted himself at second base, and Honus had to make a wide turn. At third, McGraw waited with the ball and punched it into Wagner's stomach. Honus returned to the bench. "Those guys out there are tough," said manager Clarke. "You've got to play the same way or they'll drive you back to the farm." The next time against the Orioles, Honus grounded to McGraw. As he burst toward first, he lowered his shoulder and knocked Doyle flying. The ball sailed into right field, and Wagner rounded the bases to score as Jennings and McGraw politely let him fly by unmolested. "It was the survival of the fittest," said Wagner later.

The Dutchman was highly competitive, but always congenial. He never argued with umpires. Seldom was he injured, and he had 400 or more bats for 19 consecutive years. In his later years he became a great locker room and barroom storyteller. He was a workingman's ballplayer, very popular, though he never received the adulation of the fans like Babe Ruth or Christy Mathewson. Interestingly enough, in 1910 Wagner became the first major leaguer to be paid $18,000.

John Peter Wagner was born in Carnegie on Feb. 24, 1874, the fourth of six children, five of them boys. By the age of 12, Wagner left school and joined his immigrant Bavarian father in the mines. Wagner loaded two tons of coal a day at 79 cents a ton. For five years he worked in the mines, and he later attributed the pain he had in his legs to the dampness he always felt from those days. Wagner also tried barbering with his brother Charley, and then he went to work in the steel mills. Meanwhile, he played semi-pro ball around the neighborhood.

The Dutchman got his first shot at being a professional with a team in Steubenville, Ohio, where his brother Al, called "Butts," played. For $25 a month, Honus started in left field and actually played his first game without shoes. That was 1895, and in 44 games he hit .402. He was with Ed Barrow's team in Paterson, N.J., in 1897 as an outfielder when he was sold to Louisville for $2,100. That was the big leagues, and Wagner proceeded to hit .344, .305 and .359. Louisville and Pitts-

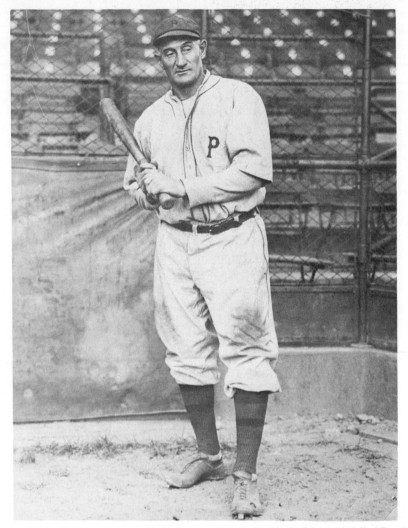

(National Baseball Hall of Fame)

Honus Wagner

burgh merged in 1899, and in his first full season in the steel city Honus led the league with .381. Clarke brought Wagner in to play shortstop in 1902, and his average dropped to .329. Quickly, however, he recovered at the plate and for seven years was over .339. It was not until his final season in 1917, when he was 43, that Wagner moved out of shortstop and took a less-demanding job at second base.

Honus' greatest fan was the Pirates' famed owner, German-born Barney Dreyfuss, who was one day older than Wagner. After never finishing lower than fourth, the Pirates dropped to seventh in 1914, the worst season Wagner ever had with a .252 average. Clarke was through as manager. Jimmy Callahan replaced him, but by 1917 the Bucs were an eighth-place club with a 51–103 mark. Callahan was fired July 1, and for three days Wagner was manager. He won his first game and then lost four consecutive games and submitted his resignation. "It wasn't for me," the Dutchman explained. "I just couldn't get mad at anybody." Hugo Bezdek, Penn State's football coach, replaced Honus. The Pirates, oddly enough, played winning ball the first 13 years Wagner was gone, and they even won a pennant in 1925.

Out of baseball after 1917, Wagner opened a sporting goods store in Pittsburgh but it eventually failed. He always was quite a hero with the politicians. James H. Duff, born nine years after Wagner in Carnegie, used him to campaign for governor in 1946. Former Mayor and Governor David L. Lawrence was one of Wagner's honorary pallbearers. With friends like these, Honus got on the "ghost payroll" and was a legislative deputy sergeant-at-arms and a fish commissioner, but he lost a bid for sheriff when he ran for political office. He also owned one of the first garages in Carnegie, selling the Cutting, Regal and Oldsmobile cars. Honus figured he sold 20 gallons of gasoline a week and used another 10 gallons for himself. "My garage didn't do too much business, but it was a convenient place for the boys to loaf and talk baseball on cold winter evenings," he said.

He was a bachelor until he was 42, when he married the former Bessie H. Smith, whose father had been a sandlot pitcher. The Wagners had two daughters.

In 1933 when Honus was out of money, Dreyfuss' son-in-law, Bill Benswanger, signed him as a Pirate coach. He became the Pirates' goodwill ambassador, and the Pennsylvania Railroad even named its station at Carnegie after him. In 1939 when baseball's Hall of Fame was dedicated at Cooperstown, Wagner—one of the first five to be admitted to the shrine—managed a team in the exhibition game. In 1955 at Schenley Park outside Forbes Field, an 18-foot, 40-ton statue of Honus hitting was dedicated. When the Pirates moved to Three Rivers Stadium, the statue followed the team.

Wagner remained in baseball and with the Pirates until his death at 81 on Dec. 6, 1955.

His plaque at the Hall of Fame reads, as if there will never be a need for a correction: "The greatest shortstop in baseball history."

Immortal Matty

... *Christy Mathewson Was Baseball's First Superstar*

Whenever Chisty Mathewson gave up more than two runs and eight hits, struck out fewer than five batters and walked more than one, he was having an off-game, one worse than his lifetime average for 16 major-league seasons.

The immortal Matty of Factoryville and Bucknell University is baseball's greatest pitcher. Those who argue for any other twirler must prove their case.

Mathewson pitched 13 consecutive years for the New York Giants with an earned run average under 3.00, eight of them under 2.20. For 12 straight seasons he won 22 or more ball games, and for three unparalleled consecutive years he won 30 or more games. In 1913 he pitched an entire month, or 68 innings, without issuing a base on balls.

As a "money player," Matty in the 1905 World Series set the standard. He won three shutout games against Connie Mack's Athletics. In all, he struck out 18, gave up 14 hits and one walk in 27 innings. Only one Philadelphia hitter reached as far as third base in the three games Matty was on the mound.

"Christy Mathewson was the greatest pitcher who ever lived," Connie

(National Baseball Hall of Fame)

Christy Mathewson

Mack exclaimed. And Gettysburg's Eddie Plank, who lost two of those 1905 Series games to Matty, called him "baseball's mightiest pitcher."

Baseball authorities agree that Matty had more control over a propelled hardball than any other pitcher who ever played the game. The statistics are as difficult to believe as Mathewson was to hit. In 1913 and 1914 he won more ball games than he issued bases on balls, 49 wins to 44 free passes. In 1908, when he won a National League record of 37 games, he walked 42 batters in 416 innings, some intentionally of course. Over a four-year stretch, he won 98 games and gave up only 116 walks. In fact, in eight of his 16 years, he pitched in more games than he surrendered bases on balls.

For a pitcher who averaged a strikeout every two innings with fastballs and curves, Mathewson's control was even more unbelievable. He was so sure of himself that he counted on throwing no more than 80 pitches, or fewer than three a batter per inning, not the usual 125 pitches a game.

"He knew exactly what you couldn't hit, and that was all you had to hit at," explained the great Cubs' second baseman Johnny Evers. Of Matty, Ring Lardner wrote: "There's a flock o' pitchers that knows a batter's weakness and works accordin'. But they ain't nobody else in the world that can stick a ball as near where they want to stick it as he can. . . . If you can't hit a fast one a inch and a quarter inside, and he knows it, you'll get three fast ones a inch and a quarter inside."

The New York *Times* said in his obituary: "On the mound, he was a master craftsman, the most consummate and brilliant artist of all time, in the opinion of many of the game's closest students."

The shock of his death at age 45 in 1925 stunned the nation. His old manager, John J. "Muggsy" McGraw, no sentimentalist, commented: "Matty was without a peer, either before or since the days he was at the height of his greatness. He had a greater variety of stuff than any pitcher I ever knew or handled. His fastball was the equal of Walter Johnson's or Amos Rusie's, his curve rivaled Nap Rucker's, he had the fadeaway down to perfection, and he utilized his knowledge of batsmen with greater effect than any twirler in the game. He possessed wonderful control, remarkable fielding ability, and was one of the finest sportsmen the game has ever known."

McGraw never took Mathewson out of a ball game. In the first place, there were few occasions to do so. Matty started 551 games in his career and completed 434 of them, almost 80 percent. In the 117 incompletions—less than an average of eight a season—Matty took himself out. He would hand the ball to McGraw, and that was it. "Matty knows as much about batters as I do," said McGraw—the ultimate compliment of the hard-bitten Giant manager who loved his star as he loved no other man. Any manager would have loved Matty, of course. Only in his first season and in his next to last season, when he had a sore arm, did Matty lose more games than he won.

Matty was the complete ballplayer. It is interesting that among the major league records he holds are those for the most put-outs and assists for a pitcher. As McGraw said, he was a remarkable fielder. He also was a fair hitter, with a lifetime average of .215 with seven home runs and 165 runs batted in. True to being a "money player," Mathewson's batting average for 32 at bats in World Series competition is .281. His Series record of 5 wins and 5 losses is deceptive. Four of his victories were shutouts. In his 102 innings of Series pitching, Matty gave up only 10 walks, struck out 48, and had a brilliant ERA of 1.15.

Mathewson hung up his spikes after the 1916 season, and his many records have been picked off ever since. Among those he still holds are the most years pitching 300 or more innings, 11; the most 30-plus wins, four seasons; the most 20-plus wins, 13 seasons; the biggest right-handed winner in National League history, 373 (tied with Grover Cleveland Alexander), and the most consecutive wins against another ball club, 24 over the Cardinals.

Matty pitched two no-hitters. He stands fourth in baseball's all-time won and loss percentage, with 373 wins and 188 losses for a .665 mark. That outshines Sandy Koufax's .655; Alexander's .642; Carl Hubbell's .621; Cy Young's .620, or Walter Johnson's .597, for example. In shutouts, Matty is third with 83, behind Johnson's 113 and Alexander's 90. He led the National League in strikeouts for six seasons and on baseball's career list ranks seventh. Matty's lifetime mark of 2505 whiffs could easily have been 1000 higher had he deliberately sought to be a strikeout king, but he pitched more for put-outs than SO's.

His 2.13 ERA over a lifetime is simply fabulous. Johnson had 2.17; Alexander, 2.56; Young, 2.63; Koufax, 2.76; Hubbell, 2.97; Lefty Grove, 3.06, and Bob Feller, 3.25.

Christy Mathewson was baseball's first superstar. He and Pittsburgh's Honus Wagner were contemporaries, but after the 1905 World Series it was Matty who had the adoration of the fans. Until Babe Ruth replaced him as a celebrity, Matty was the game's idol.

He was "a symbol of the highest type of American sportsmanship," the New York *Times* said in its front-page obituary. Unquestionably, the handsome, courteous Mathewson took the game out of its scuffy, roughhouse era and made it into the national pastime. To this day, American sports has not had a more respected gentleman-athlete. Educated and knowledgeable, though shy and soft-spoken, Matty would be a $10 million property in today's high-powered televised business of national sports and advertising. But he came before all this. In 1910, when he had a 27–9 record, he had a mere $10,000 salary from the Giants.

He was 6-foot-2 and 195 pounds. His nickname "Big Six" came from his height—the average ballplayer in his time was about 5-foot-9—and the New York fire engine called that for its six cylinders. He was a well-built version of Will Rogers, with unruly hair, a country boy's blunt face and unruffled charm. His roommate, infielder Larry Doyle, once remarked that Mathewson looked "like he meant well toward the whole world." Grantland Rice wrote, "He handed the game a certain touch of class, an indefinable lift in culture, brains, personality."

Though Matty never played ball on Sunday, he was not straight-laced. He drank occasionally, gambled a bit, did very well on the stock market, and was obsessed about playing checkers. Eight months before his death, he entered a 28-player checker match at Plattsburg, N.Y., and defeated the national champ, W. W. Banks of Chicago. He also was a fine golfer, shooting in the mid-70s.

Christy was born Aug. 12, 1880, in Factoryville, north of Scranton. He was the oldest child of a farmer. One of his two brothers, Henry, was with him on the Giants in 1906 and 1907, but pitched only 11 innings and left a lifetime mark of 0–1. Henry died in 1917 at age 30.

Nicknamed Husk, Mathewson was a sandlot pitcher at 11. By his mid-teens, he was very good. At 16, he pitched for Scranton and struck out 16 adult batters. He always had an assortment of curves and his speed was sneaky, faster than most batters thought it was.

Matty attended Keystone Academy, founded by his great-grandmother, and then at 18 in 1898 entered Bucknell to study forestry. He played semi-pro ball at the same time he was a collegiate athlete, which was permitted in those days. At Bucknell he pitched, played center in basketball, kicked for the football Bisons, was president of his junior class, served on two literary societies and was in the band and glee club. He could handle himself intellectually. After he retired from baseball, he helped cover the 1919 Series for the New York *World*, sketching questionable plays that contributed to the exposure of the Black Sox Scandal. For the 1924 Series, he wrote his own syndicated sports column.

At Bucknell, Mathewson was more famous as a football player. He was a booming punter and was a fine drop-kicker in a day when field goals meant five points. He made 65 points in his third and final season. That year he helped beat Penn State, 12–5, and got Bucknell's 10 points by two field goals, one 48 yards long, against Army in the Bisons' 18–10 loss. Matty toppled Lehigh with a 40-yard field goal, scoring Bucknell's only points in a 5–0 win. Walter Camp was so impressed that he named Matty to his 1900 All-American team, adding a twelfth slot for kicker.

It was while in Lewisburg that Matty met Jane Stoughton, the daughter of a railroad superintendent. She attended the Bucknell Institute for Women, and they were campus sweethearts. They were married in 1903 when he was with the Giants. Jane survived him by almost 42 years, dying in Lewisburg at age 87 in 1967. They had one son, Christy Jr., who studied electrical engineering at Bucknell, became an Army pilot in China in 1928, and lost his left leg in a plane crash in 1932, which also took the life of his first wife. Despite his handicap, Christy Jr. was an Air Corps lieutenant colonel in World War II. In 1950 he was burned to death in an explosion at his Texas home. At 43, young Christy had lived two years less than his father.

Matty began professional baseball in the summer of 1899 while still a Bucknell undergraduate. For $90 a month he pitched for Taunton in the New England League. Taunton went broke and Matty, with a poor 2–12 record, never received a full paycheck, but it was here that he was introduced to the fadeaway pitch.

By watching an older pitcher, Matty learned to grip the ball with two fingers and twist his wrist downward to the left as he released his pitch. Matty's incredible fadeaway broke into the fists of right-handed batters. It was an in-curve, or screwball. Matty became confident enough of his fadeaway to throw it on a full count. Batters said it was 90 percent luck when they got wood on a fadeaway. One of his catchers said Matty could hit a half grapefruit at 60½ feet with his fadeaway. Though Matty tried to teach the pitch to many other big leaguers, none ever mastered it as he had.

In the summer of 1900, Matty joined Norfolk in the Virginia League, where he had a 21–2 record and attracted attention from the Giants and the Philadelphia Athletics. Matty had his choice and took the Giants, because they had weaker pitching. He got up to the big leagues and in a few appearances failed to win and lost twice.

Mathewson left Bucknell in the spring of 1901 and rejoined Norfolk. The Cincinnati Reds claimed his contract for $100, and then the Giants traded the great Amos Rusie for him. This time Matty stuck. In fact, he opened the season for the Giants as a rookie against the National League champions, the Brooklyn Superbas, and he won, 5–3. In mid-July, Matty tossed a no-hitter against the Cardinals. By the season's end, the wonder rookie had a 20–16 record and an ERA of 1.99.

Matty slipped to a 13–18 record his sophomore season, though his ERA remained at 1.99. For the Giants, however, in mid-1902, history happened. McGraw began his 33 years as manager. Joining Matty on the club were two future Hall of Famers, catcher Roger Bresnahan and pitcher Iron Man Joe McGinnity. In 1903, his first full season under McGraw, Matty turned in a 30–13 mark. They won the pennant in 1904, but there was no World Series. In 1905 they won again, and Matty achieved national stardom with his three Series shutouts.

Though he looked like a Greek god, Matty's health was never perfect. In 1906 he was struck down with diphtheria and his record, after three seasons and 94 wins, slumped to 22–12, his poorest mark in a string of a dozen great years.

The Giants had the 1908 pennant in the bag when Fred Merkle failed to touch second base. In the play-off against Frank Chance's Cubs, Matty was bested by Three-Fingered Brown, 4–2.

Matty with his 74 wins helped put the Giants in the 1911, 1912 and 1913 World Series, but the New Yorkers came out second best in all of them. In the 1911 Series, Franklin Baker of the A's socked four-baggers off Rube Marquard and Matty to earn his fame as "Home Run" Baker.

By 1915, Matty was 35, sore-armed and tiring. He dropped to an 8–14 record and his worst ERA of 3.58. It was all over in mid-July, and his friend McGraw worked an arrangement so that Matty was dealt to the Reds to be manager. He inherited a seventh-place team in an eight-club league. In his first full season as manager, he took Cincinnati to fourth place, and then as the Reds were headed toward being a pennant winner in 1919, he joined the Army as a captain for World War I.

In an Army training session with poisonous gas, Matty was gassed. At first it wasn't bad, apparently, but many persons later thought that it led to his initial contact with tuberculosis in 1920 and his eventual death in 1925.

Matty returned to the Giants to be a coach in 1919. In mid-1920, an attack of TB forced him to be a semi-invalid and he retired to Saranac Lake, N.Y. In August of 1922 his hometown of Factoryville honored him. He recovered his health enough in 1923 to become president and part-owner of the Boston Braves. Then death came of tuberculous pneumonia on Oct. 7, 1925.

Matty died as the 1925 Series got underway, two decades after his great series. For the 1925 Series at Pittsburgh, Governor Pinchot threw out the first ball and Walter Johnson—to whom Mathewson has always been compared—took it from there and beat the Pirates, 4–1.

The nation was stunned by Matty's passing. Flags flew at half-mast in Factoryville and all businesses were closed. Matty's remains were taken to Bucknell, where he lay in state and where his son was a junior. Only 45, he should have been in the prime of life, yet he was one of America's first athletic heroes to die young. Services were held at Lewisburg Presbyterian Church and he was buried nearby, with pallbearers at the grave such as McGraw and former Pennsylvania Gov. John K. Tener, the former Chicago pitcher and once president of the National League. For a week after his death, there was a search for a will, but Matty left none.

A fieldhouse at Bucknell was planned in Matty's honor, but it never came about. A memorial gateway to the stadium was built instead. In 1936 when baseball started its Hall of Fame, the first five members, appropriately enough, were Babe Ruth, Ty Cobb, Honus Wagner, Walter Johnson and Christy Mathewson.

The One-Arm Major Leaguer

... Nanticoke's Pete Gray
Made It on Determination

Somebody may break Hank Aaron's record, as he broke Babe Ruth's career home-run mark, and perhaps there will be a pitcher who will outdo Christy Mathewson's feat of winning 30 or more games in four different seasons, but no one is likely to replace Pete Gray of Nanticoke as the only one-arm ballplayer to make the major leagues.

Gray played 77 big-league games with the St. Louis Browns of 1945. Don't laugh at that Browns' team. The year before they won the pennant, and then Gray's 1945 club finished in third place.

It is time to clear up a few misunderstandings about Pete Gray. Many fans think he was a freak with that one-arm stuff. Well, he wasn't. He was quite an accomplished ballplayer.

Gray was a fine centerfielder, though in the majors he played leftfield. Not many fans ever saw Gray make an error. His small, padless glove was a piece of stiff leather which his neighborhood shoemaker, the late Frank Wanchissen, would repatch at the end of every season. That glove today is in the Hall of Fame.

Gray would catch a ball with his left hand, flip the ball into the air as he slipped the mitt under the stump of his right arm. As the ball came

(National Baseball Hall of Fame)
Pete Gray with St. Louis Browns

down, he recaught it and made his throw. The secret of the trick was his bent little finger, injured in a childhood accident. Gray kept the finger outside his glove and was able to hook the ball with it. He credits that distended finger for enabling him to play professional baseball. His full hand is huge enough to almost hide a baseball in its grip.

In batting, Gray crowded the plate. He used a heavy 36-ounce, 36-inch-long bat, choked up a bit, and then slashed down at a pitch as if his bat were a sword. In 234 big-league times at bat, he struck out just 11 times. He never hit a home run with the Browns, but he hit some in the minor leagues. With the Memphis Chicks, he once had a double-header in which he hit seven for nine, stole six bases, and slugged a homer 390 feet.

Gray was a fine drag-bunter and quite a speed merchant. In the majors, though he hit only .218, he had 51 hits, including six doubles and two triples. He stole five bases, scored 26 runs and batted in 13. In his great 1944 season with Memphis that got him to the majors, he hit .333, had five homers, batted in 60, and tied Hall of Famer KiKi Cuyler's Southern Association League mark of 68 stolen bases.

It is more than unfair, it is inaccurate to think of Pete Gray as one of the sporting world's freaks.

At 6 foot and only 145 pounds—the same weight he was when he celebrated his 60th birthday in 1975—he was unusually strong, tremendously coordinated and, most importantly, had balance. He never thought of himself as handicapped, except that in golf he shoots in the low 80s and with two arms he could have driven balls far enough to be on the pro tour. He can whack golf balls with one arm 200 to 210 yards.

One summer he and a neighborhood pal, butcher Russ Swantko, took a drive to nearby Harvey's Lake. They stopped at a golf driving range. Pete bought a can of 25 balls. With the golf club in his one hand, he took each ball and flipped it in the air. On 25 out of 25 balls, he drove all of them straight down the range before they hit the ground. "I'll never forget that, I never will," remarked Swantko.

Besides being a fine golfer, Gray was fairly good in pool shooting, with a high run of 36 balls. He never cared for bowling or football, and never had a chance at soccer, where some one-arm men have excelled. He also is a good card player.

Gray was the pugnacious type, and competitors never took advantage of him. His one major-league brawl ended in a draw. The Browns were waiting for a train, and Gray's big, likable roommate, pitcher Jack Jakucki, dropped a dead fish into his pocket and then asked him for a cigarette. Gray reached into his pocket for the smokes, came up with the fish, and all in one motion directed his left to the jaw of Jakucki. The two fought it out in the railroad station until their teammates couldn't stand the dripping blood and stopped the fight. Thirty years after the bout, Gray and Jakucki still exchange Christmas cards.

Gray lost his right arm at age 6, falling off a delivery truck near his home and getting the arm caught in the wooden spokes of the wheel. His older brothers told him that he had been right-handed before that.

His biggest problem was keeping the rest of his body together. In his first professional game, with Three Rivers in the Canadian-American

League in 1942, he broke his collarbone making a catch. The doctors told him they didn't think he could play ball again. Actually, he got back in the line-up for the final 51 games of the season and hit .381. Even earlier as a kid, he picked up a cat who was being chased by a dog. The cat bit him on his one remaining hand, and the doctors came close to amputating it. And then there was the busted-up little finger, but Gray used that to his advantage.

He was born Peter J. Wyshner on March 6, 1915, though he post-dated that by two years to help his baseball career. He came from an immigrant Lithuanian family, and his father worked in the coal mines for 40 years. Gray's two older brothers, Joseph and Anthony, also were miners, but he never wanted anything of that.

The family lived in the Hanover section of Nanticoke, where Pete and Joe still live. The town has three sections, Nanticoke proper, Honey Pot and Hanover. Always a pleasant, friendly and usually clean neighborhood, Hanover was sports-nuts for generations. Other major leaguers, like Steve Bilko and Al Cihocki, also came out of Nanticoke. Every street when Gray was a youngster had its own team. At 7, a year after his accident, he was playing with the Lits, for Lithuanians. Sometimes the Lits were called the "Bronkos," because of the way the immigrant Lithuanians pronounced English.

From those boyhood days, Gray decided he would be a ballplayer. It ended up that baseball was the only steady job he ever held. He was a professional ballplayer from 1942 to 1952, and since then has lived on what he saved. He is a lifelong bachelor and lives frugally with his family. All have died off but his older brother Joe, and Pete keeps house

(Author)

Pete Gray of Nanticoke

for him. He took his name Gray from Joe, who had 18 professional fights as a welterweight under the odd name of Whitey Gray. Whitey once knocked out two opponents in one night at Easton.

Pete played sandlot and semi-pro ball, including Sunday baseball in the Scranton area. In 1939 he hopped a chartered bus with Nanticoke friends to go to the World's Fair. He took along his glove, made an appointment with the Brooklyn Bushwicks and signed with them for semi-pro weekend baseball. He then played two summers with a Pine Grove team, competing against clubs in Pottsville, Minersville, St. Clair and throughout the coal region. When he asked Connie Mack for a chance with the Philadelphia Athletics, Mack replied, "Son, I've got men with two arms who can't play the game." When Gray was with the Browns and they met again, Mack said, "Son, I was wrong about you. You can play major-league baseball."

The Canadian manager of Three Rivers invited him to Montreal, not knowing he had only one arm. "Where's your other arm?" he asked the blue-eyed, slim, lantern-jawed Gray when he removed his topcoat. "That's what I got," replied Gray, and he was signed anyway. Gray was on the bench for the first game, but in the ninth inning when it was tie, 1–1, he was sent up to pinch-hit. He stroked a single and won the game. That was 1942. He was with Memphis in 1943 and 1944, first hitting .289 and then .333. The management paid him $550 a month, though he was a gate-attraction.

In 1945 he went up to the Browns to play with such stars as Vern Stephens, Mike Kreevich and George McQuinn. In 1946 he was sent down to the Toledo Mud Hens, and the following season was suspended. He played with the Elmira Pioneers in the Eastern League in 1948, with the Dallas Eagles the following season, and kept going in professional ball through 1952. He had about 40 games with the House of David in 1953, and that was it.

Gray has always been a dedicated introvert. It was his fierce determination which took him to the major leagues. He asked no quarter because of having one arm. He never enjoyed publicity. He refused to have a movie made about him, or to go on television as a nostalgic celebrity. When the New York *Times* wanted to send a reporter to interview him, he told the reporter to stay home. As a player, he haggled with clubowners. His top pay was $7,000 a season, and it is obvious he was underpaid for the type of star he was.

An impatient loner, Gray keeps to himself and a few coal-cracker buddies. He is one of Nanticoke's all-time heroes, not only because of his feat of being the one-armed major leaguer, but because the town knows the warm and very real man that the modest Pete Gray is.

TOP 100 PENNSYLVANIANS IN BASEBALL

		Years	Career Record
P.	Chief Bender (Carlisle Indians)	1903–25	205–111
	Stanley Coveleski (Shamokin)	1912–28	216–141
	Christy Mathewson (Factoryville)	1901–16	372–188
	Herb Pennock (Kennett Square)	1912–34	243–161
	Eddie Plank (Gettysburg)	1901–17	304–181
	Rube Waddell (Bradford)	1897–10	194–146
	Big Ed Walsh (Plains)	1904–17	195–128
C.	Roy Campanella (Phila)	1948–57	.276
	Josh Gibson (Pgh)	1929–45	Negro League
1B.	Dick Allen (Wampum)	1964–74	.299
2B.	Nellie Fox (St. Thomas)	1949–65	.288
3B.	Billy Cox (Newport)	1946–55	.262
SS.	Honus Wagner (Carnegie)	1897–17	.329
OF.	Stan Musial (Donora)	1942–63	.331
OF.	Hack Wilson (Ellwood City)	1924–34	.307
OF.	Reggie Jackson (Wyncote)	1967–74	.267

Pitchers—Harry Coveleski (Shamokin), Bruce Dal Canton (California), Jimmy DeShong (Harrisburg), Spittin Bill Doak (Pgh), Fritz Dorish (Swoyersville), Fred Frankhouse (Port Royal), Gunboat Harry Gumbert (Elizabeth), Nelson King (Shenandoah), Ron Kline (Callery), Albert "Sparky" Lyle (DuBois), Pat Malone (Altoona), Jon Matlack (West Chester), Sam McDowell (Monroeville), Doc Medich (Aliquippa), Joe Page (Cherry Valley), Togie Pittinger (Greencastle), John Quinn (Hazleton), Ken Raffensberger (York), Mike Ryba (Delancey), Bobby Shantz (Pottstown), Bob Shawkey (Brookville), Willie Sherdel (Hanover), Curt Simmons (Egypt), Bucky Walters (Phila), John Montgomery Ward (Bellefonte).

Catchers—Steve O'Neill (Minooka), Carl Sawatski (Shickshinny), Ossee Schreckengost (Phila), Gene Tenace (Russellton), Mike Tresh (Hazleton), Jimmy Wilson (Phila).

First Basemen—Steve Bilko (Nanticoke), Rip Collins (Altoona), Jake Daubert (Llewellyn), Harry Davis (Phila), Dick Gernert (Reading), Mickey Vernon (Marcus Hook).

Second Basemen—Glenn Beckert (Pgh), Max Bishop (Waynesboro), Bucky Harris (Pittston), Dutch Knabe (Carrick), Bobby Lowe

(Pgh), Marse Joe McCarthy (Germantown), Danny Murtaugh (Chester), Eddie Stanky (Phila), Pete Suder (Aliquippa), Mickey Witek (Luzerne).

Third Basemen—Les Bell (Harrisburg), Jumping Joe Dugan (Mahanoy City), Jimmy Dykes (Phila), Don Hoak (Roulette), Whitey Kurowski (Reading), Bill McKechnie Wilkinsburg).

Shortstops—Joe Boley (Mahanoy City), Charley Gelbert Jr. (Ambler), Dick Groat (Swissdale), Billy Hunter (Punxsutawney), Hughie Jennings (Pittston), Eddie Miller (Pgh), Billy Myers (Enola), Bobby Wallace (Pgh).

Outfielders—Rocky Colavito (Temple), Dom Dallersandro (Reading), Bobby Del Greco (Pgh), Rap Dixon (Steelton, famed early black slugger), Del Ennis (Phila), Tito Francona (Aliquippa), Buck Freeman (Catasaqua), Carl Furillo (Stony Creek Mills), Al Gionfriddo (Dysart), Pete Gray (Nanticoke), Greg Gross (Goldsboro), Fielder Jones (Shingletown), Danny Litwhiler (Ringtown), Barney McCosky (Coal Run), Pat Mullin (Trotter), Danny Murphy (Phila), Ron Northey (Mahanoy City), Jimmy Ripple (Export), Hank Sauer (Pgh), Amos Strunk (Phila), Chuck Tanner (New Castle), Frank Thomas (Pgh), Vic Wertz (York).

TOP 35 PHILADELPHIA ATHLETICS

		A's Yrs.	Career Record
MG.	Connie Mack	1901–50	9 pennants
P.	Chief Bender	1903–14, 17	205–111
	Lefty Grove	1925–33	300–141
	Eddie Plank	1901–14	305–181
	Rube Waddell	1902–07	194–146
C.	Mickey Cochrane	1925–33	.320
1B.	Jimmy Foxx	1925–35	.325
2B.	Eddie Collins	1906–14	.333
3B.	Frank "Home Run" Baker	1908–14	.307
SS.	Jack Barry	1908–15	.243
OF.	Socks Seybold	1901–08	.293
OF.	Bing Miller	1922–26, 28–33	.312
OF.	Al Simmons	1924–32	.334

P. Jack Coombs, George Earnshaw, Herb Pennock, Ed Rommel, Bobby Shanz, Rube Walberg.

C. Frankie Hayes, Wally Schang.

1B. Harry Davis, Stuffy McInnis, Dick Siebert.

2B. Max Bishop, Pete Suder.

3B. Jimmy Dykes, George Kell, Hank Majeski.

SS. Joe Boley, Eddie Joost.

OF. Sam Chapman, Mule Haas, Indian Bob Johnson, Wally Moses, Elmer Valo.

TOP 35 PHILADELPHIA PHILLIES

		Phillies Yrs.	Career Record
MG.	Eddie Sawyer	1948–59	1 pennant
P.	Grover Cleveland Alexander	1911–17, 30	373–208
	Jim Bunning	1964–67, 70–71	225–184
	Steve Carlton	1972–74	133–105
	Robin Roberts	1948–61	286–245
C.	Jimmy Wilson	1923–28, 34–38	.284
1B.	Dick Allen	1963–69	.299
2B.	Dave Cash	1974	.290
3B.	Mike Schmidt	1973–74	.247
SS.	Granny Hamner	1944–58	.262
OF.	Chuck Klein	1928–33, 40–44	.320
OF.	Richie Ashburn	1948–59	.308
OF.	Big Ed Delahanty	1888–01	.346

P. Harry Coveleski, Jim Konstanty, Claude Passeau, Eppa Rixey, Chris Short, Curt Simmons.

C. Bill Killefer, Stan Lopata, Andy Seminick.

1B. Frank McCormick, Eddie Waitkus.

2B. Dutch Knabe, Tony Taylor.

3B. Willie Jones.

SS. Dave Bancroft, Larry Bowa.

OF. Gavvy Cravath, Del Ennis, Danny Litwhiler, Ron Northey, Lefty O'Doul, Harry "The Hat" Walker, Cy Williams.

TOP 35 PITTSBURGH PIRATES

		Pirates Yrs.	Career Record
MG.	Danny Murtaugh	57–64, 67, 70–71, 73–74	2 pennants
P.	Babe Adams	1907–26	196–140
	Wilbur Cooper	1912–24	216–178
	Elroy Face	1953–68	104–95
	Vernon Law	1950–67	162–147
C.	Manny Sanguillen	67, 69–74	.300
1B.	Al Oliver	1969–74	.293
2B.	Bill Mazeroski	1956–72	.259
3B.	Pie Traynor	1920–37	.320
SS.	Honus Wagner	1900–17	.329
OF.	Roberto Clemente	1955–72	.317
OF.	Paul Waner	1926–40	.333
OF.	Willie Stargell	1962–74	.283

P. Jack Chesbro, Dave Giusti, Bob Friend, Deacon Phillippe, Rip Sewell.

C. Smokey Burgess, Al Lopez.

1B. Cholly Grimms, Dale Long, Gus Suhr.

2B. Rennie Stennett.

3B. Debs Garms, Richie Hebner, Don Hoak.

SS. Dick Groat, Arky Vaughn, Glenn Wright.

OF. Matty Alou, Max Carey, Fred Clarke, KiKi Cuyler, Ralph Kiner, Lloyd Waner.

6

BOXING

Pugilistic Pennsylvania

. . . There Was Greb, McGovern, Conn and Loughran

Joe Palooka, the most magnificent pugilist of them all, came out of Pennsylvania. A mountain is named for him south of Wilkes-Barre, the birthplace of his creator, Ham Fisher.

Palooka was the epitome of the nonpareil, clean-cut American boy. That his name has come to stand for the stumblebum club fighter is a case of this generation's disrespect for the legendary. A far lesser figure, but a real one, was Harry Greb, the "Pittsburgh Windmill" and truly the greatest fighter Pennsylvania ever produced. "Prize fighting ain't the noblest of arts, and I ain't its noblest artist," snarled Greb. Joe Palooka was incapable of such cynicism.

All told, Pennsylvania has turned out 19 world champion boxers, including champs who won in two divisions, Terrible Terry McGovern and the incomparable Greb. In one incredible 13-month period in 1940–41, Western Pennsylvania had five of the world's eight reigning champions: Billy Conn, light-heavyweight; Billy Soose, middleweight; Fritzie Zivic, welterweight; Sammy Angott, lightweight, and Jackie Wilson, featherweight. No other section of the United States has ever had so many champions in the sweet science at one time.

"There ain't any more enthusiastic fight fans anywhere in the world than these Pennsylvania coal miners," remarked Mickey Walker, the Toy Bulldog, after he lost his welterweight crown in Scranton to Pete Latzo in 1926. Observed Art Rooney Sr., of the Pittsburgh Steelers, who was an amateur fighter in his youth and did some boxing promotion: "You had working people, like steelworkers and coal miners, and they liked the fights and turned out good fighters. Name any good-size Pennsylvania town and it was a good fight town. Boxing was exciting in Pennsylvania until television closed it up." Agreed Fritzie Zivic, "This was a real good state for boxers, plenty of action."

Jack Dempsey, for example, rode the train and from January 22 to February 13, 1919, had bouts in Harrisburg, Reading, Easton and Allentown, all first-round knockouts for him.

The New Years Day fight card of 1922 showed Jack Zivic winning one of four bouts at Pittsburgh's Motor Square Garden. Lew Tendler turned in another victory in Philadelphia. Harrisburg, Scranton, Shenandoah, Allentown and Beaver Falls all had professional boxing matches that day. Meanwhile, Harry Greb was over in Cincinnati, Ohio, beating up on somebody legally.

The four decades before World War II were boxing's greatest years in Pennsylvania. Almost every week there were pugilistic attractions in at least 10 towns for the fight crowd. Philadelphia's most famous artist, Thomas Eakins, caught the flavor of ringside in his 1899 oil painting, "Between Rounds."

The Pennsylvania list of 19 world champs:

Light-heavyweight—Philadelphia Jack O'Brien (b. Joseph Hagan), 1905–12; Battling Levinsky (b. Barney Lebrowitz) of Philadelphia, 1916–20; Harry Greb of Pittsburgh, 1922–23; Tommy Loughran of Philadelphia, 1927–29; Billy Conn of Pittsburgh, 1939–41, and Harold Johnson of Philadelphia, 1961–63.

Middleweight—Frank Klaus of Pittsburgh, 1913; George Chip (Chipulonis) of Scranton and New Castle, 1913; Harry Greb, 1923–26; Teddy Yarosz of Monaca, 1934, and Billy Soose of Farrell, 1941.

Welterweight—Harry Lewis (b. Harry Besterman) of Philadelphia, 1909–13; Pete Latzo of Colerain and Scranton, 1926–27, and Fritzie Zivic of Pittsburgh, 1940–41.

Lightweight—Jimmy Goodrich of Scranton, 1925, and Sammy Angott of Washington, Pa., 1940–42.

Featherweight—Terrible Terry McGovern of Johnstown, 1900–01, and Jackie Wilson of Pittsburgh, 1941–42.

Bantamweight—Terrible Terry McGovern, 1899, and Tony Marino of Pittsburgh, 1936.

Flyweight—Midget Wolgast (b. Joseph Loscatzo) of Philadelphia, 1930.

The late Nat Fleischer in 1969 ranked his all-time ten boxers in eight divisions. Nine Pennsylvanians made the select company: Philadelphia Jack O'Brien was second among the light-heavyweights, Tommy Loughran, fourth, and Battling Levinsky, sixth. Harry Greb was third in the middleweight division and Frank Klaus, sixth. Harry Lewis was the sixth-ranking welterweight. Lew Tendler, who never won a title, was the ninth lightweight. Terry McGovern was No. 1 featherweight. Midget Wolgast—not to be confused with the light-heavyweight Ad Wolgast— was the eighth flyweight.

There are a few oddities about Pennsylvania's boxing history. The Commonwealth never produced a heavyweight champion. Ezzard Charles, Sonny Liston, Joe Frazier and Muhammad Ali all either fought with Pennsylvania backing, resided here at times or trained here, but they were not Pennsylvanians. Angelo Dundee, the gregarious trainer and cornerman for Ali, came from South Philadelphia. Zach Clayton, the first black boxing referee in the nation and the chairman of the Pennsylvania Boxing Commission, came out of Philadelphia's Simon Gratz High School to be an early-day black professional baseball and basketball player. Clayton refereed such championship bouts as the 1951 Walcott–Charles and the 1974 Ali–Foreman fights.

Philadelphia Jack O'Brien, though only 158 pounds, had no-decision bouts with Jack Johnson and Marvin Hart and lost to Tommy Burns and Sam Langford. He beat Bob Fitzsimmons for the light-heavyweight crown, lost to Stanley Ketchel and Johnson in another bout, and then went into vaudeville. Edward "Gunboat" Smith came out of Philadelphia orphanages and though only 170 pounds was a "white hope" heavyweight prospect. Before World War I, Gunboat, a Pacific Fleet champ, beat Jess Willard, Battling Levinsky and Sam Langford, but lost to Georges Carpentier and Jack Dempsey and never got the crown. Frank Moran, a 205-pound giant from Pittsburgh, was one of boxing's first big men. His specialty was his "Mary Ann," an overhead right smash that sent 24 opponents into dreamless slumber. Moran had no-decision bouts with Willard and Gunboat Smith and lost a 20-round title fight in Paris in 1914 to Jack Johnson.

Leo Houck, of Lancaster, in 20 years went from a flyweight to a heavyweight and fought many of the big names, including Harry Greb, before he became the Penn State boxing coach from 1922 to 1949. Steve Hamas, the 11-letter winner at Penn State and a great fullback, was a native of New Jersey. He defeated Max Schmeling in 12 rounds in 1934 in Philadelphia, but in a return bout was knocked out.

Tommy Loughran, born in Philadelphia in 1902, remains one of boxing's greatest masters. He had 227 fights in 19 years, lost only 23 and was knocked out just twice. Though only 5-foot-11 and 175 pounds, he was so quick, clever and tough that he took on the heavyweights and defeated Jack Sharkey, Max Baer and Jim Braddock, all champions. He gave up a record 86 pounds to Primo Carnera and lost a close 15-round decision to him. Loughran beat such tough, smaller alley cats as Harry Greb and Mickey Walker in his amazing career.

Light-heavyweight champ Harold Johnson, like Loughran, had fights in the heavyweight division. Freddie Beshore of Harrisburg got as far as to be knocked out by both Joe Louis and Ezzard Charles.

And then there was Billy Conn, the bully boy from Pittsburgh who entered the pros with no recognized amateur experience. On June 18, 1941, at the Polo Grounds before 54,487 fans, Conn in the 13th round had the heavyweight championship within his grasp. On the referee's scorepad it was Conn 7 rounds to 5; a judge had it Conn, 7–4–1, and the second judge had it 6–6. It was then that the handsome Conn, a veteran of only seven years, tried to get cute with the slugger who was two inches taller and 30 pounds heavier. Conn sent a left and a right to Louis' head in an attempt for a knockout. Louis counterpunched a left to Conn's face. Conn hooked a left to the body and another left to the head. Louis smashed two rights to the chin and body, nailed Conn with another right to the chin, then another, and scored with an uppercut and finally a right to the jaw. Taking still one more on the jaw, Conn dropped to the canvas. It was 2:58 of the 13th round. The great Joe Louis later said that Billy Conn gave him the toughest fight of his career.

In the famous return match of June 19, 1946, at Yankee Stadium before 45,266 fans, Louis knocked out Conn in eight rounds. The postwar Conn was a different man, and it was the most dismal fight of a career in which Conn had 60 wins, 19 of them by knockouts, and 10 losses. The only two times Conn was knocked out were by Louis. Yet those Louis–Conn paychecks were great. Conn got almost $400,000 for the two fights.

The Louis encounters unfortunately block out the rest of Billy Conn's story. He was light-heavyweight champion for two years until he retired undefeated from that division. He defeated such great fighters as Fritzie Zivic, Tony Zale and, twice each, Fred Apostoli and Gus Lesnevich. He took Monaca's Teddy Yarosz two out of three bouts. Conn left the ring for good in 1948, putting his last two opponents to sleep in the ninth round. Ever since he has been a Pittsburgh celebrity, the gutsy Irishman who was almost the Cinderella Kid.

Four great heavyweight fights have been held in Pennsylvania. The famed first Tunney–Dempsey fight of 1926 drew 120,757 with a $1.9 million gate in Philadelphia. That was the fight Gene Tunney decisioned Jack Dempsey and took the crown. Jersey Joe Walcott had three bouts here. At Forbes Field in 1951 he knocked out Ezzard Charles in the seventh round and took the title. He kept the crown with a decision over Charles in Philadelphia on June 5, 1952, but then that September 23 in Philadelphia before 40,372 fans the famed Rocky Marciano knocked out Walcott in the 13th round to be champ.

Pennsylvania has had some top fighters who never won titles.

Lew Tendler probably was the best. Some considered this 5-foot-7, 135-pound lightweight the supreme left-hander in boxing history. He started throwing punches on Philadelphia street corners as a 12-year-old newsboy. He never was an amateur, but started in the pros for $1.50 a fight. After a 15-year career, which ended in 1928, Tendler had 168 bouts but only 11 losses. Twice he lost brawls to the great Benny Leonard. From 1932 until 1970, the year of his death, Tendler had a popular restaurant in Philadelphia.

An unknown named Preston Brown of Philadelphia's Broadway Athletic Club must have been a great one. Brown was one of the early fine black boxers. Weighing only 125 pounds, he once announced in 1913 to an audience that he would take on all comers. Six professionals stood up. Brown knocked out five and decisioned the sixth for an evening's work.

Billy Petrolle, the "Fargo Express," was a native of Berwick. Petrolle fought the toughest lightweights but never got a crown. Albert "Buck" Crouse, a Pittsburgh Irishman who lived from 1891 to 1956 and was a pal of Art Rooney's, had the frightening experience of fighting George Chip, Ad Wolgast, Harry Greb, Battling Nelson and Stanley Ketchel. Gil Turner, of Philadelphia, turned in 29 straight victories, 25 of them by knockouts, and then came up against Kid Gavilan in Philadelphia and was beaten for the welterweight title. Rockey Castellani was a tough, Zivic-like welterweight from Wilkes-Barre and had some bloody fights with Sugar Ray Robinson. Tony Baldoni, a Wilkes-Barre middleweight, had a better punch than a record. Charley Scott and Sugar Hart were two Philadelphia welterweights with some class in their division. Middleweight champion Joey Giardello did much of his fighting from Philadelphia, but was a native of Brooklyn, N.Y.

Most of Pennsylvania's champions were in the heyday of boxing, or before 1950, when each division was stocked with rugged characters.

Frank Klaus went up against Carpentier, Ketchel and Greb. Battling Levinsky took on Carpentier, Tunney and had ten tough bouts with

Jack Dillon. Sammy Angott fought Willie Pep, Bob Montgomery, Fritzie Zivic, Sugar Ray Robinson, Henry Armstrong, Ike Williams, Beau Jack and Lew Jenkins, all champions. George Chip fought Greb four times. This 158-pounder of Lithuanian stock knocked out Pittsburgh's Klaus for the title in 1913 and then in a return match knocked him out again. Billy Soose from Farrell beat Tami Mauriello and Tony Zale. Tommy Yarosz at the height of his career in the 1940s went 38 fights without a loss. Tony Marino of Pittsburgh in 1936 held the bantamweight crown just 33 days. The following year, after a loss in Brooklyn, the 25-year-old Marino died of a cerebral hemorrhage.

And then there was Terrible Terry McGovern.

McGovern, born March 9, 1880, in Johnstown, was only 5-foot-4 and 128 pounds, but probably was "the greatest little man the ring ever knew," as the New York *Times* said in his obituary. McGovern held both the bantamweight and featherweight titles. He fought in boxing's wild days from 1897 to 1908 and even then was called "a terror." His strategy was to jump from his corner at the sound of the bell and start slugging. The little guy won 81 fights, 33 of them by knockouts. In one stretch, he knocked out 12 men, 10 of them in the first three rounds. He lost only three fights, and he was knocked out only twice, both times by Young Corbett. McGovern lives as hard as he fought. He moonlighted in three Broadway shows, and when he died of pneumonia at age 37, George M. Cohan was one of his pallbearers in Brooklyn.

But none compared to Harry Greb. Perhaps nobody in boxing history compared to Harry Greb.

He held both the light-heavyweight and middleweight titles and lost only eight bouts out of 294. But what was most incredible is that he fought the last 86 fights of his life blinded in the right eye. In a 1921 non-decision match with Kid Norfolk, he lost the use of the eye. But even with only one good eye, he went on to beat Gene Tunney for the light-heavyweight crown, defend it against Tommy Loughran, and then topple Mickey Walker for the middleweight title.

Greb actually sent out Christmas cards in 1925, the year before his untimely death, with the greeting: "I am anxious to defend my laurels against any man. I will meet any light-heavyweight or heavyweight as fast as they can toe the mark. In all my years of campaigning, I have barred no man. I am willing to go on short notice. The opponent can write his own terms, and it will be first-come, first-served."

That was Greb, 5-foot-8 and 158 pounds, but he fought Gene Tunney five times, while Jack Dempsey would have nothing to do with him. Moody and truculent, he would fight in barrooms just to keep busy. One of his greatest brawls was in a New York alley with Mickey

Walker, who proclaimed that "professionals shouldn't fight civilians," but he never considered Greb civil. It is strictly myth that Greb once gave his own mother a black eye.

Greb was called "the rubber man with perpetual motion," a guy who had the style of an electric fan. "A tireless fighter with an inexhaustible supply of energy, stamina and strength," the New York *Times* said. Often he gave up 20 to 30 pounds to an opponent. Oddly enough, his one weakness was that he lacked a great punch, but he made up for that by slapping, cuffing, smacking and butting in an unorthodox fashion that never followed the rules.

The first time Greb fought Tunney he outpointed him in 15 rounds by cutting him to pieces. In their next four bouts, Tunney never let him get near. He later said he danced so fast that Greb even missed him with his spit. Yet Tunney loved the man. He was a pallbearer for Greb's funeral and called him a great competitor.

Greb was born June 6, 1894, in Pittsburgh. He came from a German family whose original name was Greb spelled backward, or Berg.

He was a cut-up in his private life too. He enjoyed the Broadway lights, chorus girls, and good whiskey. "There are two things Harry Greb loves more than eating, and fighting is one of them," they said.

At 31 he was dead. He previously had a cataract removed from his good eye. Then he was in an automobile accident, of all things. He underwent an operation in Atlantic City for the removal of a fractured bone from his nose, and died Oct. 22, 1926, from surgery. Unlike many fighters, he had money. He liked to bet on the fights. Knowing how good Tunney was from personal experience, he reaped a reported $60,000 on bets from the first Tunney–Dempsey fight.

Harry Greb is a legend. As the late John Lardner wrote, publicists for rookies still ascribe their would-be champions as "faster than Greb, fiercer than Dempsey, and better to his mother than Whistler."

Harry Greb, the Pittsburgh Windmill

Pardon Me, It's Zivic

... *Fritzie Was the Ring's Greatest Brawler*

"You can't be a dirty fighter if you say, 'Pardon me,' " explains Fritzie Zivic to all who want further elaboration on how he choked, held, butted, hit below the belt, and worked with the laces of his gloves while practicing the manly art of self-defense.

"Whenever I had the opportunity and the occasion presented itself, I always said, 'Pardon me,' " related Zivic of his tactics with Henry Armstrong, Bummy Davis, Sugar Ray Robinson, Billy Conn, Lew Jenkins, Jake LaMotta, Beau Jack, Sammy Angott, Freddie "Red" Cochrane and the other pugilists he tangled with during an 18-year career in the golden age of American boxing.

Pittsburgh's Fritzie Zivic was the welterweight champion of the world from Oct. 4, 1940, when he took the title away from a surprised Hammering Henry Armstrong in 15 rounds, until he lost his crown to Cochrane in 15 rounds on July 29, 1941. He held the title through 11 fights.

But it is not as a champion nor as one of boxing's most prolific workmen that Zivic's laurels rest. In the annals of the ring, there has never been a greater brawler than this 5-foot-9, 147-pounder. Not

(Author)

Fritzie Zivic

gifted with the great ability of a Harry Greb, the pugnacious Fritzie had
to make it to the top with Greb-like tenacity and roughness.

Zivic had 230 credited professional fights, though he thinks the actual
number exceeds 300. Everytime he jumped through the ropes, he staged
a "pier-sixer," the fight fraternity's term for a brawl.

He always had a good punch—he won 80 of his fights by knockouts.
And he could take a punch—he was kayoed only five times, an amazing
record considering the sluggers he met. He was quick and he had an
abundance of savvy, but otherwise he was not overly endowed with
natural pugilistic talent.

He came up as a street fighter and always remaining one, busting
heads to win a paycheck. He was a pro when the business had more
great fighters than ever before or since. The working stiffs of Western
Pennsylvania loved him, for they recognized him as one of their own.

Nobody in the ring was badmouthed as much as Zivic. Triple title winner Armstrong, whom Zivic decisioned once and knocked out once, called him "just a nasty fighter, just a foul fighter." Billy Conn, his fellow Pittsburgher, decisioned Zivic and said, "That was like going to college for five years, just boxing him ten rounds." Conn was four years younger, two inches taller and ten to 25 pounds heavier.

Yet however uncouth the Zivic style was, Fritzie was never disqualified in a professional bout. He actually won a major fight in 1940 when Bummy Davis was disqualified in the second round for fouling him.

Zivic left the ring in 1949. Today he wears the trophies of his former trade proudly. His left ear is cauliflowered, the result of his using his good left hand too often to jab or to hook and then to hold, leaving that side of his noggin open for the other fellow's right. His flattened nose has a crease in it as wide as the Allegheny. But at 62 in 1974, his weight was 140 pounds, his stomach flat, his eyes sparkle, and his speech clear. He wears a hairpiece, and he doesn't look like an ex-pug at all.

He is a self-educated, fairly well-read man, with a library of a few thousand books, art hanging on the walls, and a den with memorabilia of his boxing past.

Zivic lounges in his suburban Pittsburgh home with all the comforts of the successful bourgeoise. He even has a 95-pound Doberman pinscher named Duke who won a ribbon in a dog show. Duke's trophy is cherished by Zivic almost as much as his gold-plated title belt encased in glass over his bar.

The old brawler is not exactly a man of means. At least $80,000 of his savings were lost in an unhappy venture to operate a small Pittsburgh sports arena. He was a salesman and a house painter, and today is a boilermaker doing "climbing work" in the construction of Western Pennsylvania power plants. He also is a master of ceremonies and after-dinner speaker, who shows old fight films and provides chatter that never fails to entertain. The one thing Fritzie doesn't do is to talk tough. With his pixie-like grin and exuberant gabbiness, Zivic is anything but the cliched, pitiful, washed-up prize fighter.

He was married early in his career in 1932 to a neighborhood girl, the former Helen Stokan. To celebrate his tenth anniversary, he knocked out an opponent in Pittsburgh who had decisioned him a month earlier. Fritzie and Helen have three children, all of whom went to college. Fritzie Jr. played the backfield for the University of Cincinnati and today owns seven restaurants in Connecticut. Charles graduated from Penn State and is a drug salesman. Janis has her master's degree from Pittsburgh and is in personnel work in San Francisco. There are four grandchildren, including a 14-year-older who wants to be a golfer and a 1-year-older named Fritzie III. "Of all the kids," said Mrs. Zivic, "it was Janis who most had Fritzie's competitive instincts." "Yes," said Fritzie, "she might have done well in the ring if she had had a punch."

The family is wryly amused by father's reputation as the dirtiest fighter of all time. Even Mrs. Zivic jokes about the ease of handling him because, "I know where to use the knee."

He was born Ferdinand Zivic on May 8, 1913, in a Croatian family in Lawrenceville, on the Pittsburgh East Side by the mills. He was the youngest and the tallest of the "Five Fighting Zivics." Dad worked in the mill to support five sons and three daughters. Then he got a saloon, which with true Zivic enterprise he turned into a speakeasy during Prohibition.

Pete Zivic won an Olympic gold medal in 1920 as a flyweight. He turned pro, as did Jack who also made the U.S. Olympic boxing team. Jack, now dead, knocked out Lew Tendler in 1925. Joe and Eddie also were boxers. And then came Fritzie, fighting his way up off the streets like his older brothers and training in Jack Metz's local boxing palace, the Willow Club. There were Polish, Irish, Serbian and Croatian mill kids in the neighborhood, all eager to fight with or without gloves. Few were the weeks, Fritzie recalls, that a kid either didn't take a punch in the nose or give one.

From those beginning days, Zivic learned a principle he maintains to this day—no grudges. Bodily damage and facial rearrangement were considered all in a night's work to Fritzie, with no malice, or "resentment" as he terms it, intended.

In 1929 he started in amateur fights. The Motor Square Garden in East Liberty held Monday night bouts, four to ten-rounders. Some nights the crowd got as large as 1000. Fritzie worked his way up, and then had some bouts in the Duquesne Garden in the fancier Oakland section of Pittsburgh. He turned pro in 1931, and by 1933 was established when he had eight knockouts in 14 fights and was undefeated for the year.

Zivic hit the limelight in his Dec. 27, 1936 bout with Conn at the Duquesne Garden. The house was 11,000 and Zivic's purse was $2,500. He and Billy each put up a $1,000 forfeit that his weight would be 150 pounds and Conn's 160. "An honest butcher's scale," in Zivic's words, certified that the boys made their weights. Then Fritzie went to the men's room. For fun, he reweighed himself and the scale showed 147½. The bigger Conn took him in 10, but Zivic didn't agree with the decision.

For 14 years Zivic fought eight or more fights annually. In 1938 he

To Paul B. Berns
your Pal
Fritzie Zivic

fought 22 times, including four times in August. Few top professionals ever kept a schedule the equal of Zivic's. That is an explanation of why he lost 65 fights, or much more than most world champions ever lost in their careers.

The one off-year for Fritzie was 1937 when he turned in a 6–1 record. He was down 57 days with pneumonia, so sick that he was given the last rites.

In 1940 at the age of 27, Zivic was at his peak. He had 11 wins, including five by knockouts, and two losses. The key win was at Forbes Field in a non-title go with the popular Western Pennsylvanian Sammy Angott, the lightweight champ. Pittsburgh's Dapper Dan Club staged the match, with a $5,000 purse for Angott and the winner to meet Armstrong for the welterweight crown. With Armstrong watching, Zivic decisioned Angott. Six weeks later in New York, with the odds favoring Armstrong by six to one or more, Zivic went into his first 15-rounder. He was conditioned to go 40 rounds if need be. Armstrong in the first five rounds beat him unmercifully. Then Zivic began to brawl, bloodying Armstrong as the champ had never been before. In the last round, Zivic decked the master who in his career lost only 22 times in 175 fights and was knocked out only twice.

Fritzie won the crown and a mere $3,400 for what was one of the toughest fights in the annals of boxing. Three months later, on Jan. 14, 1941, they were rematched and once again Armstrong was the favorite. This time Zivic kayoed him in 12 rounds, retaining his title and taking back to Pittsburgh $25,000. But the glory was shortlived. On July 29, 1941, in Newark, N.J., a town and state Zivic still mistrusts for boxing decisions, Freddie Cochrane outpointed him in 15 rounds to grab his title. A year later in New York, Zivic beat Cochrane, but Freddie had previously lost the crown. Interestingly, Armstrong couldn't forget Zivic, and finally caught up to him in 1942 to decision the Pittsburgher.

After 1943, Zivic won more than he lost, but the chances for a title and big money grew dimmer. Champions like Beau Jack and Sugar Ray Robinson took wins over Zivic, and so did tough Jake LaMotta. Jake and Fritzie had four brawls, with the older Fritzie winning once against the bull-like future middleweight champ.

Finally in 1949, after two wins over unknown competitors, the 35-year-old Zivic retired. He took the gloves, trunks and shoes he wore in his title championship with Armstrong and bronzed them for posterity.

"I loved fighting," said Zivic. "Hell, I would have been in the mill if it weren't for that. Just to toughen my hands, I once worked two weeks in the mill for 75 cents an hour. That wasn't for me. I got out of there fast."

7

WRESTLING

Grapplers' Grip

... Pennsylvania Mat Men Excel

"Bethlehem is wormy with wrestling fans," sportswriter Red Smith announced in 1973. It was the appropriate metaphor, not only for Bethlehem but also for the Lehigh Valley and for much of Pennsylvania. The worm comes in all sizes, it crawls, it endures, it is hard to destroy, it is absolutely essential and it is little appreciated. So are wrestlers and wrestling fans.

Superb in many sports, the Lehigh Valley is simply tremendous in wrestling. In six years, 1970–75, it has had six natives win seven national collegiate wrestling titles. Invariably its schoolboys cop a state-wide crown or two. Furthermore, it is the home of Lehigh University, which has not had a losing wrestling season since 1944 and has won 20 Eastern team championships, or more than anyone else.

The zest for wrestling, of course, extends beyond the Lehigh Valley. There are places like Bellefonte, Clearfield, Lock Haven, Waynesburg, Washington, Cannonsburg, Muncy, Suburban Philadelphia, Hollidaysburg and Hummelstown, among others, that get emotional about wrestling too.

The fact is that Pennsylvania is the biggest wrestling state in the nation.

In 1971 Pennsylvania overtook Wisconsin as the nation's top state in schoolboy wrestling participation. In 1974 the Commonwealth had 475 high school and 306 junior high wrestling teams, comprising 32,000 wrestlers. Next to girls basketball, schoolboy grappling is the fastest growing sport in Pennsylvania. The Pennsylvania Interscholastic Athletic Association has had to align its member schools into "A" and "B" classifications for district, regional and finals competition—resulting in what is surely the most intense and dramatic individual championship tournaments in the state.

In the postwar's 30 years, 1946–75, at the National Collegiate Athletic Association wrestling championships, Pennsylvania produced 36 title winners, including Ed Peery who won three times and seven other Pennsylvanians who won twice. In 1971, 1972 and 1973, Pennsylvania won three of the ten weight classes; in 1974, two, and in 1975, three again.

Typically, Pennsylvania showed its stuff at the 1975 NCAA championships held at Princeton, N.J. Three winners were John Fritz (Bethlehem), 126 pounds for Penn State; Jim Bennett (Corry), 142 pounds for Yale, and Mike Lieberman (Allentown), 177 pounds for Lehigh. There were 400 wrestlers from 118 colleges, and the Pennsylvania boys made their usual superlative showing.

Fritz, the Penn State captain out of Liberty High School, had to defeat the defending champion, Pat Milkovich of Michigan State. Milkovich, in turn, had beaten Craig Helmuth (Chambersburg), a Gettysburg College freshman who had a 24–1–1 record. In that same tough division, the remarkable Jimmy Carr (Erie) was edged by a single point. Though only a freshman at Kentucky, Carr was seeded second to Milkovich.

Bennett, a former PIAA champ, was not even seeded in the 142-pound division, so all his wins were upsets.

Mike Lieberman was another surprise at 177 pounds. In the semifinals he upset Bill Shuffstall (Conneaut Lake), who had had a 16–2 year for Slippery Rock State College. Mike's freshman brother at Lehigh, Mark, also an Eastern champion, missed making the quarter-finals of the 167-pound class when he was decisioned by a point.

Joe Carr, Jimmy's older brother, had a 29–0–2 record as a sophomore at Kentucky. He made it to third place in the NCAA's 167-pound rankings. Terry DeStito (Enola) was 15–0–1 for Lehigh and was the only grappler to win the top award at two consecutive Eastern championships. With 81 mat victories in a four-year collegiate career, DeStito was the winningest Lehigh wrestler in history. He handled all comers, from 167 pounds to heavyweight. At the NCAA championships, he was a light 209-pound heavyweight, giving up 75 pounds to some opponents. Even with the odds against him, DeStito came in fifth, losing his crucial match in overtime no less.

Lehigh finished fifth in the NCAA team rankings, while Penn State was tenth. In the top 20 for the 1975 regular season, five Pennsylvania schools—Lehigh, Penn State, Slippery Rock, Pitt and Clarion State—were among the national leaders.

The all-time collegiate pinning champion is a Pennsylvanian, Wade Schalles of Hollidaysburg. Two-time NCAA champ for Clarion State, Schalles set a mark of 106 pins in his college career in which he won 153 matches. A 1969 PIAA champ, Schalles was an unorthodox, crowd-pleasing grappler who won national crowns at 150 and 158 pounds and lost only five times in four years of college mat work. Schalles was incredible at the NCAA tournaments. In both the 1972 and 1973 national championships, he pinned four of his five opponents, two of them within a minute. His two decision wins were by easy 8–3 and 9–2 scores.

The 126-pound Jimmy Carr is another spectacular wrestler. A ghetto boy—one of the Commonwealth's first great black wrestlers—he grew up in a family of 16 children. In 55 matches for his Erie high school, he lost just two bouts and both were in regional competition. As a junior he won the state title—that is, after he was on the Olympic team. In international matches, he was 1–2, but he was only 16 years old, the youngest American to ever wrestle on the Olympic team. Carr in 1974–75 wrestled for the University of Kentucky, where his brother, Fletcher Carr Jr., is coach. The excellent 167 pounder on the team is a third brother, Joe Carr.

Undoubtedly the most amazing Pennsylvania wrestling story is that of the Peerys of Pittsburgh. There is really nothing like it in the annals of American collegiate wrestling. A father and two sons, and each won the national wrestling title three times—an oddsmaker would give a billion to one on that probability and feel comfortable.

Rex Peery, the father and long-time University of Pittsburgh wrestling coach, won three national titles as an undergraduate back in Oklahoma. Then his older son Hugh at Pitt won three titles, and finally his younger son Ed won three.

The ninth and final Peery championship came the night of March 30, 1957, appropriately enough at Pitt where the NCAA championships were held that year. As he had been in his previous two NCAA championship bouts, Ed was trailing. He was up against the quick Harmon

Leslie of Oklahoma A & M, and dropped behind by a 2–6 count. At the end of the regulation nine minutes, the hollow-cheeked, beetle-browed Peery was down 6–7, but got the tying point for riding time, or top position. In overtime, the two were tie again, 2–2, and up came the critical decision. It was unanimous for Peery, who the previous year had defeated Leslie by a close 7–5.

The Pitt Fieldhouse crowd went wild with cheers as Ed Peery's arm was raised in triumph. A wrestling match cannot be closer than one that finishes 9–9 with a referee decision. It was the toughest match Ed Peery ever had, but the win meant that he had duplicated the rare achievements of his brother and father.

Records are made to be broken, but the Peery family record might not be.

Rex Peery, born in 1910 in Stillwater, Okla., the son of a coal miner, was two-time state schoolboy champion of Oklahoma. For Oklahoma State University, at 5-foot-6 and 118 to 135 pounds, he won the national championships in his sophomore, junior and senior years, his last title in 1935. Rex never lost a collegiate match. The one loss he suffered in his entire career came in the open AAU trials for the 1936 Olympic Team, but he still earned an alternate position on the team. When Rex took his first national crown, he knocked off Joe Puerta, the defending champ from Illinois. He won his last championship by pulling a reversal in the semi-finals to avoid a defeat, and then in the finals he pinned his opponent.

Hugh Peery, born in 1931 in Stillwater, Okla., was twice the Oklahoma schoolboy champion and once, as a sophomore, the runner-up. At 5-foot-5 and 115 pounds, he came to Pitt when his father took over as coach in 1949. Hugh swept the national crowns of 1952, 1953 and 1954. He was one of the finest wrestlers on his feet that his father ever saw. In the semi-finals in his senior year, Hugh defeated an Olympic champion. In his 55 college bouts, he lost one match, that to Bob Homan of Penn State, 4–2, but the next year he took Homan, 18–8. Hugh made the 1952 Olympic Team, and in Helsinki he defeated Egyptian and Swedish wrestlers before bowing to a Russian.

Edwin Peery was born in 1935 in Stillwater, Okla., just as his father was preparing to enter the critical semi-finals of the NCAA championship in his senior year. Ed went to high school at Shaler Township and was the Pennsylvania schoolboy state champ in his sophomore and junior years. In his senior year, he lost the title by a referee's decision to Dean Seese of Clearfield. The 5-foot-6 and 123-pound Ed went on to Pitt, where he won the 1955, 1956 and 1957 national titles, as well as the Eastern championships twice. Like Hugh, he lost one match in

Wrestling's Rex Peery

(Author)

college, that in his junior year. Like his father, he won an alternate position on the 1956 Olympic Team. Ed, said his father, had as much heart as any wrestler he has ever seen. He had the Peery quickness, knowledge, determination and balance, as well as strength and stamina, to win over the nation's best.

Dr. Hugh Peery today is a dentist in Pittsburgh. Ed Peery for the past 15 years has been head coach of the U.S. Naval Academy wrestling team. Each of the boys has three children, and Ed's one son is a wrestler.

Wrestling as intercollegiate competition began at the University of Pennsylvania in 1900. Rex Peery was into it as a collegian in its pioneering days. He became one of the first well-trained coaches. For five years he coached in some small Oklahoma high schools and then spent nine years at Tulsa Central High School, producing a team record of 71–5–2.

Rex Peery moved on to Pitt, where in 16 seasons as head coach he had a record of 116–42–3. He stepped down in 1965 after his Panthers had won 13 national individual titles, six of them by his own two sons, of course.

Pennsylvania schoolboy wrestling started to grow rapidly at the end of World War II, but Pennsylvania collegiate wrestling was strong before the schoolboy program was well-organized statewide. The NCAA championships began in 1928, and Lehigh had a winner, John Engel, in 1931. Penn State swept four Eastern championships as early as 1918–21. The Nittany Lions' overall record for 1909–74 is 369–92–21. The famed Dr. Charlie Speidel coached from 1927–64, with four years off for World War II, and produced a mark of 191–56–13. By 1950, Franklin and Marshall, Lock Haven State, Gettysburg, Indiana State University, Pitt and Wilkes had solid wrestling reputations.

The surge of the state colleges in recent years has been remarkable. Bloomsburg, Clarion and Slippery Rock all produced national champions in the early 1970s. Clarion had four: Garry Barton (Erie), Wade Schalles (Hollidaysburg), Don Rohn (Hellertown), and Bill Simpson (Gaithersburg, Md.). Clarion had wrestling from 1946–50 and then dropped it for lack of interest. Its present athletic director, Frank Lignelli, put Clarion back into collegiate wrestling in 1959 and through the 1973–74 season it had a 169–31 mark for dual meets. Robert Bubb, a Lock Haven native and a Pitt wrestler under Rex Peery, took charge in 1966 after coaching at Tyrone High School. Bubb has had a winning record at Clarion ever since.

Pennsylvania has had the very best in collegiate wrestling coaches. The same is true at the schoolboy level, and wrestling is one sport

Dan Muthler, Navy champ from Jersey Shore

where the quality of coaching has a direct effect on the quality of performance.

Thanks mainly to Doc Speidel, Penn State between 1918–73 won 15 Eastern team championships and had 106 individual champs, or more winners than any other Eastern college. Bill Koll took over the Nittany Lions in 1965 and kept them winning. From Fort Dodge, Iowa, Koll wrestled for Iowa State Teachers and in the 145-pound division won the NCAA crown three times, 1946–48. He also was on the 1948 Olympic team. Koll, incidentally, has his doctorate in education.

Hubert Jack, now retired in Grove City, earned a national reputation for taking once-unknown Lock Haven State to the top. Grey Simons, a native of Virginia, was the nation's best 115 pounder for Lock Haven three times, 1960–62, while Lock Haven's Len DeAugustino in 1953 and Bill Blacksmith in 1966 also won NCAA crowns.

John Reese, a PIAA finalist at Kingston, put little Wilkes in the big-time. Taking over in 1953, Reese has produced three undefeated seasons and 13 Mid-Atlantic team titles. The Wilkes Colonels have not had a losing season since 1954.

Coach William Sheridan of Lehigh (1885–60) is the legend in Pennsylvania wrestling. For 41 years, or 1911–51, he guided the Engineers. He had six undefeated seasons and won 13 Eastern titles. Little Billy had only five losing seasons, just one of them in his last 30 years at Lehigh.

Sheridan grew up near Loch Lomond, Scotland, and as a fatherless boy got into professional wrestling to earn money. He slipped back into the amateur class to win the equivalent of the 126-pound division in Scotland, throwing nine opponents in an average of 2:05 minutes, it is said. Then he won Scotland's featherweight and lightweight divisions and claimed the championship of the entire British Isles. In all, he won a record 74 wrestling tournaments in Scotland. He emigrated to Ontario, Canada, and within six weeks had the professional title there. In 1910 he arrived in Philadelphia and took up boxing. He practiced at Andy Ryan's Gym at Seventh and Vine Sts. In his first bout, with Kid Broad, Billy took a right on the jaw and was knocked stone-cold and out of boxing forever. He wandered over to the Penn gymnasium, watched the collegians work out, and got on the mat and pinned everyone from lightweight to heavyweight.

Lehigh started wrestling in 1909, and in 1911 it signed Sheridan as coach. His technique was simple. He taught his squad the fundamentals and then let them wrestle. "He didn't believe in calisthenics," said his 1934 national champ, Ben Bishop. "If you want to be a wrestler, you get on the mat and wrestle your head off. It seemed to work." Many of the toughest bouts were Billy's boys wrestling for positions on the team.

When Sheridan came to the Lehigh Valley, only Liberty High School had wrestling. He talked other school districts into getting the sports, and meanwhile was himself a local school director for 18 years. He coached at the Olympics and Pan American games, ran summer wrestling camps, talked up wrestling from coast to coast, and built the Engineers a national reputation.

Lehigh started out more interested in football, but then its gridiron fortunes floundered. In 1927–33 the Lehigh football record was 19–40–4, while Sheridan's grapplers were 51–6–1. Ever since, Lehigh has been a wrestling school. Even basketball was downgraded. In the past 30 years, the college has had only four winning basketball teams. Its 1974–75 season was the worst among the major colleges, 1–23, and its resigning head coach blamed the school's emphasis on wrestling for that.

Gerry Leeman succeeded Billy Sheridan in 1952, and turned in 18 winning wrestling seasons in 18 years, including undefeated marks in 1957 and 1961. Thad Turner, of Philipsburg, became coach in 1970 and continued the Engineers' winning ways on the mat. Turner as a young wrestler under Coach Leeman was twice team captain and copped the most outstanding wrestler award at the 1961 Easterns.

Lehigh gets some of its talent from New York and New Jersey, but most of its top wrestlers are Pennsylvania boys. Its winning 1974–75 squad had 18 Pennsylvanians out of 36, with eight of them from the hometown Allentown-Bethlehem area.

While the Peerys stand alone for father-sons achievement, there are many other Pennsylvania families that have had great success too. Len, or "Gus," DeAugustino, of Grove City, was the schoolboy state champ and then national champ. His son Mike at North Allegheny High was two-time PIAA 112-pound king, 1974–75. Mike's sophomore brother, Scott, lost the PIAA 119-pound crown in 1975 in overtime. Don Maurey, of Clearfield, was schoolboy state champ too. His son Steve, of Altoona, took a title in 1974, only to lose in 1975 in a high-scoring preliminary match to Scott DeAugustino. The older Maurey brothers were fabulous. Jim and Don each won a schoolboy title, but Gerry took honors four times—an incredible feat for a high schooler. The three Maureys wrestled at Penn State, but oddly enough none ever won a national championship.

Dr. James Conklin, of Waynesburg, was a four-time state schoolboy champ back in the 1930s, while Mike Johnson came out of Lock Haven to win the title four times before wrestling his college days at Pitt. Stanley Mousetis was a schoolboy king and won the Easterns for Frank-

(Lehigh University)

Tom Sculley, Lehigh national champ

lin and Marshall. His son Tim matched him with a state title. Mousetis today is a prominent referee and coach, producing outstanding wrestlers at Washington High School.

Here is a list of Pennsylvania-born national champions since 1941, with their hometowns, weights and colleges: Richard DiBattista (Ardmore), 1941–42, 175 lbs., Penn. George Lewis (Farrell), 1948, 125 lbs., Waynesburg. Anthony Gizoni, (Washington), 1950–51, 121 lbs., Waynesburg. Len DeAugustino (Grove City), 1953, 137 lbs., Lock Haven State. Hudson Samson (Wilkinsburg), 1953, 191 lbs., Penn State. Joe Solomon (Cannonsburg), 1954, 167 lbs., Pitt. Larry Fornicola (Bellefonte), 1955, 137 lbs., Penn State.

Ed Peery (Shaler Twp.), 1955–57, 123 lbs., Pitt. Ed DeWitt (Chartiers Twp.), 1956, 167 lbs., Pitt. Tom Alberts (Waynesburg), 1957, 167 lbs., Pitt. John Johnston (Clearfield), 1957, 130 lbs., Penn State. Paul Powell (Lock Haven), 1958, 123 lbs., Pitt. Ed Hamer (Philipsburg), 1959, 167 lbs., Lehigh. Arthur Baker (Erie), 1959, 191 lbs., Syracuse, also a noted football player.

Larry Lauchle (Muncy), 1961, 130 lbs., Pitt. Arthur Maugham (Cannonsburg), 1963, 115 lbs., Moorhead State, Minn. Kirk Pendleton (Bryn Athyn), 1963, 157 lbs., Lehigh. Jim Nance (Indiana), 1963 and 1965, heavyweight, Syracuse, also All-American football player. Bill Stuart (Suburban Phila.), 1965, 137 lbs., Lehigh. Bob Kopnisky (Shaler Twp.), 1965, 157 lbs., Maryland. Greg Ruth (Bethlehem), 1965–66, first 165 lbs. and then 160 lbs., Oklahoma. Veryl Long (Washington), 1965, 147 lbs., Iowa State.

Bill Blacksmith (Lemoyne), 1966, 145 lbs., Lock Haven State. Gobel Kline (Beaver Springs), 1969, 152 lbs., Maryland. Geoff Baum (Allentown), 1970–71, first 190 lbs. and then 177 lbs., Oklahoma State. Stan Dziedzic (Allentown), 1971, 150 lbs., Slippery Rock State. Andy Matter (Upper Darby), 1971–72, 167 lbs., Penn State.

Garry Barton (Erie), 1972, 134 lbs., Clarion State. Wade Schalles (Hollidaysburg), 1972–73, first 150 lbs. and then 158 lbs., Clarion State. Dan Muthler (Jersey Shore), 1973, 142 lbs., Naval Academy. Don Rohn (Hellertown), 1973, 134 lbs., Clarion State. Floyd Hitchcock (Wyalusing), 1974, 177 lbs., Bloomsburg State. Tom Sculley (Bethlehem), 1974, 134 lbs., Lehigh. John Fritz (Bethlehem), 1975, 126 lbs., Penn State. Jim Bennett (Corry), 1975, 142 lbs., Yale. Mike Lieberman (Allentown), 1975, 177 lbs., Lehigh.

Recent Olympic Team members: ReAugustino, 1952, 136 lbs. DeWitt and Lauchle, both 1970, 171 lbs. and 125 lbs. respectively. Ruth, 1964, 154 lbs. James Carr (Erie), 1972, 114.5 lbs.

BASKETBALL

8

The Mighty Macs

... *Little Immaculata Made Hoop History*

It was 15 of the nation's top basketball teams versus Pennsylvania's little Immaculate College at the 1975 tournament of the Association of Intercollegiate Athletics for Women. All the big guns were against the three-time champion Mighty Macs.

In the three rounds to get to the finals, Immaculata was unsurprisingly consistent. By nine points or better, the Mighty Macs knocks off bigger Kansas State, undefeated Wayland Baptist College of Texas and California State of Fullerton.

Then in the finals, the pressure descended as everyone knew it would, on defending champion Immaculata. The challenger, Delta State of Mississippi, was undefeated in 27 games. Its 6-foot-3 All-American, Lusia Harris, probably was the nation's top woman basketball player. The Mighty Macs had no one in height to compare to her, and Lusia zipped through a 32-point night with 16 rebounds. Yet Immaculata hung on. With eight minutes left, the Pennsylvanians were only two points behind, but then they missed five consecutive shots. Yet on the floor, the Mighty Macs outscored Delta State with five more field goals, but they gave the challengers 18 more attempts at the free-throw line. That made the difference, and Delta State took the crown, 90–81.

In four years, 1972–75, Immaculata College was three times number-one in women's basketball and once number-two. In the short annals of the now fastest-growing team sport in America, that is the standard. And in Pennsylvania collegiate basketball history—male or female—nobody has outdone the Mighty Macs.

Sports glory came shockingly quick and unexpected to the Catholic girls liberal arts school.

"We do not want the image of a sports college," said Immaculata's president, Sister Marie Antoine, in 1975, yet it is sports that has made the college known even to Pennsylvanians let alone the rest of the nation.

The school was opened in 1921 as the first and only college of the Servants of the Immaculate Heart of Mary. It has a magnificent 390-acre campus with gray stone and red-tiled buildings overlooking the Pennsylvania Turnpike. Its neighbors, West Chester State, Cheyney State and Villanova University, are well established, and until basketball put it in the spotlight Immaculata was a rather isolated, small sectarian school at Frazer with 525 full-time undergraduate Catholic women. Suddenly it emerged from a cloistered existence to national headlines, and the college's leadership naturally has ambivalent feelings about that.

The Mighty Macs tell an amusing story indicative how much fame, though not yet fortune, has come their way.

In 1974 they copped their third successive title by bumping off Kansas State, Indiana University, William Penn College and Mississippi College in the 16-team AIAW tournament. Meanwhile UCLA, winner of nine of the past 10 male National Collegiate Athletic Association crowns, got dumped by North Carolina State. The UCLA coach, John Wooden, was dismayed and huffy about his loss of national honors.

"If UCLA wins next year, they'll be the Immaculata of men's basketball," CBS sports correspondent John Phillips cracked to the Mighty Macs. "Yes," replied one of the girls, "and if they win, John Wooden will be the Cathy Rush of men's basketball too."

Wooden retired in 1975 with the top male team in the nation. Cathy Rush had the number-two team in the women's ranks. There was one feat of Mrs. Rush's, however, that Wooden never duplicated. She was pregnant in both 1973 and 1974 as her Mighty Macs headed for national titles. Not only did she give birth to two sons, Eddie and Michael, but the latter was born two months after the 1974 glorious triumph. Even Knute Rockne couldn't do that for Notre Dame football.

And in the prosaic matter of won-loss records, so cherished in coaching circles, Mrs. Rush is up on national male leader Wooden too. His 29-year career mark in college basketball was 667–161, or .806. Mrs. Rush's five-year record for 1971–75 was 97–7, or .933.

No Pennsylvanian is likely to catch Mrs. Rush either. The retired Harry Litwack was 356–183, or .660, for 22 years at Temple. Charles "Buzz" Ridl, a native of Irwin who retired in 1975, had a 19-year career record at Westminster and Pitt of 313–174, or .641. Through 1974, John Manning at Duquesne was .642 and John Bach at Penn State, .576. The late Ken Loeffler, a native of Beaver Falls, had possibly the finest years in Pennsylvania male collegiate basketball at La Salle in 1950–55, but his 145–30 record made .829. There are all sorts of high school marks. The late John Goepfert for 34 years at Mahanoy City High won 27 championships and was 803–179, or .818.

Perhaps Mrs. Rush's closest rival is, ironically, another woman, Pat Wallace of the Lancaster Catholic High girls team. A guidance counselor by profession, Miss Wallace in 1960–75 led the Crusaderettes to a 226–31 mark, or .879. In one stretch over 1973–74, they had 53 straight wins. Pennsylvania started the statewide girls championship in the 1972 school year, and Allentown Catholic won. Lancaster Catholic took it the following season with a 27–0 record and was in the top four in the 1974–75 school year with a 27–2 mark, while Allentown Dieruff High won the title. Dieruff was the first public high school to be state girls champion. The success of the Catholic girls was not accidental, because the parochial schools were into girls sports, with fairness and emphasis, long before Pennsylvania's public schools. In fact, a measure of Immaculata's success is the way it draws on a supporting parochial system.

Immaculata is the modern equivalent of the old Carlisle Indian School for its smallness, its spirit, its competitiveness, and its contribution for focusing national attention on Pennsylvania.

Pennsylvania plays a lot of basketball, but seldom is the Commonwealth recognized nationally, as it invariably is for its football and wrestling. Contrary to many Pennsylvanians' opinion, the hoop game in California, Indiana, Illinois, North Carolina and Massachusetts, to cite a few states, has been better over the years.

There have been big Pennsylvania stars, like Wilt Chamberlain, Paul Arizin, Maurice Stokes and Tom Gola. There have been some nationally respected figures, such as Harry and Mendy Rudolph, of Wilkes-Barre. Harry, the father, was a great referee and before his death was president of the Eastern Basketball League. Mendy, the son, marked his 22nd season as a National Basketball Association official in 1975.

Pennsylvania has had some fabulous teams, like Philadelphia's old Sphas and Warriors and the Wilkes-Barre Barons in the professional ranks, and Penn, Temple, Villanova, La Salle, St. Joseph, Philadelphia Textiles, Pitt, Duquesne, St. Francis and Cheyney among the college boys. But the calibre of stardom and team play goes up and down yearly. The Commonwealth has not had a collegiate powerhouse since 1954–55, when La Salle won national and then runner-up NCAA champion, or since the Warriors won the NBA title in 1967. Villanova lost the 1971 NCAA crown by six points to UCLA, and then was deprived of its ranking because its star, Howard Porter, was accused of signing a prior pro contract. Temple took the National Invitational Tournament in 1938 and 1969 and Duquesne in 1955. Villanova was runner-up in the NIT in 1965 and Duquesne in 1940 and 1954, and that has been about it.

Pennsylvania basketball is modestly good at all times, infrequently superb. In the Philadelphia and Pittsburgh areas, it is always competitive and popular. Beyond that, the rest of the nation notices Pennsylvania basketball only when it is blinded by brilliance.

Immaculata broke the mold. Beyond the lustre of its record—including a 35-game winning streak, the longest in the history of women's college basketball—the Mighty Macs have indelibly etched their name in the annals of sports for being the pathbreaker and the first great national women's champion. Others will follow, but Immaculata was the spectacular first.

It began in 1971 when Cathy Rush, then 22, was hired as coach. A native of Atlantic City, where she had been a fair basketball player, Cathy graduated from nearby West Chester State. Along with East Stroudsburg State, Slippery Rock State and a few others, West Chester is one of the leaders of Pennsylvania collegiate girls basketball. Cathy played two seasons for the Rams and then switched to gymnastics, in which she excelled, for two years. She also is a fine golfer, incidentally.

Cathy is married to Ed Rush, a native of Flourtown, also a West Chester graduate, and who for six years refereed in the NBA and then went to the American Basketball Association. Ed and Cathy operate a summer basketball camp in the Poconos. They and their two sons live near Immaculata, and Mrs. Rush is able to call herself "a full-time mother and a part-time coach."

Cathy took the Immaculata post after teaching a few years because she wanted an "easy, little part-time job, low-key and relaxing." With the winners she has had and the national attention, the job has been anything but low-key. Championship teams must work hard. Drilling fast breaks and pick-and-roll and outlining strategies, Coach Rush conducts lively but intensive practice sessions. Wearing earrings and usually a warm smile, the slim, 5-foot-7, blond Cathy is more lighthearted at practices, however, than her serious players. She is the exact opposite of the stereotyped stern tyrant of the hardwoods. She is relatively indifferent to the fame that has come her way, nor does she seek to promote her own feminine charm and beauty that the outside sports world takes to. Her desire is that the Immaculata girls win all the attention for their play on the court.

(Immaculata College)

Immaculata's Coach Cathy Rush

The nickname "Mighty Macs" had not been coined when Mrs. Rush came aboard. The college had volley ball, tennis and field hockey, as well as basketball. Its 1970 record in basketball was 5–5. Cathy turned that into 10–2 in her first season, and since then basketball has been "the sport" at Immaculata.

Coach Rush started off with some good talent. Her 1971 captain was Pat Walsh, who in 1973–74 became Immaculata's assistant coach. For the 1975 season, Pat accepted the head coaching job at Princeton.

Theresa Shank, now Theresa Grentz, is the second coach Mrs. Rush put into the college ranks. Theresa, of Glenolden, became the mentor at St. Joseph's College. She was the 6-foot star of the 1971–72–73–74 teams, certainly the greatest woman basketball player in Pennsylvania history to date. Averaging in one season as many as 22 points a game, Theresa could outplay any other girl center in the nation. In the 1974 championship quarter-finals against Indiana, the Mighty Macs got a 60–56 victory because Theresa scored 23 points and pulled down 20 rebounds. The next night against big William Penn, she popped 18 points and got 18 rebounds. In the finals against Mississippi College, she scored another 18, and the championship was Immaculata's. Always a playmaker, Theresa's scoring was limited by her eagerness to rebound, set up plays and pass off.

The first national championship came in 1972 when the name "Mighty Macs" was born as the Rushites turned in a 24–1 record. In 1973 they outdid that with a perfect 20–0 mark, a second national championship, and Cathy's reward as Coach of the Year.

The pressure was on for 1974, but the Mighty Macs came through with a 20–1 record, a third national title, and Mrs. Rush's second Coach of the Year citation. Immaculata went through a 12–1 regular season in 1974 by averaging 63 points for 32-minute games (in 1975, women's basketball adopted the 40-minute game). There was not a close win in the batch. The one loss came at Flushing, N.Y., to Queens College, a heartbreaking 57–56 defeat—and the saddened Immaculata nuns noted that it happened on Ash Wednesday.

Immaculata's success happened to coincide with the historic change in women's basketball. The age-old sissy sport of girls toss-ball went out as Cathy Rush took over the Mighty Macs in 1971. The traditional contest nationally of six girls playing a half-court type game was replaced by the five-girl team on a full court with a 30-second clock to keep the game lively. The change made girls basketball exciting, competitive and a genuine sport. The girls were no longer oddities in a rather patronizing exhibition. Similarly, the new game fitted into Cathy Rush's talents for organizing a well-coached, hard-driving, play-conscious team. Mrs. Rush developed teams that could average better than a basket a minute.

Immaculata does it all on a basketball budget of merely $9,000. It offers no athletic scholarships, but attracts many fine players because of its and Coach Rush's reputations. For the 1975 team, 25 girls tried out and 12 made the varsity. On that team were seven Pennsylvanians, three girls from New Jersey and two black girls, one a transfer student, from Michigan.

The average height of the 1975 team was 5-foot-8, with freshman center Dolly Van Buskirk, of Downington, the one 6-footer. Unlike men's basketball, height usually is not a critical factor in the women's game. Because there is seldom more than a foot difference between the tallest and shortest girls on the court, the girls play is not distorted by oversized giants who dominate the backboards. Experience is a factor, and Coach Rush went into the 1975 season disadvantaged with two seniors, one junior, three sophomores and six freshmen on her squad.

The Mighty Macs are better than good, they are interesting.

Marianne Crawford was selected first-team All-American in 1975. A 5-foot-6 guard from Upper Darby, she played organized basketball since the sixth grade. In her junior and senior years at Archbishop Prendergast High School, Marianne was on undefeated teams that won the Catholic League titles. She recruited herself to Immaculata and kept her unbeaten ways on the 1973 team. She can spin a ball, dribble behind her back and through her legs, make steals, set pickoffs, and be almost perfect at the foul line. One of her talents is to play the 30-second clock down to the last tick—a vital skill in the 40-minute girls game where scores often are close. Because of her informal practice garb and her hustle, Marianne has been described as "a dead-end kid Leo Gorcey in bloomers."

Helen Canuso, a 5-foot-7 freshman from Holland, Pa., was the other guard on the 1975 team. She was a track star for Archbishop Wood High School, one of five athletic sisters. In the 1975 Maryland game on national television, Helen made seven of eight shots from the floor and, in all, tallied 19 points. A key figure on the 1972–75 teams was 5-foot-11 Rene Muth from Broomall and Villa Maria Academy. Rene was noted for her consistency, her refusal to let pressure bother her, and her good-natured outspokenness. "Don't call me a jock," she told sports-writers who were impressed with her athletic prowess.

It has all been very exciting at Immaculata, and for good reason. The victories and national championships have been sweet, but so has been the fun of pioneering modern women's basketball. The Mighty Macs in 1975 became the first girls college team to play at the Palestra, and they

(Immaculata College)

All-American Marianne Crawford

beat St. Joe's. They also were the first on national television, defeating Maryland, 80–48. That was an odd game. They embarrassed themselves with 29 turnovers, but they startled many viewers by hitting 47 percent of their shots from the floor. And then on Feb. 22, 1975, they became the first women's team to win a college basketball game at Madison Square Garden. Before 11,919 fans, they beat Queens, 65–61, and that was an especially pleasing triumph for the Mighty Macs. "When you're good, people will come to see you play," Coach Rush told the New York *Times*, and with all the aplomb of a John Wooden.

TOP 50 PENNSYLVANIANS IN BASKETBALL

F.	Paul Arizin (Phila), Villanova Warriors	6–4
	Tom Gola (Phila), LaSalle, Warriors, Knicks	6–5
	Pete Maravich (Aliquippa), LSU, New Orleans	6–5
	Earl "The Pearl" Monroe (Phila), Bullets, Knicks	6–4
	Maurice Stokes (Pgh), St.Francis, Rochester Royals	6–7
	Jack Twyman (Pgh), Cincinnati Un., Royals	6–6
C.	Wilt Chamberlain (Overbrook), Kansas, Warriors	7–1
	Theresa Shank Grentz (Glenolden) Immaculata	6
	Tom McMillen (Mansfield), Maryland	6–11
G.	Fred Carter (Phila), Mt.St.Mary's, Bullets, 76ers	6–3
	Bob Davies (Harrisburg), Seton Hall, Royals	6–1
	Dick Groat (Swissvale), Duke, Ft.Wayne Pistons	6
	Geoff Petrie (Springfield), Princeton, Portland	6–4
	Guy Rodgers (Phila), Temple, Warriors	6
	Norm Van Lier (Midland), St. Francis, Chicago Bulls	6–1

Centers—Len Chappell (Portage), Wake Forest, Milwaukee. Larry Foust (Phila), LaSalle, Ft. Wayne. Joe Holup (Swoyersville), Geo. Washington, Syracuse Nats. Willie Sojourner (Germantown), Weber St., N.Y. Nets

Forwards—Mike Bantom (Phila), St. Joe, Phoenix Suns. Ernie Beck (Phila), Penn, Warriors. Chuck Cooper (Pgh), Duquesne, Boston Celtics. Bryan Generalovich (Farrell), Pitt, Johnstown Pros. Matt Goukas (Phila), St. Joe, 76ers, Bulls. Wayne Hightower (Overbrook), Kansas, San Francisco and Denver pros. Billy Knight (Braddock), Pitt, Indiana Pacers. Pete Kramer (Camp Hill), Duke. Jack Marin (Farrell), Duke, Bullets, Buffalo. Julius McCoy (Farrell), Mich.State, Sunbury Mercuries. Cas Ostrowski (West Wyoming), Wilkes-Barre Barons. Dick Ricketts (Pottstown), Duquesne, Rochester Royals. Ray Scott (Phila), Portland Un., Detroit Pistons. Whitey Von Neida (Ephrata), Penn State, Lancaster Red Roses. Jim Washington (Phila), Villanova, 76ers, Buffalo.

Guards—Marianne Crawford (Upper Darby), Immaculata. Francis "Chink" Crossin (Luzerne), Penn, Warriors. Walt Hazzard (Overbrook), UCLA, Lakers, Seattle. Pat Hennon (Wampum) Pitt. Wali Jones (Overbrook), Villanova, 76ers, Milwaukee. Red Klotz (Phila), Villanova, Phila. Sphas, Bullets, Washington Generals. Stu Lantz (Uniontown), Pistons, Lakers. Hal Lear (Overbrook), Temple,

Warriors. Freddie Lewis (McKeesport), Arizona State, Indiana
Pacers. Bill Melchionni (Phila), Villanova, N.Y. Nets. Larry Miller
(Catasaqua), North Carolina, Carolinian pros. Barry Parkhill (State
College), Virginia, Virginia Squires pros. George Senesky (Mahanoy
City), St. Joe, Warriors. Willie Somerset (Farrell), Duquesne, N.Y.
Nets. Dave Twardzik (Middletown), Old Dominion, Virginia Squires.
Hubie White (Phila), Villanova, Warriors.

(New York Knicks)

Earl "The Pearl" Monroe

(Philadelphia Warriors)

Guy Rodgers

Fred Carter   (Philadelphia 76ers)

Norm Van Lier

9

HOCKEY

The Green Bay of
the Ice Game

. . . Hershey Loves God,
Country, Chocolate and
Flying Pucks

The car with hockey fans headed down the "Hershey Road," or Route 422, into what is called "Hershey." There were two bumper stickers on the back: "Hershey Bears" and "God Has Everything Under Control." Just as the fans got to their seats at the Hersheypark Arena, the lights dimmed. Mitch Grand, the organist, started, "The Star-Spangled Banner," and the fans actually sang it—probably the only place in America where the audience does not stand slack-jawed for the national anthem.

When the last echo of "the home of the brave" bounced off 17,000 square feet of ice and up 100 feet to the cork-lined concrete roof, the chocolate-brown and white jersey Hershey Bears were ready for action. "Knock 'em on their heinies!" the fans shouted who had the stickers on his automobile. "Get good and mad this time, you bums!"

Hershey, Pennsylvania. Technically it does not exist. The municipal name is Derry Township, population 16,045, east of Harrisburg, west of Palmyra, north of Elizabethtown and south of suburbia, the Blue Mountains and the coal-crackers. Between the Mason-Dixon Line and

218

the St. Lawrence Seaway, this must be the oddest place for a hotbed of hockey, but it is.

Hershey is the Green Bay of hockey. It has the most successful minor-league franchise of any sport in America.

From the time in 1938 when Hershey entered professional hockey, more than 5 million fans have paid their way into the Hersheypark Arena to see their beloved Bears. Milton S. Hershey himself, the Chocolate King, would stand in line for a ticket and then march up to the press box to watch the game. If he had guests, he bought them tickets. And one of the arena managers used to sit up there with a pad, marking down each time a puck flew into the spectators or when a hockey stick was splintered.

Frank S. Mathers is now president and general manager. He was one of hockey's most brilliant coaches for 17 years, 1956–72, and when he stepped down after 666 home games, sportswriter John Travers added up that 3,860,526 fans had watched the Bears at Hershey in that era, an average of 5795 a game. Since the arena seats 7286 and the record hockey crowd was 8703, the Bears invariably play to an almost full house.

In 1963 when the Bears were considered for a National Hockey League franchise, along with its rivals Baltimore, Cleveland and Pittsburgh, Hershey easily was outdrawing these big cities in minor-league competition.

It does not make sense that Dutchmen and coal-crackers would be such hockey enthusiasts, especially in a section of Pennsylvania famous for its conservative, quiet life-style that shuns emotionalism. Mr. Hershey was an ardent golfer—he put five golf courses in his little town and Ben Hogan once was the pro at the Hershey Country Club. The candy millionaire delighted in chasing a golf ball around, but he was the grandson of a Mennonite bishop and he never quite understood why his neighbors were so aroused by watching outsiders violently pursue a hockey puck over ice. "If that's what they want, I'll give it to them," he used to say about projects that had strong public support. So he built a hockey dynasty unrivaled in the United States.

Nobody in American hockey has ever matched the Hershey Bears for continuous success, in the game or at the box office. It was the winning hockey, in fact, that made such stalwart fans of the Dutchman from Harrisburg, Lancaster, Manheim and Annville and the coal-crackers from Pottsville, Tremont, Schuylkill Haven and Tower City.

The Bears joined the American Hockey League in 1938 and immediately won a division title with a 31–18–5 record. Through the 37th season that ended in the spring of 1975, the Bears won an AHL record, nine division crowns, five Calder Cups and 17 second-place finishes. Second only to Providence in years in the league, Hershey is first in games won. The Bears have gone to the play-offs an amazing 33 out of 37 seasons. Five times they took the Cup—1946, 1957, 1958, 1968 and 1973—and eight times they were the losing finalists. Just as important, the Bears finished last only once, in 1949, and in only five other years did they lose more games than they won. Overall, the Bears have won 1195 games, lost 1021 and tied 279, for a .539 mark through the 1974–75 season.

In the 1958 season, the Bears did the impossible. They ended in fourth place with a 32–32–6 record, so average that they scored 200 goals and had 202 goals scored against them, that is how average they were. But Coach Mathers drove them through the play-offs. They whipped Cleveland and Buffalo, the top teams in the league, and became the AHL's only fourth-place club to ever win the Calder Cup.

Pennsylvania is not known for hockey, but it should be. In 1975 it became the first American state to have five professional teams in play-off competition—Johnstown Jets and Philadelphia Firebirds in the North American League, the Hershey Bears in the AHL, and the Pittsburgh Penguins and Philadelphia Flyers in the National Hockey League. The Jets won their title and the Flyers, of course, took their second consecutive Stanley Cup.

Philadelphia fooled with hockey for years. The old Philadelphia Arena at 46th and Market Streets opened in 1920 and featured such losers as the Rockets and Ramblers. The Firebirds in the NAL are a descendant, but a winning team, and not to be confused with the defunct Pottstown Firebirds who had two glorious seasons, 1969–70, in winning the Atlantic Coast Football League.

The Spectrum went up in 1967 and in came the NHL Flyers. With Coach Fred Shero, these "Broad Street Bullies" in 1974 became the first NHL expansion team to go all the way, in only seven years, and take the Stanley Cup, beating the awesome Boston Bruins. They repeated in 1975, this time against the Buffalo Sabres. Theirs was a new style of scrambling play, with heroes like Bobby Clarke, Dave Schultz and Bernie Parent. Schultz in the winning seasons became the most penalized player in hockey history, while Clarke is the game's top forward and Parent is the super goalie. Philadelphians went wild—680,280 for 40 home games at the Spectrum in the 1974–75 season, and motorcades that brought out two million people when their skaters returned with the trophy. A new folklore sprung up over three seasons when Kate Smith sung "God Bless America" and the Flyers responded with an amazing

43–3–1 record when she sang. The Flyers are Philadelphia's darlings as no other team has been since Connie Mack's great pennant winners of 1929–31.

The Penguins are an offshoot of the old Pittsburgh Hornets of the AHL. The Hornets had some good teams. In fact, Frank Mathers starred on the Hornets' Calder Cup winners of 1952 and 1955. The Penguins have not grabbed glory yet like their Turnpike rivals, the Flyers, but in 1974–75 they had their first winning season and were the NHL's third top scoring team.

Johnstown is an odd place for hockey, but it has always been a great sports town. Eleven pro football players are from the area. For 24 years it had the minor-league baseball Johnnies, where Joe Cronin, Vern Stephens and others broke in.

In 1941 Johnstown had a season in the old Eastern Hockey League. It used a rink that is now a warehouse. In 1950 the 4100-seat Cambria County War Memorial was opened, and Johnstown was back in hockey. Strong business backing from leaders such as Charles Kunkle Jr., Howard Picking Jr., B. T. DuPont and the late publisher Walter Krebs kept the ice game in Johnstown. There is enthusiastic support for the 37 home games, with an average attendance of 2800. Coach Dick Roberge played 17 years with the team and President Don Hall was with him on that line for 12 years. In off-season Roberge is a golf pro and Hall a stockbroker. Executive Director John Mitchell has been in Johnstown 12 years. All three are now naturalized American citizens.

Hershey's love affair with madness on ice started back in 1930 when Charles F. Ziegler and John B. Sollenberger talked Mr. Hershey into putting ice in his Convention Hall. The hall is now the Hershey Museum, but in those days was used for religious gatherings by the Brethren and Mennonites. Ziegler was president of Hershey Estates and Sollenberger succeeded him.

The first hockey game was played Feb. 18, 1931, with the Penn Athletic Club defeating Villanova, 5–4, before a packed house of 1800 in what was known as the Ice Palace. Porter Waite, an automobile dealer, played for Villanova, and the following season he brought his Swarthmore A.C. to use the Ice Palace as home ice. That November 19, Swarthmore played the Crescent A.C. of Brooklyn, and Russ and Lloyd Blinco, a pair of brothers from the paper mills of Grand Mere, Quebec, were on the ice for Crescent. Lloyd "The Bull," a hard-driving center, was persuaded to stay in Hershey. He stayed for 40 years, or until he retired as president of the Bears. Short and tough, with a face that absorbed thousands of elbows, Blinco set up Hershey's "birddog" system throughout Canada. Former players and scouts recommended young talent, and Blinco would get the lads to Hershey and send $50 back to the birddog. Later Hershey became affiliated with the Boston Bruins, Detroit Red Wings, Pittsburgh Penguins and Buffalo Sabres, and even more good players came to Chocolate Town.

In the winter of 1932–33, Hershey established its own amateur team, the famed B'Ars, that lasted until the professional club was formed for the AHL in 1938. The name, Hershey B'Ars, did not last, however. New York sportswriters insisted that B'Ars had an obvious commercial connotation with the world-famous sweet produced at Hershey, so a second vowel had to be added and that is how the name Bears originated. To introduce the new name, a real bear was acquired. The bear was kept in a cage in the team locker room before games, and players poked him with their hockey sticks. By the time the trainer wheeled the bear out on the ice before the fans, the animal was blazing mad. That didn't work. So Hershey brought in a bear who had been trained to skate. The crowd awaited this wonder, only to see a bear who kept falling on his behind or relieving himself on the ice. After that, Hershey put a bear or two in its zoo, and devotees could visit the mascot there.

Ziegler and Sollenberger talked Mr. Hershey into building the world's first modern ice arena. His architect-engineer, D. Paul Witmer, a farm boy from Elizabethtown, had built many of Mr. Hershey's projects, including his magnificent Hotel Hershey. Witmer took him the initial plans for the arena to seat 5000. Mr. Hershey, though no great hockey fan, looked them over and said, "You better make it a little bigger." Witmer increased the capacity by a third.

Hersheypark Arena is one of the great landmarks of the sporting scene. It has a standard-size rink of 200 by 85 feet, which was unusually large for the 1930s in the United States. Its five-section reinforced concrete roof is only $3\frac{1}{2}$ inches thick, arched to rest on lead plates. What is particularly pleasing is that there is not a bad seat in the place. As a world-traveling millionaire with one of the most recognizable names in America, Mr. Hershey often went incognito, only to have some unknowing restaurant maitre d's put him at the table in the corner behind a pillar. When he had Witmer in 1929 build him the hotel, he gave him a picture postcard of a 30-room Mediterranean hotel he and his wife had enjoyed and told Witmer to "blow it up" to 200 rooms. For the sake of the Spanish style, the plans were cut to 170 rooms. The great circular dining room has no obstructions. That was Mr. Hershey's order. Witmer had a pillar in the middle, but Mr. Hershey said he would rather pay extra to have the roof supported by an additional truss than have that post get in the way of anyone's view. The same order went out for the far bigger arena, and there is not an interior pillar to be seen.

The new arena opened Dec. 20, 1936, for the old amateur Bears. Better than 6000 fans were there. The clock had ticked only 1:28 and Blinco on a breakaway scored the first goal to be recorded in the new palace. The score ended Bears 3 and the New York Rovers 2.

As the professional Bears, Hershey played its first game in the arena on Nov. 5, 1938. The great Frankie Brimsek was in the nets for the Providence Reds. Hank Lauzon, the first pro player ever signed by Hershey, was the Bears' goalie. Before a 6000 crowd again, Hershey won, 2–1. Blinco, who had been the amateur star, retired before ever turning pro. Lauzon, interestingly, became the first of many Bears players to make Hershey his permanent home. Mainly a defenseman for eight years, Lauzon was All-League twice. He married into the Reese Peanut Butter Cup family.

It was in that first pro season that Mr. Hershey sought to test two new soap bars, "Hershey Mechanic Soap" and the famous "Hershey Cocoa Butter Soap." He decided to give a bar of each to every fan who passed through the turnstile. Sollenberger warned him that soap bars could become flying objects. "There isn't any Dutchman going to throw away 10-cent bars of soap," said Mr. Hershey. In the second period, a Bears player was sent to the penalty box. The fans were irrate. One soap bar went flying out over the ice. Then another, and finally hundreds. "The Soap Storm," it was called. Mr. Hershey never gave away free gifts at a hockey game again.

The Chocolate King (1857–1945) did not live to see his Hershey Bears in their prime.

The fine trainer, William Henry "Scotty" Alexander joined the team in 1946. A native of Aberdeen, Scotland, he trained two Calder Cup teams at Buffalo and four at Hershey before he retired in 1973. Little Scotty in a game against Buffalo once had to be rushed in as a substitute goalie. Only a few minutes elapsed before the Buffalo forwards zipped by the Hershey defensemen, Scotty panicked and got his stick caught in his own net, and Hershey surrendered the strangest goal in its history.

Mathers took over as player-coach in 1956. He played with Pittsburgh, 1948–55, and with Hershey, 1956–61, and continued on as the Bears coach through the 1972–73 season. One of the greats in all of hockey, Mathers as a player, coach and club president has been with six Calder Cup champions. He was an all-league defenseman six times. He played 799 games in 14 seasons in the AHL. Big and strong at 6-foot-1 and 182 pounds—with the looks and build of Gordie Howe—the

Frank Mathers

(Hershey Bears)

southpaw Mathers was one of the smoothest defensemen to ever take a puck away from an opponent. Invariably in position, he used every trick he knew but that of unnecessary violence. He spent only 636 minutes in the penalty box, or less than a penalty for every two games he played.

Mathers was born March 29, 1924, in Winnipeg. He was a junior in the New York Rangers organization, but turned pro with the Toronto Maple Leafs. Meanwhile, he was a football fullback for the Winnipeg Blue Bombers in the Grey Cup and also played for the Ottawa Rough Riders. An all-around athlete, he shoots golf in the low 80s. In World War II, he was a pilot with the Canadian Air Force. Mathers wanted to be a left-handed dentist and had three years of college before hockey captured his fancy. Though it worked out best for his career, he had only 23 games in the big-time with the Maple Leafs.

Mathers became business manager as well as coach of the Bears in 1962, then general manager in 1968, and finally, leaving coaching behind, president in 1973. In going to the top of the Hershey organization, he turned down numerous NHL coaching offers. Ironically, four former Bears players in 1974 were NHL mentors—George "Red" Sullivan with Washington, Floyd Smith with Buffalo, Marc Boileau with Pittsburgh and Don Cherry with Boston.

For such a sophisticated, courteous person, Mathers had some of the toughest hockey teams of all time. Larry "The Rock" Zeidel and Obie O'Brien had assault charges filed against them for a game in Buffalo. Born Lazarus Zeidel, he was Hershey's only Jewish player. From 1955–62, The Rock fought all comers. In one game against Springfield, Zeidel led associates up into the stands after unruly fans. In the 1959 Calder Cup against the old Cleveland Barons, 412 minutes of penalties were assessed for seven games, Zeidel getting his share. "That wasn't a hockey series. It was more like World War III," Mathers exclaimed. "There hasn't been a series in hockey anywhere to match it for brutality."

While Hershey never had an angrier Bear than Zeidel, it has had a cage full of colorful players—Ralph Keller, Barry Ashbee, Wally Kilrea, Red Sullivan, Dunc Fisher, Lorne Ferguson, Arnie Kullman, Willie Marshall, Gene Ubriaco, Jack McKenzie, Bobby Perreault, Gil Gilbert, Bobby Leiter and Mike Nykoluk, to name a few.

Though it lacks the bright lights of the big towns, Hershey has excellent living conditions and most players regret leaving the club when their time is up. Keller, now coach at Fort Wayne, established a beauty parlor in Hershey. Kullman, a Bears star for 13 years, made his permanent residence in Hummelstown. McKenzie and Marshall married sisters from Palmyra.

The hometown flavor of Hershey, the closeness of living conditions and the availability of ice time are part of the secret why the Bears are successful at hockey. Players stay in condition. Team spirit is high. Wives know each other. And there is plenty of practice time. In fact, the Bears probably practice more hours than any other professional team in America. Around the league it is known that the Bears invariably are "up" for the play-offs, since they get through long seasons without many of the distractions and disadvantages most other pro athletes suffer.

The greatest Bear was the "Big Bear," Mike Nykoluk. He looked like a battle-hardened, venerable Indian chief, this 5-foot-11, 209-pound former high school fullback from East Toronto. He played 16 years in the AHL, 14 of them with Hershey, or 969 Bears games. Nobody was ever in a Hershey uniform longer. He played when he was bloodied and beat-up. In the Calder Cup finals, he even played with a broken toe. "He's like Stan Musial, that popular," wrote Travers. "It's not just that he gives 150 percent all the time, but he's a magnificent man."

Nykoluk became an American citizen, living in Hershey with his wife Dolly and four children. When he would skate onto the ice, organist Mitch Grand would play, "Hello, Dolly." Mike's last game was on March 29, 1972, and 7486 fans screamed their admiration for the big-shouldered guy. Nykoluk and his Bears' teammate, Barry Ashbee, went on to be Fred Shero's assistant coaches and played a major role in the Flyers' Stanley Cup championships.

When Mathers left the coaching bench, he signed Chuck Hamilton, who had played for him eight years, to manage the 1973–74 season. "It's the break of a lifetime," exclaimed Hamilton. A graduate of Carleton College with additional studies at Elizabethtown College, Hamilton shares Mathers' studious nature. The trait is not unbecoming for winning hockey. In his first season, Hamilton took the Bears to second place and then won the Calder Cup.

The little town where they believe in God, sing the national anthem, munch on chocolate bars and love the Hershey Bears had one of its greatest nights on Jan. 5, 1975. The Wings of the Soviet arrived on their American tour. Seven of the Russians had skated on the 1973 World Cup champions and the 1972 Olympic silver medal teams. This was a tough outfit in the top division of Soviet hockey. On their American visit, they kept their winning ways. And then they came to capitalistic Hershey.

The Bears were up for the Russians. Before 7273 cheering onlookers, including Gov. Milton J. Shapp and Harrisburg's Mayor Harold A. Swenson, the locals swept into a 6–1 lead in the first period. The

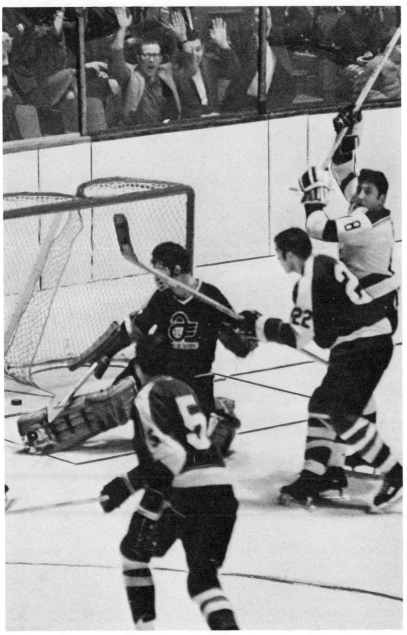

(Harrisburg *Patriot-News*)

Mike Nykoluk (8) scoring for Hershey

(Hershey Bears)

Mike Nykoluk

Russians knotted the contest, 6–6, in the third period. Then Billy Inglis and Bernie Lukowich hit back-to-back goals within 42 seconds. Both players ended up with three goals, or the "hat trick." When the final buzzer sounded, it was Hershey 10, the Soviets, 7.

"Our guys went right up the ice and took it to 'em," explained Coach Hamilton. And that's the way it has always been in the Green Bay of minor-league hockey.

BILLIARDS 10

Perfectionists with a Cuestick

... *The Great Mosconi Leads the Pack*

"Don't ask me why, but Pennsylvania is the top state in the nation for billiards," said Jim Rempe as he prepared for the opening of the new Pabst-Brunswick Pro Billiard Tour, appropriately enough launched at Penn State University in 1974. "Maybe it's because in Pennsylvania you stay indoors so much."

Pennsylvania is not that much an indoor-sport state. It has, after all, more licensed hunters and fishermen than any other state in the nation. Yet it also has the nation's most enduring tradition for great pool shooting.

The checklist of Pennsylvania names on billiard's all-time honor roll is impressive: Willie Mosconi and Andrew Ponzi, both of Philadelphia; Onofrio Laurie, Jimmy Caras and Jim Rempe, all of Scranton; Joe Balsis, of Minersville, and Louis Butera, of Pittston, are just seven of the most prominent names.

The pool hall used to be "the neighborhood man's country club," in the words of five-time world champion Jimmy Caras. In the working towns, especially of Eastern Pennsylvania, the pool hall was the gathering spot for relaxation, camaraderie and sporting competition. Arnold

Willie Mosconi

Palmer and Joe Namath, among other Pennsylvanians, grew up knowing how to use a cuestick. The big cities had neighborhoods as tightly
knit as the small towns. In the early 1800s when Pittsburgh was still a
borough, there was a record of a $500 fine levied for operating a
billiard hall. South Philadelphia, the home of Mosconi, has been a
hotbed for billiards for generations, in part because the game is as
attractive to the ethnic crowd as it is to the tuxedo set. When John
O'Hara wanted a short story to reveal how domestic troubles can dis-
tract a man's mind, he used the setting of a pool room. "Straight Pool"
tells how a fellow cannot sink 50 balls unless he concentrates only on
the game. For O'Hara himself, pool was his best sport. He once ran 26
balls.

Mosconi, born June 27, 1913, ranks with Willie Hoppe and Ralph
Greenleaf in the Big Three of American billiards. Hoppe, now dead,
was a New Yorker who in his later years played out of Drexel Hill.
Greenleaf, also deceased, played many of his tournaments in Pennsylvania.

Nobody outdid Mosconi. He was world champ 11 times in the 14
years between 1941–55 that official competition was held. Just a little
man, 5-foot-7 and 165 pounds, Mosconi in his prime was as high-
strung, meticulous and dramatic as any American athlete on the scene.
He said that Greenleaf used to play position to within two inches of
where he wanted the ball, but he shortened that to an inch.

He once ran 150 balls in 19 minutes. In an exhibition match in 1954,
he established the world's record by running 526 balls, or better than 37
racks. What is so astounding is that good positioning after breaking a
rack of 14 balls is at least 10 percent luck, as Caras believes.

Mosconi took the world title in 1941, a year in which 50 times he
had runs of 100 balls or more, and the odds of sinking 100 straight are
about one in 25. He rewon the title in 1942 and held it again in
1944–45 and 1947–48. In 1949 he lost the crown to Caras. Then
Mosconi was champ again, 1950–53 and 1955. In 1947 on the old,
king-sized 5-foot-by-10 tables, Mosconi and Caras set the world's
tournament mark for runs of 127 each. The standard tournament table
of 4½-feet-by-9 was adopted in 1950, making runs longer but the
players infinitely more vulnerable and tense. In the 1956 unofficial
world title, Mosconi's opponent played a safety in the first frame. Wizard Willie then took to the table and sank all 150 balls in the sudden-
death game. Jimmy Moore, of Albuquerque, never had another chance
to use his cuestick.

Mosconi was the oldest of six children, the son of the nation's third-
ranking bantamweight boxer during the World War I era. When the

elder Mosconi lost a chance at the title, he quit boxing and opened a five-table billiard parlor in South Philadelphia. Two of Willie's uncles were vaudeville dancers. They were headliners at the Palace 58 times, but Willie didn't want that kind of a career. Much to his family's dislike, he was in billiard competition at 6 and by the time he was 18 he was a professional. He was the Philadelphia champion and fourth-ranking national player at 20. Had he failed, he would have completed an apprenticeship in the upholstery trade.

In the early days of the Depression, young Mosconi teamed up with the invincible Ralph Greenleaf to play a circuit of big-city hotels. The nervous but colorful Greenleaf was famed for wearing down opponents. His hair was slicked with grease and parted in the middle, and he played in formal evening garb. Young Mosconi didn't give the edge to the old champion in either style or determination. Greenleaf topped him in matches, 57 to 50, but after that Mosconi was the big name in the game.

Mosconi said he once beat Greenleaf, 150 to minus-11, because the old pro kept scratching the cueball. At a Times Square tournament against Greenleaf which started at 8 p.m., Mosconi watched him break the rack. Then Willie got up and ran 125 straight balls. He had tickets for the 8:30 p.m. performances of "Abie's Irish Rose" a few blocks away, and was in his seat when the curtain went up.

"I was aggressive, mostly because I figured if a man didn't have confidence in his playing he ought to get into something else," said Mosconi. "The point is once you get the table you don't ever want to give it back. You can destroy a man in this game if he has to sit on the sidelines while you run 100 balls at a time."

Mosconi calls billiards "a prestige game," and he plays it neatly clad in a jacket. The green-baize table, he says, may be recreational for the husband, wife and kids in the suburban game room, but to the tournament player it is torture.

Caras was born in Scranton in 1910, the son of a hat cleaner. He lives today in suburban Philadelphia. At 17 Caras defeated Greenleaf in an exhibition match and was called the "Boy Wonder of the Billiard World." At 26 in 1936 he became the game's second youngest player to win the world title by defeating Erwin Rudolph. He won again in 1938, 1939, 1949 and 1967. In his last championship, when he was 56, he lost his first match but then swept 11 straight to take the crown in St. Louis. In his career, he competed for 12 world titles and won five of them.

Talkative and friendly, Caras is good at conversation to cover the tension that blankets billiards. "Sometimes they go in, sometimes they

(Brunswick)

Jimmy Caras

don't," is a favorite expression of his when a ball hangs on a pocket edge and doesn't drop. When a competitor starts playing a ball at a time, instead of programming his play for five successive balls, Caras notes, "If you're not a good thinker in this game, you don't run balls."

The patented Caras trick is the "machine gun," where he lines up 15 balls and in seven seconds caroms them into a side pocket.

The prime age for great billiard players is between 35 and 55, though the current ranks have many successful younger players. The late Onofrio Laurie, of Scranton, was excellent, though at 81 he was no longer a serious tournament player. Louis Butera, a native of Pittston, is in his

(Harrisburg *Patriot-News*)

Jim Rempe

late 30s and was world champion in 1973. Joe Balsis, in his early 50s, came out of Minersville but now makes his home in Los Angeles. Balsis was world champ in 1966 and won the U.S. Open title in 1968 and 1974, the latter year with an exciting 200–199 victory over Jim Rempe.

Rempe, born Nov. 4, 1947, in Scranton where he still resides, is one of the sparkling upcoming players. He is the son of a retired dairy route manager and grew up in a duplex, where his aunt nextdoor had a grocery store and pool table. From ages 6 to 13, Rempe was hitting the cueball. At 13 he began a serious apprenticeship of two years in Downtown Scranton pool halls, learning and perfecting his game. By 16 he was confident enough to consider himself a "30 to 40 ball man," meaning he could maintain runs of that size fairly consistently.

He is 6-foot-2, unusually tall for a billiard player, and at 160 pounds is in top athletic condition. On the surface he is relaxed, but he admits that tension can get to him as it does every billiard player. He has the stamina necessary to compete. In the opening of the Pabst-Brunswick pro tour in 1974 at Penn State, Rempe was on his feet for 40 minutes to sink 120 balls in succession. Twice he used four-ball combinations.

Rempe's match against Steve Mizerak at Penn State was billiards at its best. Mizerak, a blond, 30-year-old school teacher from Perth Amboy, N.J., was the U.S. Open champ from 1970 through 1973. He was headed for a fifth straight crown in August of 1974 until Rempe knocked him off. At Penn State they met again. The left-handed Mizerak opened up a 114–77 lead and then Rempe ran 45 balls, stopped only when a 2-ball hung on a pocket. Mizerak regained a 143–133 lead until Rempe left him caught in a pack of balls. Back at the table, Rempe was ready to sink the final 17 balls, but he missed a long, high-bridge shot to the far corner pocket. Mizerak finished the game off for a 150–133 triumph. Caras, watching the competition, acclaimed Rempe as one of the brightest of the new stars.

Popular with young spectators, Rempe gives a cool and orderly performance. When just starting in the professional world in 1971, he won his first three tournaments. Then at the 1972 U.S. Open, he never really got a chance when opponents like the old ace Irving Crane, had runs of 128, 90 and 60 against him. At the 1974 U.S. Open in Chicago, Rempe already had ten major championships in four years of pro competition. He seemed ready to explode into the headlines when he missed what appeared to be a routine angle shot at a side pocket. The ball popped out, and his fellow Pennsylvanian, Joe Balsis, defeated him by as close a score as billiards can have, 200–199.

For Jim Rempe there is possibly 30 years more of competition ahead. The challenge remains to clean the table of balls.

11
HORSES

The Finest Standardbreds in the World

. . . *Pennsylvania Trotters and Pacers Are Unrivaled*

Pennsylvania isn't a one-horse state. It is the standardbred horse capital of the world, and many of its finest athletes are four-legged.

In 1974 a new record was written when all ten of the $100,000 major standardbred stake races were won by horses bred or sired in Pennsylvania. It was a clean sweep of the big money. Among the victories were Lana Lobell-sired Armbro Omaha in the Little Brown Jug; Keystone Gabriel out of the Hempt Farms in the $117,000 purse of The Colonial at Philadelphia's Liberty Bell Park, and Christopher T, sired at Hanover Shoe Farms, in the Hambletonian, the Kentucky Derby of harness racing.

Pennsylvania produces 2000 to 2500 quality standardbred racehorses a year. No other state comes close to matching this. It is no surprise, then, that invariably Pennsylvania horses lead the field, as in 1974 with such winners as Boyden Hanover, Spitfire Hanover, Waymaker, Surge Hanover and Keystone Presto, to name some other oatburners who garnered $100,000 or more for a mile's trot or pace.

The 1974 Harness Horse of the Year was Delmonica Hanover, a 5-

236

year-old mare bred in Hanover, owned by Meadow Lands, and a career winner of 45 races. She has won more than $700,000 and is the first American-owned horse to win France's pestigious Prix D'Amerique at Vincennes.

The two legends of harness racing, Dan Patch and Greyhound, were from Indiana, though Dan Patch holds the all-time pacing mark at the Allentown Fair. But most of the other great horses to pull a sulky have come from Pennsylvania. Steady Star, the grandson of Tar Heel and great-grandson of Adios, was the fastest standardbred who ever lived, with the mile record at 1:52. Bret Hanover was the world's fastest pacer with a time of 1:53. Bullet Hanover held six world records. Max Hempt's Stenographer held 11 world records and was trotting's greatest filly.

Pennsylvania's breeding statistics are awesome. Bye Bye Byrd at the Hempt Farms has sired 42 horses who did the mile in two minutes or less, including 25 who won $100,000 purses. Albatross, at Hanover Farms, won 59 out of 71 contests and was out of the money only once in his three-year racing career. An absolute sensation, Albatross was horse of the year twice, 1971–72, and is history's leader in track earnings for the industry, $1.2 million. A great-grandson of Adios and Tar Heel and with a track record better than both combined, Albatross could command $5,000 stud fees when he entered service. Tar Heel, the pride of Hanover, won 35 of 60 races as a two and three-year-old and was out of the money only ten times. At 26 in 1975, this senior citizen had stud fees of $15,000, simply because he is the world's greatest and leading money-producing sire whose progeny have earned more than $22 million. Tar Heel is the daddy of such big winners as Bret, Romeo and Romalie Hanover.

Adios (1940–65) was the greatest stallion in all of racing history, including the thoroughbred division. His progeny reaped $20 million, a figure since surpassed by Tar Heel's offspring but in a day of larger purses and inflation. Adios—nicknamed "Big Daddy"—was the first standardbred stud to have a $15,000 service fee. Pennsylvania courts ruled that the state sales tax must be collected for each successful ejaculation. "Tail is retail," the horsemen said disappointedly. Adios in 1965 produced 32 foals at a cost of $480,000, and the sales tax, then at five percent, was $24,000 net. With the sale of his yearlings, Adios was giving Pennsylvania $50,000 a year in tax revenue. "When it came to taxes, Adios never said neigh," Governor Milton J. Shapp once quipped. The Adios, a $109,000 stake race at The Meadows Racetrack near Washington, Pa., Big Daddy's home, is in his honor.

Pennsylvanians, native or adopted, have been among the biggest

(*Harness Horse* Magazine)

Tar Heel of Hanover Farm

names in the harness racing business. Among the horsemen with national reputations have been the late L. B. Sheppard, John F. Simpson, Sr., Delvin G. Miller, Max Hempt, Levi Harner, the late Mahlon "Shoe Wizard" Haines of York and Hambletonian winner Jimmy Arthur of Hollidaysburg.

Golfer Arnold Palmer may be an upcoming horseman. He had a one-third ownership of Spitfire Hanover, the 1974 Yonkers Trot winner. Charley Keller, the former Yankee outfielder, has a horse farm in Maryland, but gets most of his breeding done over the line in Pennsylvania. Art Rooney, of the Pittsburgh Steelers, invests in both standardbreds and thoroughbreds and has a horse farm in Maryland too. Wilt Chamberlain, the basketball giant from Overbrook, profited from his investment in harness horses.

The Pennsylvania Standardbred Sale at the Farm Show Arena each November in Harrisburg is the richest horse market of its kind in the world. At the 36th annual sale in 1974, some 687 trotters and pacers changed hands for $7,857,400. Italian buyers put up $60,000 for a broodmare, and that was a modest price compared to what some yearling colts brought.

Pennsylvania has the nation's biggest outdoor show, the Devon Horse Show, each May, and the biggest indoor show, the Pennsylvania National, each October. In addition to standardbreds, the Commonwealth has considerable breeding and raising of Quarter, Appaloosa, Tennessee Walking, American Saddle Bred, and Morgan horses.

In actual racing itself, Pennsylvania is still behind other states. The Commonwealth did not get its first modern betting race, in harness racing again, until June 7, 1963, when Liberty Bell Park opened. Only in 1974 did it get Sunday racing. County fairs, however, had non-betting sulky racing in the last century. Allentown, Reading and York were on the old grand circuit. Dan Patch's enduring record at Allentown dates back to 1905.

The lack of in-state competitive racing is one reason Pennsylvania has had such few drivers. Levi Harner, of Bloomsburg, is the most famous. The son of a fairgrounds sulky racer, Harner has earned almost $3 million on the circuit, winning 20 percent of the 15,000 times he wheeled out. His son Eldon is a driver too.

Del Miller is the most prominent of the living drivers, trainers and owners. Born in California in 1913, he was raised on his grandparents' farm at Avella and today owns the Meadow Lands Farm. A 5-foot-6, 158-pounder, he was one of the greatest drivers of all time, with 1600 victories, 17 world records, 50 races at two minutes or under, a Hambletonian triumph, and $6.2 million in earnings.

Thoroughbred, or flat, racing was last to Pennsylvania and has only a limited tradition here, but perhaps its most famous jockey is a Pennsylvanian. Bill Hartack came out of Black Lick and went the way of horses because he was too small to work in the coal mines. He and Eddie Arcaro are the only jockeys to win the Kentucky Derby five times. A bachelor and a southpaw, Hartack rode the first of more than 4000 winners in 1952. Unmatched in flat racing, he was the leading jockey three consecutive years, 1955–57, and he has won more than $26 million in purses. "You either know what you are going to do when you go out on the track or you don't know," the notoriously candid Hartack has said. "You either ride a horse good or you ride him bad. Good isn't good enough for me. I've got to be better. That's the way I'm built."

It is ironical, too, that some of the most noted thoroughbred owners have been Pennsylvanians. The Wideners of Philadelphia produced Hialeah Park, the 5½ straightaway furlong at Belmont Park called the "Widener Chute," and the very much appreciated 1929 court decision that permits tax write-offs for breeding and racing, keeping horsemanship the sport of kings. The Phipps and Mellons of Pittsburgh are other famed thoroughbred dynasties. The greatest horse of them all, Man o' War, as well as his son War Admiral, was owned by Samuel D. Riddle, a textile manufacturer from Glen Riddle. The president of the Rose Tree Hunt Club, he purchased Man o' War at the Saratoga Sales for a mere $5,000. Big Red (1917–47) was stabled in Lexington, Ky. The latest hopeful is Dick Allen, baseball's slugger from Wampum who grew up with horses and now has a trainer's license and a thoroughbred farm at Perkasie. "To play in the World Series or to develop a good horse, I can't think of which would give me more pleasure," he said.

Pennsylvania is the standardbred capital of the world because it is here that the top of the breed are sired, bred and raised. The finest horse-farm nurseries are here mainly because of the quality of horsemanship in Pennsylvania, and that is attracted to the southern half of the Commonwealth because of the climate and nutritious limestone soil that makes it fabulous horse-raising country.

The world's largest breeding farm for racehorses is in southern Adams and York counties, not in California, Kentucky or Texas. The Hanover Shoe Farms has an international reputation.

The Lana Lobell Farms, founded in 1961 by the Leavitt family, also is in Hanover. The Hempt Farms in Silver Spring Township, started in 1946, completes the big-three in horse nurseries. The Meadow Lands Farm near Washington, the U. C. Steele Farms at Bloomsburg, the new Allwood Stable near Hanover, the Double J Farm of Joseph J. Cignetto at Mechanicsburg and the Dana Irving Farms at Oxford are others. It is these farms, plus a few smaller ones, that makes horse-raising a multi-million-dollar industry in Pennsylvania.

Hanover Farms has as near an arcadian setting over a ten-mile radius as any landscape artist could hope to paint. In the rolling pastures, the colts and fillies run and roughhouse at play like schoolkids. In the spring during the six months before they are weaned, the foals romp with their mares. There are always horses in the field, some frisky in their youth and others statuesque in their maturity.

It is a breeding business. Hanover does no training and has no racing stable. Its orange and blue are farm colors, not racing colors.

"We are raising athletes, and they all become aware of that pretty early in life," said Murray Brown of the Hanover staff. "Some will dog it, of course, but they know their purpose. They are outside almost all the time, roughing it to get the strength they will need to endure the stresses of racing."

Hanover Farms is seven miles from the Mason-Dixon line in rich, limestone country. Neighboring farmers raise fruit, cows and corn in the high-mineral soil. Spread out for 400 acres, encompassing what was once 33 separate farms, Hanover at its peak in mid-May will have as many as 1850 horses. No other breeding farm for racehorses anywhere equals in size or productivity this farm. It has 15 resident stallions and 300 broodmares. As many as 700 outside mares are shipped in each year to be bred. Some 400 horses are born at Hanover each foaling season between November 1 and mid-June. These standardbreds have their birthdays set at November 1—two months earlier than the thoroughbreds. Two Novembers later they will be sold for an average of $18,000 per colt or filly. Their racing careers can last for 13 years, between ages 2 and 14. A less nervous and a more sure breed than the thoroughbred, the standardbred often is a glutton for track work. One of the top studs at Hanover, the big bay Lehigh Hanover, a son of Adios, made 30 starts as a 2-year-old and had 75 starts in his three-yeaᵣ career before he became a father of 16 offspring with 2-minute miles.

Stud fees at Hanover range from $2,000 to $15,000. There is a double sales tax, first on the stud service and then on the sale of the yearling. Ninety-five percent of the standardbreds are born at night, and within 48 hours almost all of them are healthy enough to be insured. To watch over their upbringing, Hanover Farms has two full-time veterinarians, eight foremen and 100 farm hands.

The late Lawrence B. Sheppard, one of the most remarkable figures in Pennsylvania sports, started the breeding farm.

(*Harness Horse* Magazine)

L. B. Sheppard with Dean Hanover

Sheppard was born in Baltimore, Md., in 1898, the 13th child and seventh son of Harper D. Sheppard. "I was out of a second litter. Dad married three times, had 15 kids. My mother was the former Henrietta Dawson Ayers," L. B. once said, speaking of his lineage in a horseman's lingo.

H. D. Sheppard and Clinton N. Myers started the Hanover Shoe Company in 1899. Myers was a horseman, but he was more interested in raising some of the nation's best English setters and in breeding gamecocks for a sport long popular in rural Pennsylvania. Young L. B. was a grade-school pupil in Hanover and got his first horse at 11 so he could haul shoes to the first Hanover retail store in York.

Sheppard went to Haverford College, ran a tourist horse pack at Yellowstone National Park in the summers, and went on to the University of Virginia Law School. He became a lawyer, but never practiced. He also was a Navy pilot in World War I. His only son, Larry Jr., a World War II pilot, was killed in his private plane in 1949 when he hit a powerline at Villanova in returning from the Roosevelt Raceway.

Sheppard purchased his first racehorse, the gelding Peter Manning, in 1925. The next year Peter Manning set the trotting record at the Reading Fair which still stands. The breeding farm, as a corporate entity apart from the shoe company, was established in 1926. When his father and Myers left on a vacation, young Sheppard played Hercules and cleaned out the stable. "I immediately did what I had longed to do," he said. "I sold the whole works, every lousy horse. When Dad came home, he saw red, but didn't say much. I told him that he and Mr. Myers couldn't part with any horse, no matter how bad, and as a result had a stable full of critters not worth a damn."

Much as he loved horses, Sheppard was a realist about them. He regarded them as among the dumbest beasts on earth, and often said so.

With an empty barn, Sheppard proceeded to buy the entire stable of the late A. B. Coxe of Paoli, the coal baron. He got 69 horses for $150,000. Among them was Miss Bertha Dillon, who became the first mare to have three daughters to run the mile in two minutes. Her one daughter, Hanover's Bertha, was the first mare to win the Hambletonian. That was 1930, and seven years later Bertha's daughter, Shirley Hanover, won it too. With the package, Sheppard got a fine stallion in Dillon Axworthy, and then he bought Guy McKinney, who that year, 1926, had won the first Hambletonian. Thus the famed Hanover bloodline was established.

Possibly 5000 various Hanover surnamed horses have come off the farm, many to the winner's circle and quite a few to fortune as well.

Sheppard's favorite was Dean Hanover, who is one of about 40 great horses buried at the farm. L. B.'s daughter, Alma Sheppard Tolhurst, as a 13-year-old raced Dean Hanover against the clock on the "Big Red Mile" at Lexington, Ky., and set a world record for a woman driver at 1:58½. Then Sheppard took him in competition and drove him to four world records, two of which still stand.

An alert, lively, quick-witted gentleman, Sheppard was a daring horse-trader. Del Miller bought the great Adios from the Warner Brothers Farm of Hollywood movie fame for $21,000. Sheppard wanted Adios and wrote a personal check to Miller for $500,000—at that time the record in the harness racing business. Eventually, L. B. divided the ownership of Adios with Miller and Max Hempt. It was a typical gesture of Sheppard, who had a well-earned reputation for being a check-grabber when friends gathered to talk about furthering the breed.

Hempt is a giant of a man, 6-foot-7 and 275 pounds. An all-around athlete at Camp Hill High School, Hempt became a road-builder who plays polo for fun. With his family, he also runs one of the nation's finest breeding farms. His stallions Bye Bye Byrd, Hickory Pride and Harlan Dean, all with Hanover blood, have produced progeny who have earned in excess of $22 million. Hempt takes an active role in the Carlisle Fair and has a national name for his enthusiasm in supporting all aspects of harness racing.

When racing was approved in Pennsylvania, Governor David L. Lawrence, a lifelong Democrat, named Sheppard, a lifelong Republican, as the first chairman of the Harness Racing Commission. Beyond his interest in shoe manufacturing and harness racing, Sheppard before his death in 1968 was the leading citizen of Hanover. He was president of the school board, a waterworks commissioner, a founder and director of the hospital, president of the Boys Club, president of the trust company, and even publisher for a time of the Hanover *Evening Sun*. His three surviving daughters, Mrs. Charlotte DeVan, Mrs. Patricia Winder and Mrs. Tolhurst, have bred a fourth generation Sheppard bloodline interested in Hanover horses.

In 1951 Sheppard hired a young hot driver and trainer named John F. Simpson, who came out of South Carolina and as a young man had ridden the first of his 88 standardbreds to pass the two-minute mark. "My Birthday" started Simpson off until today he is the fourth ranked driver for lifetime two-minute miles. He drove winners in the Hambletonian, Little Brown Jug, the Messenger, the Kentucky Futurity and the Fox Stake. Simpson Sr. and his older son, Simpson Jr., are the only father-son combination ever to win both the Hambletonian and the Kentucky Futurity. Sheppard took a liking to Simpson when he asked him in 1949 to train Imperial Hanover, purchased for $81,000. Simpson brazenly said the horse was a bust. He reluctantly gave in to Sheppard, but Imperial Hanover still was a bust. Yet so impressed was L. B. with Simpson's horse sense that he hired him on, and now the 55-year-old former driver and trainer is his successor as president. In few other sports can athletes like a Sheppard or a Simpson move into the executive office with such surety, but great horsemanship requires managerial ability as well as skill at the reins.

(*Harness Horse* Magazine)

John F. Simpson Sr. driving Bullet Hanover

APPENDIX A

Pennsylvania Interscholastic Track Records

Event	Class A	Class B
100-yd Dash	9.5 Tony Darden (Norristown 75)	9.8 Earl Brown (Middletown 72)
220 Dash	21.2 Don Webster (Kennett 61) Orin Richburg (Westinghouse 64) Wm. Clugston (North Penn 69) Jim Scott (Carlisle 69)	21.4 Gary Risch (Freeport 69)
On Curve	21.7 Bill Johnston (Chichester 70)	22.2 Earl Brown (Middletown 72)
440	47.8 Larry Floyd (W.Mifflin 69)	49.1 Smittie Brown (Coraopolis 67)
880	1:52.7 Chas. Norelli (Emmaus 73)	1:56.2 Sam Bair (Scottsdale 64) Dennis Bohlayer (Twin Valley 69)
Mile	4:11.1 Jerry Ritchey (N.Allgh. 67)	4:17.6 Bob Snyder (C.Fulton 74)
2-Mile	9:11.9 Mel Boyd (Ringgold 74)	9:20.5 Terry Wile (Kane 73)
120 High Hurdles	14.0 Levi Porter (Westinghouse 67)	14.2 Mike Shine (Youngsville 72)
180 Low Hurdles	18.7 Jan White (Harrisburg 66)	19.3 Mike Shine (Youngsville 72)
High Jump	6–9.75 Dan Goodyear (Red Lion 74)	6–9 Bill Fitz (Greencastle 72)
Broad Jump	23–9 Ron Coleman (Grove City 63)	23–7 Gene White (Bristol 69)
Pole Vault	14–2.5 Mark Mondschein (Haverford 70)	13–11 Dave Strein (Catasauq. 74)
12-lb. Shot	66–5.5 Ron Semkiew (Baldwin 72)	60–11 Dick Hart (Morrisville 61)
Discus	182–3.5 Erwin Jaros (N.Penn 65)	180–7 Ty Higgins (L.Moreland 70)
Javelin	230–0 Ray Mushinski (Ambridge 69)	223–3 Bob Cummins (Grove City 72)
Triple Jump	48–0 Maurice Peoples (W-B GAR 68)	47–1 Gene White (Bristol 69)
880 Relay	1:27.8 Abington 1965	1:30.6 Darby Twp. 1972
Mile Relay	3:16.8 Wissahickon 1970	3:23.0 Coraopolis 1967
2-Mile Relay	7:47.0 N. Allegheny 1970	8:00.7 North East 1968

APPENDIX B
Pennsylvania Sports Hall of Fame

The Pennsylvania Sports Hall of Fame was organized in 1958 and made its first selections in 1963. It was launched by the late George E. Bellis, activities director for the Pennsylvania American Legion; Joseph Scott, now president of the Philadelphia Flyers, and the late John B. Sollenberger, president of Hershey Estates. There are now 20 chapters with a total membership of more than 3000. The following are its selections, 1963–74.

1963

Connie Mack—Grand Old Man of Baseball, manager of A's for 50 years
John "Hans" Lobert—Star infielder and manager from Williamsport
Jim Thorpe—Greatest all-around American athlete of all time
Chuck Bednarik—All American Penn center, All-Pro Eagles linebacker
Roberta Rank Bonniwell—Philadelphian on 1928 U.S. Olympics gym team
Barney Ewell—Olympics 100-meter dash champ from Lancaster
Glenn Killinger—All-American at Penn State, West Chester State coach
Stan Musial—Donora slugger and one of baseball's finest
Arnold Palmer—The living legend in golf from Latrobe
Harold "Pie" Traynor—Hall of Fame third sacker for Pirates

1964

Honus Wagner—Greatest shortstop of all time, from Carnegie
Paul Waner—Hall of Fame outfielder with Pirates
Harry "Haps" Benfer—Albright College's greatest football player
Barney Berlinger—Penn grad in Olympics decathlon
Pete Dimperio—Outstanding Westinghouse High coach for 19 years
Charles "Rip" Engle—Penn State mentor for 16 years, from Elk Lick
Del Miller—One of the top harness racing drivers of all time
Anne B. Townsend—A star and president of State Field Hockey Assn. for years
Steve Van Buren—Greatest running back in Eagles history
Stewart Holcomb—Outstanding football coach, including at W & J

1965

Bert Bell—Commissioner of NFL and one of its founders
Christy Mathewson—Factoryville lad who became one of baseball's finest

George Bellis—Allentown batboy who devoted a lifetime to Pa. sports

Roy Campanella—Three times most valuable player, from Philadelphia

Chick Davies—Almost 30 years hoop coach at Duquesne and Homestead High

Jimmy Dykes—Great third baseman and noted manager, from Philadelphia

Jimmy Foxx—Famed slugger for Connie Mack

Robert "Lefty" Grove—One of baseball's top southpaws for A's

Clark Hinkle—Led nation in scoring at Bucknell, later pro standout

Bill Hollenback—Penn All-American fullback and Penn State coach

Johnny Lujack—Great football triple-threat from Connellsville

E. E. "Hooks" Mylin—Coached at Lebanon Valley, Bucknell and Lafayette

Frank "Butch" Snyder—Erie bowler and a great in its early days

1966

Glenn "Pop" Warner—Carlisle, Pitt and Temple famed coach

Dr. John "Jock" Sutherland—Coach at Lafayette, Pitt and Steelers

Art Rooney—Founder and president of Pittsburgh Steelers

Bob Allman—Finalist in Eastern wrestling three years, and blind

Tommy Davies—Pitt All-American halfback, later a coach in Pennsylvania

Johnny Woodruff—Connellsville black who set Olympic 800-meter record

Les Bell—World Series third sacker for Cardinals, from Harrisburg

Eddie Gottlieb—Developed pro basketball with Philadelphia Warriors

Billy Conn—Colorful Pittsburgh fighter, almost heavyweight champ

Charley Gelbert—Great shortstop, Lafayette baseball coach

Jim Daniell—Mt. Lebanon star, captained first Cleveland Browns team

George Munger—One of the great Ivy League coaches at Penn

Robin Roberts—Finest modern-era Phillies pitcher

Henry "Hinkey" Haines—Red Lion all-around athlete at Penn State

Tommy Loughran—Great light-heavyweight champ from Philadelphia

1967

Wilbur Cooper—Won 202 Pirate games, more than any other lefthander

Duffy Dougherty—Famed Michigan State skipper from Barnesboro

Bob Davies—Star basketball player at Seton Hall and in pros

James Henry—Noted athletic director at LaSalle College for years

Charles "Pop" Kelchner—Dean of baseball scouts

John B. Kelly—Won U.S. single scull championship 1919–20

Andy Kerr—Carlisle High grad and noted Colgate coach

Dr. Hobart Light—Outstanding Penn football player

Joe "Ducky" Medwick—Star of the Cardinals' Gas-House Gang
Mike Wilson—All-American under Jock Sutherland at Lafayette
William "Tiny" Parry—Noted Lebanon *Daily News* sportswriter
Ed Pollock—Sports scribe with Philadelphia *Bulletin* for 40 years
Carl Snavely—Respected coach at Bucknell, Cornell and North Carolina
Maurice Stokes—Great basketballer at Westinghouse, St. Francis and
    pros
Leo Weinrott—Long-time Philadelphia football official
Johnny Weismueller—Olympic champ and movie star from Windber

1968

George "Whitey" Kurowski—Cards' third baseman from Reading
Charley Trippi—Collegiate and pro football great out of Pittston
Fritzie Zivic—Welterweight champion and notorious brawler
Willie Mosconi—One of billiards' greatest, out of Philadelphia
J. K. "Poss" Miller—Penn football, basketball and baseball star
Tom Gola—LaSalle's most outstanding basketball player
Paul Arizin—Villanova's greatest basketball star
Bob Duffy—Football great at Lafayette, later Philadelphia lawyer
Joe Hill—Lebanon lawyer on undefeated 1932 Colgate team
Eugene "Shorty" Miller—One of Penn State's earliest and finest QBs
Bob Higgins—Great Penn State end and coach
Aldo "Buff" Donelli—Duquesne star, later Duke and Columbia coach
Bill McKechnie—One of baseball's brainiest managers
Ray Mueller—Ironman catcher, started in Harrisburg, resides in
    Steelton
Lloyd Waner—Younger brother of Paul, "Little Poison" for Pirates
Curt Simmons—Phillies Whiz-Kid pitcher who helped win 1950 pennant

1969

Charley Berry—Lafayette end, A's catcher, famed umpire
Harold "Doc" Carlson—Won 367 games as Pitt hoop coach for 31 years
Vic Emanuel—Harrisburg Tech, Gettysburg, Pottsville Maroons star
Bob Friend—Won 191 games for Pirates as star right-hander
Dick Groat—Most Valuable Player for 1960 pennant-winning Pirates
Jack Kelly Jr.—Duplicated his father as a great oarsman
Duke Maronic—Went from Steelton to Eagles as star guard
Ed McCluskey—Farrell High School's famed basketball coach
Jack Twyman—One of pro basketball's greatest out of Pittsburgh
Art Wall—Pennsylvania amateur champ to a Masters winner
Helen Siegel Wilson—State golf champ five times, Philadelphia champ,
    11 times

1970

Josh Gibson—Great Pittsburgh catcher in Negro National League
Harry Greb—All-time best Pennsylvania boxer
George V. Kenneally—Captained Pottsville Maroons, 1926–28
Francis "Reds" Bagnell—Maxwell Award winning Penn tailback
Henry Benkert—At Rutgers, leading national scorer in 1924
Lloyd S. Blinco—Hershey Bears captain and general manager
Tom Brookshier—Five-time All-Pro defensive back for Eagles
Dick Button—Six-time world skating champion, won nationals at
    Hershey
Paul V. Costello—Gold medal rowing winner, 1920–24–28
Jim Crowley—One of Four Horsemen, Pennsylvania boxing commis-
    sioner
Elroy Face—Won 17 straight games as Pirates reliever in 1959
George "Lefty" James—Cornell coach out of New Cumberland
Ralph Kiner—Home run king for Pirates
John Michelosen—Pitt quarterback, later Pitt and Steelers coach
George H. Newmaster—World trap shooting champ

1971

Bruce Brubaker—World fly-casting champion from Camp Hill
Stanley Coveleski—Great Cleveland pitcher from Shamokin
Billy Cox—Fielded third base as well as anyone in history
Bill Dudley—Triple-threat halfback with Steelers
Roy Engle—Center and 1933 Penn captain, played all but 17 minutes in
    3 years
Nelson Fox—From St. Thomas, made 2663 major league hits
Joe Fulks—Early superstar with Philadelphia Warriors
Cal Hubbard—Tackle and fullback with Geneva College
Herb Pennock—Masterful pitcher, later general manager of Athletics
George Senesky—St. Joe's All-American guard, famed with Warriors
Bucky Walters—Won 198 National League games
Hack Wilson—Great Ellwood City slugger with Chicago Cubs
Joseph C. Zacko—Leading Pottsville sportsman and historian.

1972

Richie Ashburn—Speedster won two batting titles with Phillies
Henry T. Bream—Great field-goal kicker and coach at Gettysburg
Raymond T. Frey—Lebanon Valley great, early basketball high scorer
Frank W. Gustine—Popular Pirates third baseman
Wilbur "Fats" Henry—Immortal W & J and Pottsville Maroons tackle
Leo Houck—Fought 12 world champs, then Penn State boxing coach
Stan Jones—Out of Lemoyne to Maryland and Chicago Bears

Eddie Plank—Gettysburg star and American League's top southpaw
Ken Raffensberger—Native of York and 12 years as major league
    pitcher
Francis X. Reagan—Penn's answer to Tommy Harmon
Vic Sexias—Finest Pennsylvania tennis player since Tilden

1973

Joseph G. Crowley—Noted Pennsylvania football official
Dave DeFilippo—Coached Pottstown Firebirds 1969–70 championships
Edward "Scrapper" Farrell—Great at Muhlenberg and high school
    coach
Rick Gilbert—Lancaster state diving champion three times, Cornell
    coach
Stan Hitz—Four-time national handball champion out of Harrisburg
Dr. William "Skip" Hughes—Coached St. Francis hoopsters to glory
Danny Murtaugh—Pirates pennant-winner from Chester
John M. Ogden—Oxford pitcher to major leagues, discovered Dick
    Allen
Gil Reich—Quarterback great out of Steelton
Truett "Rip" Sewell—One of the Pirates' most colorful pitchers
Frank Sinkovitz—Out of Harrisburg, defensive captain of Steelers
Sol "Woody" Wolf—Famed Lock Haven coach and broadcaster
Roberto Clemente—The perfect baseball player
Harry O. Dayhoff—Won 12 letters at Steelton, 12 at Bucknell
Bing Miller—Athletics right fielder with career average of .312

1974

Chuck Cooper—Duquesne great, one of the four first blacks in NBA
Earle Edwards—Greensburg native, coached North Carolina State
Glenn H. Horst—All-around Lancaster and F & M athlete
Walter "Bull" Levine—Captained Lock Haven's 1925 national champs
Harry Litwack—Two-time Temple captain, its greatest basketball coach
Danny Litwhiler—Superb big-league fielder from Ringtown
Tony Margio—Speedboat racer from Harrisburg
Joe Schmidt—One of greatest linebackers, from Pittsburgh
Joseph C. Scott—President of Philadelphia Flyers
Frank Thomas—Native Pittsburgher who played for Pirates
Chuck Drulis—Great guard for Temple and Chicago Bears
Bill Jeffrey—Coached Penn State soccer 27 years, 154–24–29 record
Bob Peck—Famed Pitt center from Lock Haven

ATHLETES INDEX

(Location of illustrations is indicated by page numbers in italics.)